MW00659237

FREE SPEECH

Why do we protect free speech? What values does it serve? How has the Supreme Court interpreted the First Amendment? What has the Court gotten right and wrong? Why are current debates over free expression often so divisive? How can we do better? In this succinct but comprehensive and scholarly book, Len Niehoff and Thomas Sullivan tackle these pressing questions. *Free Speech: From Core Values to Current Debates* traces the development and evolution of the free speech doctrine in the Supreme Court and explores how the Court – with varying levels of success – has applied that doctrinal framework to "hard cases" and current controversies, such as those involving hate speech, speech on the internet, speech on campus, and campaign finance regulation. This is the perfect volume for anyone – student, general reader, or scholar – looking for an accessible overview of this critical topic.

Len Niehoff is Professor from Practice at the University of Michigan Law School, where he teaches First Amendment and media law. He has practiced First Amendment law for almost forty years, representing journalists and media outlets in numerous cases. He is the author of more than 100 publications.

Tom Sullivan is President Emeritus and Professor of Law and Political Science at the University of Vermont. Previously he served as Provost at the University of Minnesota and Dean at the University of Minnesota and University of Arizona law schools. He is the author of twelve books and over seventy-five articles and essays.

Free Speech

FROM CORE VALUES TO CURRENT DEBATES

LEN NIEHOFF
University of Michigan Law School

E. THOMAS SULLIVAN
University of Vermont

CAMBRIDGE
UNIVERSITY PRESS

CAMBRIDGE
UNIVERSITY PRESS

University Printing House, Cambridge CB2 8BS, United Kingdom

One Liberty Plaza, 20th Floor, New York, NY 10006, USA

477 Williamstown Road, Port Melbourne, VIC 3207, Australia

314–321, 3rd Floor, Plot 3, Splendor Forum, Jasola District Centre, New Delhi – 110025, India

103 Penang Road, #05–06/07, Visioncrest Commercial, Singapore 238467

Cambridge University Press is part of the University of Cambridge.

It furthers the University's mission by disseminating knowledge in the pursuit of education, learning, and research at the highest international levels of excellence.

www.cambridge.org
Information on this title: www.cambridge.org/9781108830577
DOI: 10.1017/9781108902380

First published 2022

A catalogue record for this publication is available from the British Library.

Library of Congress Cataloging-in-Publication Data
NAMES: Sullivan, E. Thomas, author. | Niehoff, Leonard M., author.
TITLE: Free speech : from core values to current debates / Thomas Sullivan, University of Vermont; Len Niehoff, University of Michigan Law School.
DESCRIPTION: Cambridge, United Kingdom ; New York, NY : Cambridge University Press, 2022. | Includes bibliographical references and index.
IDENTIFIERS: LCCN 2021056496 (print) | LCCN 2021056497 (ebook) | ISBN 9781108830577 (hardback) | ISBN 9781108822138 (paperback) | ISBN 9781108902380 (epub)
Subjects: LCSH: Freedom of speech–United States.
CLASSIFICATION: LCC KF4772 .S85 2022 (print) | LCC KF4772 (ebook) | DDC 342.7308/53–dc23/eng/20211223
LC record available at https://lccn.loc.gov/2021056496
LC ebook record available at https://lccn.loc.gov/2021056497

ISBN 978-1-108-83057-7 Hardback
ISBN 978-1-108-82213-8 Paperback

For my wife, Lisa, and our son, Jordan

– Len Niehoff

For all my students I have taught for over four decades

– Tom Sullivan

Contents

Acknowledgments

Professor Niehoff wishes to thank Dorothy Kryskowski of the University of Michigan Law School for her invaluable assistance in the preparation of the manuscript of this book. He also thanks his research assistants, Renee Griffin (class of 2021, University of Michigan Law School) and Rachel Carpman (class of 2021, University of Michigan Law School), for their hard work. In addition, he extends his thanks to the University of Michigan Law School for its support of this project through summer funding grants. Finally, he wishes to express his appreciation to the law students in his First Amendment and Media Law courses over the past thirty years, where many of the ideas explored here were discussed and tested.

Professor Sullivan wishes to thank his research assistants, Anders Newberry (class of 2020, Vermont Law School), Katie Conroy (class of 2021, University of Minnesota Law School), and Eric Tucker (class of 2022, Duke University Law School). He also thanks Leslie Black Sullivan for her support and encouragement throughout this project. In addition, he extends his appreciation to Scott Dewey, research librarian at the University of Minnesota Law School Library, and to colleagues at Cambridge University Law Faculty, the Law Library Staff, and to President David Ibbetson of Cambridge University's Clare Hall College for their advice and support during a visiting faculty appointment at the University of Cambridge.

Introduction

Debates about free expression are a fixture of everyday discourse. Discussions of free speech issues abound, not just on college campuses and in law schools, but also in the workplace, in living rooms, around dinner tables, at social events, and in the popular media. Those conversations explore such issues as whether a professional football player has a right to protest during the national anthem, whether the government has the power to restrict the speech of people with extremist views, whether someone should be able to express dissent by burning the flag, whether "political correctness" results in objectionable self-censorship, whether campaign contributions should count as speech, and whether the media deserve the protections that the First Amendment provides or abuse those privileges in order to spread "fake news." Mainstream debates even delve into such exotic questions as whether the President has to let people with whom he disagrees participate in his Twitter feed and whether the First Amendment gives a baker the right to refuse to make a cake for a gay wedding that he opposes on religious grounds. Across all of these issues, people recognize that speech matters but also has consequences.

Unfortunately, these discussions often make little progress in advancing understanding. One of the principal reasons for this stalemate is that views of free expression tend to fall into two categories. And those two views see things very differently.

The first view, which we call "absolutism," reflects a strident antagonism toward any externally imposed limitation on an individual's freedom to say whatever he or she likes. Proponents of this view often use the language of liberty, as in the colloquial "it's a free country." They also often use the language of rights, as in the commonly invoked (and frequently misattributed) quotation: "I disapprove of what you say, but I will defend to the death your right to say it."

The absolutist view has merit and appeal. It has the virtues of clarity and commitment. It has a respectable intellectual pedigree, having been embraced by many historic champions of freedom. Indeed, as we will discuss, the Supreme Court of the United States has over time taken a fairly absolutist view of free speech. This perspective has a point: freedom of expression brings with it serious challenges, but they pale in comparison to those that would follow if we empowered the government to dictate what a person may say or think.

Proponents of this view frequently claim support in the First Amendment and point to it as a source of authority. If the analysis proceeds no further, then the absolutist view can take on a descriptive character. "I have the right to say what I want because the First Amendment guarantees it."

This common framing of the absolutist view puts aside such questions as whether so expansive a principle makes any sense, whether it aligns with the other goals of a rational and compassionate society, and whether it has outworn its welcome and should be revisited – as laws in a constitutional republic can be. A critic could even accuse it of circular reasoning: "I have the right to do this because I have the right to do this." The absolutist view need not amount to mere description and circularity, but it often does.

Whatever the virtues of absolutism, it faces a serious challenge. If pressed, most absolutists will acknowledge that they are less absolute than they claim and that exceptions do and must exist. They will agree that no one has a right to threaten another with bodily harm or to commit blackmail, fraud, bribery, or extortion, even though speech plays a central role in each of those activities.

People who argue against absolutism often invoke the famous observation of Justice Oliver Wendell Holmes that no one has the right to cry "Fire!" in a crowded theater. The example is not a particularly good one, because the vast majority of speech does not result in certain, immediate, and dangerous panic. Still, it has become a comfortable and resilient cliché in these discussions and the central point holds: no workable principle of free expression can immunize *all* speech from government restriction.

That is where the absolutist's problems begin. After all, if a principle of free expression must give way to some exceptions, then why not this one, and that one, and this one? If the law bars the possession of child pornography, then why not also the possession of racist propaganda? If hate speech causes suffering and contributes nothing of value to public discourse, then why can't the law punish it just as it does threats and blackmail? If the First Amendment doesn't get in the way of an injunction against speech using someone else's trademark, then why does it get in the way of an injunction against speech that portrays women as inherently less intelligent or that denies the reality of the Holocaust? And so on and so on.

Absolutists find themselves with a dilemma. On the one hand, a civilized society cannot embrace a model of free expression that admits of no exceptions. On the other hand, at some point a principle riddled with holes ceases to be much of a principle at all. Absolutists justifiably worry about exceptions watering down the First Amendment until only a weak and ineffectual tonic remains. Still, they cannot defend a free speech principle that allows no compromises.

We call the chief view that competes with absolutism the "relativist" view. In sum, relativists believe that the principle of free expression should yield as necessary to accommodate other countervailing interests and values. Proponents of relativism often use language of balancing and proportionality. This approach has found support in other countries; for example, the European Court of Human Rights often assesses the right to freedom of expression by balancing it against other rights, like privacy and dignity.

Most relativists will acknowledge that free expression matters. But they will also resist the absolutist's view that it matters so much that other considerations become marginal or irrelevant. Relativists believe that we need to weigh free expression against other things that we think are important, like protecting people against discrimination, providing redress for hateful speech, preserving public safety, maintaining sexual decency, affording individuals a zone of privacy, safeguarding personal reputation, and so on. They also believe that, in this weighing process, we should not put so heavy a thumb on free expression's side of the scale.

Proponents of the relativist view in this country sometimes claim a basis in laws other than the First Amendment, like the Equal Protection Clause of the Fourteenth Amendment, which guarantees equality under the law regardless of characteristics like race. Indeed, legal scholars have quarreled over which of these two constitutional principles should have primacy when they conflict. In the United States legal system, the First Amendment generally has prevailed, particularly in recent years, though not invariably.

Often, however, relativists base their views less in the law than in appeals to countervailing values, consequential harms, and common sense. "Why do people who want to overthrow the government have any rights under the Constitution they propose to usurp?" "Why should we allow neo-Nazis to hold public rallies that cause emotional injury and contribute nothing worthwhile to the exchange of ideas?" "Why must we permit a speaker on our campus who wants to express views that will deeply offend our students and make them feel unsafe and unwelcome here?" These questions have genuine moral force and implicitly ask whether existing First Amendment doctrine has gotten things right or has gone too far.

Proponents of the relativist view maintain that protection for free expression afforded by current United States law is excessive and unjustifiable. They say that First Amendment doctrine has lost sight of other compelling interests and has lost touch with our deeply held intuitions about what makes for a fair, just, welcoming, open, and healthy society. They contend that our laws need to provide greater protection against speech that every sensible person understands causes harm.

And that is where the relativist's problems begin. It is one thing to speak out against an idea or an expression of it. But it is something else altogether to translate that disapproval into a law that is clear, understandable, appropriately tailored, and reaches *only* the speech that our society wants to prohibit.

Laws come with benefits but also with costs. Relativists have struggled to translate their (legitimate) concerns and (honorable) impulses into laws where the good done clearly outweighs the damage. Unfortunately, to use Justice Frankfurter's memorable phrase, some of these efforts "burn the house to roast the pig."[1] Courts repeatedly have struck down laws against hate speech for just that reason: they go too far in what they constrain and the expressive casualties are too great.

Furthermore, regardless of their skepticism about free expression, relativists understand the importance of due process. To comply with basic notions of fairness, a law must put someone on reasonable notice of what it does and does not proscribe so he or she can act accordingly. It turns out, however, that defining a category of prohibited speech with that level of clarity presents extraordinary challenges.

The Supreme Court's prolonged (and arguably still unsuccessful) struggle to define "obscenity" offers a case in point, but numerous examples exist. For instance, many people would sympathize with the impulse to pass a law that punishes speech "promoting cruelty toward animals," but writing such a law in terms sufficiently clear to satisfy due process proves unexpectedly difficult. The simple phrase just quoted seems clear enough on its face, but if it appeared in a statute how would someone know whether the prohibition included an instructional bow-hunting video, or a documentary about bullfighting, or a pamphlet advocating for the declawing of housecats, or an advertisement for dog shock collars?

It might seem as though absolutists and relativists should not struggle as much as they do to find common ground. After all, to some extent their positions are simply a matter of degree. Absolutists must acknowledge that things other than speech also count and, therefore, they must allow for exceptions. Relativists cannot wholly dismiss the importance of free expression and, therefore, they must admit that regulating it poses unique difficulties. One would think that debates over free expression would routinely find their way toward shared territory and would progress accordingly. It has not worked out that way.

To some extent, the cause for this intransigence lies in the fact that conversations about free expression are usually conversations about something else as well. People often differ deeply and irreconcilably about how much value to place on the something else they are discussing. Flag-burning provides an excellent example. Debates over whether an individual should have the right to burn the American flag as an act of protest tend rather quickly to become arguments over the importance of the flag, the people who have died defending it, and respect for the flag as a credential of patriotism.

In recent years, advocates of the rights of minority groups frequently have protested decisions to allow speakers who espouse racist and other discriminatory viewpoints on a college or university campus. Within this context, debates over free expression almost immediately shift to arguments over whether the school

[1] Butler v. Michigan, 352 U.S. 380, 383 (1957).

administration places sufficient importance on the concerns of the targeted group. What begins as a discussion of free speech swiftly transforms into a discussion of such matters as structural discrimination, group isolation, and institutional commitment. Those who take a skeptical view of First Amendment doctrine may even question why the discussion *began* as one about free speech rather than as one about the targeted group's concerns.

A book on free expression cannot change this dynamic. Free speech serves as a vessel. People always will argue over the relative value of its cargo. We obviously cannot rank in importance the infinite variety of subject matters under discussion and would not presume to try. So, to the extent public discourse about free expression cannot progress because the disputants fix themselves in immovable positions about the various underlying subject matters, we can offer little beyond Tolstoy's trenchant observation that "people have eternally been mistaken and will be mistaken" and so perhaps a bit of humility is in order.

We are firmly convinced, however, that there is another reason why conversations about free expression often prove unproductive. In our view, many people do not have four tools that are critical to an informed and useful discussion of free speech. The first is an understanding of the core values that underlie the protection of freedom of expression. The second is a working knowledge of the legal doctrine that the United States Supreme Court has developed over time and of the basic principles that have emerged from that doctrine. The third is a recognition of the problems and counterintuitive results that necessarily follow from our embrace of those values and principles. And the last is an acknowledgment of the grave risks that we take when we depart from those principles and abandon the values they serve.

In many conversations about free speech, the absence of these tools results in an unfortunate and unproductive reductionism in both camps: the absolutists think of free expression as just about everything while the relativists think of it as just another thing. Our public discourse around free expression has suffered greatly as a result. We think access to these four tools can help us do better. This book seeks to provide it, with a focus on United States law.

This book strives to help readers achieve a stronger, clearer, and more nuanced understanding of free expression. It seeks to foster a better comprehension of what's at stake when our laws limit free expression and also when they don't. Although the book traverses a variety of challenging fields – political philosophy, Supreme Court history, legal doctrine – we have labored to make it interesting and accessible to any intelligent reader.

We view this as a work of scholarship but especially of *public* scholarship, intended to facilitate conversations between thoughtful people about an important collection of questions: Why do we protect free expression? Do we afford it too much protection, or not enough? How has the Supreme Court thought about it for the past couple hundred years? What has the Court gotten right and when has it fumbled? How should we think about free expression when other important values come into conflict with it? Should we create exceptions? For what kinds of speech? How should we fashion them? Can we create exceptions without inadvertently compromising protection for speech that we think matters? What free expression problems continue to challenge us? How might they be solved? Are they solvable at all, or are they an unavoidable consequence of a selection of certain values and principles? What do the approaches of other countries have to teach us about free expression? If the United States is exceptional in its protection of free speech, is that a source of pride, or trouble, or both?

We have a great deal of territory to cover in this book. Because we have written it for a broad audience, we have tried to pass through the terrain expeditiously and with a minimum of detours. We have forgone some fascinating side roads as a result, but we believe that, just as the perfect can become the enemy of the good, the comprehensive can become the enemy of the comprehensible.

This book has four parts.

Part I considers the core values that underlie protection for free expression. We review the most important and persuasive of the theories of the value of free expression that have been advanced. We begin with theories that treat free expression as an instrumental good – that is, as having value because it promotes something else, like truth-finding or informed participation in the democratic process. Then, we consider theories that treat it as an intrinsic good – that is, as having value in itself, for example because it constitutes a core component of human dignity and individual autonomy.

Part I also considers two other value-related ideas. The first is that free expression stands in close – but perhaps sometimes subtle – relation to other values and so can help shed light on their importance. To return to an example cited earlier, limitations on free expression raise concerns about due process that have much broader application. In this sense, free expression has not just instrumental and intrinsic value but instructional value as well. Our struggles with free expression can help us understand other things that matter a great deal to us.

The second point is that our society has come to embrace free expression as a public good that transcends existing legal parameters. In other words, our society finds the values that drive free expression so morally compelling that it applies them even when the law of the First Amendment does not require it. Thus, people often invoke freedom of expression as a value (or even as a "right") in circumstances where First Amendment doctrine does not control the outcome, such as when the entity seeking to limit the speech is a private one rather than a state or federal government actor.

It is tempting to dismiss those invocations of the First Amendment as simple misunderstandings of law. We believe, however, that they reflect something much more complex, deeper, and more interesting. As a society, free expression has moral force that works well beyond the limitations of legal doctrine. Our embrace of free expression therefore is reflected not just in the law but also – and perhaps as importantly – in a layperson's "Everyday First Amendment."

The Everyday First Amendment provides guidance as to how members of our society should deal with each other as human beings. It is driven by a normative vision, not a legal one. This dynamic helps explain why debates about free expression prove so challenging: they are often less conversations about what *the law is* than they are conversations about *what we think is right* in a deep moral sense.

In Part II, we turn our attention to legal history. We discuss the evolution of the Supreme Court's thinking about free speech over three periods: prior to 1919, from 1919 to 1963, and from 1964 to the present. These three periods reflect a history of increased protection for speech – even speech that may seem highly logical to want to suppress. Along the way, we show how the extraordinarily protective principles that emerged over time relate to the values discussed in Part I.

Then, in Part III, we discuss in greater detail the basic principles that flow from this body of case law: a powerful hostility toward prior restraints and content-based regulations; a deep suspicion of laws that are vague; a grave concern about laws so broad that they reach speech we want to protect as well as speech we want to limit; and an imperative to afford breathing space to speech, such that we end up protecting some speech that may not deserve it in order to make sure we protect all the speech that does. We explain how these first principles advance the values explored in Part I of the book. And we show why these principles so commonly result in the invalidation of laws aimed at speech, including speech we may think of as having little or no merit or even as being corrosive to our society.

Finally, we consider some of the exceptions to First Amendment protection that the Court has identified. In the 1942 case of *Chaplinsky* v. *New Hampshire*,[2] the Court famously listed as such exceptions "the lewd and obscene, the profane, the libelous, and insulting or 'fighting' words." We show that over time the Court has interpreted these exceptions very narrowly and has extended substantial protection to a great deal of speech that people would intuitively think should fall outside the shelter of the First Amendment. The narrowing of these exceptions was, however, a natural consequence of the core values discussed in Part I and the basic principles discussed in Part III.

Part IV of the book explores some of the challenges that trouble our current First Amendment jurisprudence and our debates over free speech. These include such issues as campaign finance, speech in the education context, hate speech, and online speech. The legal and moral complexity of these issues has led to a good deal of confusion among members of the general public – and occasionally among Supreme Court justices.

In Part IV, we discuss why the core values and basic principles that underlie our free speech jurisprudence make these free expression issues so difficult. And we

[2] Chaplinsky v. New Hampshire, 315 U.S. 568 (1942).

explain why departing from those values and principles to address current challenges (while understandably tempting) may lead us into even greater dilemmas.

In the pages that follow, we spend much of our time considering legal doctrine. Before getting there, however, we begin in the first chapters with a foundational question of political and moral science: Why do we protect free expression, anyway?

PART I

Core Values

1

Instrumental Value Arguments for Free Speech

Hard cases raise hard questions. Take, for example, *Snyder* v. *Phelps*.[1] That case involved picketing by protestors from the Westboro Baptist Church on public grounds near the funeral of Marine Lance Corporal Matthew Snyder, who died in Iraq in the line of duty. His father, offended by the demonstrators' signs, sued Westboro for intentional infliction of emotional distress and other claims. A jury awarded him millions of dollars in damages, but the Supreme Court found the speech protected and reversed the verdict.

The members of Westboro make up a small congregation based in Kansas. They believe that God hates the United States for its tolerance of homosexuality and punishes it through military losses and casualties. They convey their beliefs in virulent and uncompromising terms. For example, the picket signs they carried near Matthew's funeral included such slogans as "America is doomed," "God hates the USA," "Thank God for 911," "You're going to hell," and "Thank God for dead soldiers."

The Supreme Court acknowledged that Westboro's speech was hurtful and had added to the "already incalculable grief" of Matthew's father. It further recognized that, while Westboro thought America was morally flawed, "many Americans might feel the same about Westboro." And it conceded that Westboro's "contribution to public discourse" was probably "negligible."

The Supreme Court nevertheless found the speech protected. Furthermore, the Court did not treat Westboro's expression as if it occupied the borderlands of the First Amendment, having somehow crept across the line into safe territory. To the contrary, it located Westboro's speech right at the center of First Amendment protection. When the Supreme Court decides a case involving a close legal question, the vote is often five to four; in *Snyder*, it ruled in favor of Westboro by a vote of eight to one. The Court did not view *Snyder* as a hard case.

[1] Snyder v. Phelps, 562 U.S. 443 (2011).

Cases like *Snyder* v. *Phelps* understandably lead people to ask why our constitutional doctrine gives such strong and expansive protection to freedom of speech, especially to speech that appears to contribute nothing worthwhile to public discourse. It is a valid question. The speech at issue in that case had nothing to recommend it. And *Snyder* is just one of many cases where courts have protected speech that seems obviously to have little or no merit and to do much more harm than good.

Some answers to the question of why we give broad protection to free expression depend on the idea that speech is a good in itself. We look at those arguments in Chapter 2. We call those "intrinsic value" arguments.

The arguments we examine in this chapter make a different point. They contend that we afford such extensive immunity to speech because of other values that it serves. In other words, the theories we look at here focus on freedom of expression as an essential tool in achieving something else. We call these "instrumentalist" theories.

The most widely acknowledged and durable of the various instrumentalist theories argues that free expression is valuable because it provides a means to help us (both as individuals and as a society) discover the truth. Finding the truth, in turn, enables us to do lots of things that we think are very important: make better decisions about our lives; provide better guidance and counsel to others; be better parents and partners and citizens; offer better contributions to debate within our deliberative democracy; achieve better government; and so on. As the Supreme Court declared in *Bose Corp.* v. *Consumers Union*, the First Amendment "presupposes that the freedom to speak one's mind is not only an aspect of individual liberty – and thus a good unto itself – but also is essential to the common quest for truth and the vitality of society as a whole."[2]

The most famous and enduring articulation of the truth-finding theory comes in the dissenting opinion filed by Justice Oliver Wendell Holmes in *United States* v. *Abrams*.[3] We should note at the outset that the majority decision in *Abrams* reflects a very different approach to free speech than we have today. Indeed, viewed through our current lens, the outcome in *Abrams* seems almost unthinkable.

In that case, five individuals printed and circulated pamphlets that were critical of President Woodrow Wilson, condemned capitalism, and urged workers to join in a general strike. By contemporary standards of public discourse, these materials seem like garden variety political hyperbole that is unlikely to result in much of anything, let alone to threaten national security. Today, we encounter on a regular basis speech that is more toxic and incendiary.

In our current legal and political environment, the notion that the defendants could go to prison for making such statements is incomprehensible. Nevertheless,

2 Bose Corp. v. Consumers Union of the United States, 466 U.S. 485, 503 (1983).

3 Abrams v. United States, 250 U.S. 616 (1919).

the defendants were criminally charged under the federal Espionage Act, convicted, and sentenced to twenty years of incarceration. A strong majority of the Supreme Court – seven justices – upheld this result.

Justice Holmes crafted an opinion that has so carried the favorable judgment of history that people who refer to it sometimes forget that it was a dissent. Even First Amendment scholars occasionally struggle to remember who wrote the majority opinion. Ironically, the author was Justice John Hessin Clarke, who usually voted with Holmes and whose record generally reflected a progressive point of view. In this case, Clarke and Holmes dramatically parted company.

Holmes himself had not always been a great friend of the First Amendment. To the contrary, in *Patterson* v. *Colorado*,[4] he wrote an opinion upholding a newspaper editor's contempt conviction for printing articles and cartoons insulting the Colorado Supreme Court. In *Fox* v. *Washington*,[5] he wrote an opinion upholding the defendant's misdemeanor conviction for printing an article in praise of nudity. And in *Schenck* v. *United States*,[6] he wrote an opinion upholding the defendant's conviction – under the Espionage Act – for distributing a circular that was critical of military conscription and that encouraged resistance to the draft. We take a closer look at some of these cases in Chapter 6.

A substantial body of scholarship, including Thomas Healy's book, *The Great Dissent*, has explored how and why Holmes changed his mind.[7] Multiple factors appear to have had an influence: friends and fellow judges lobbied him; he studied the work of European legal and political philosophers; and he grew concerned with overzealous efforts by the federal government to stifle dissent. For our purposes, the critical fact is that, starting with *Abrams*, his position on free expression took an entirely different course, and, as a result, he wrote arguably the most important opinion in the history of the First Amendment.

The central passage in Holmes's dissent begins with a trenchant observation about human nature: "Persecution for the expression of opinions seems to me perfectly logical." Holmes acknowledged that when people have strong convictions they naturally want to embed their beliefs in law and to "sweep away all opposition." He pointed out, however, that today's certainties have an unsettling tendency to become tomorrow's absurdities. As Holmes poetically put it, "time has upset many fighting faiths." In sum, no matter how firm our beliefs, and our corresponding antagonism toward dissent, we must leave room for the possibility that we could be wrong. Our theory of free speech must leave room for it as well.

Holmes explained his theory through the use of a metaphor that courts and scholars have come to describe as "the marketplace of ideas." "The ultimate good

4 Patterson v. Colorado, 205 U.S. 454 (1907).
5 Fox v. Washington, 236 U.S. 273 (1915).
6 Schenck v. United States, 249 U.S. 47 (1919).
7 Thomas Healy, The Great Dissent (2013).

desired," he said, "is better reached by free trade in ideas [and] the best test of truth is the power of the thought to get itself accepted in the power of the market." In this model, we allow as many differing ideas as possible to compete for our allegiance. We analyze, debate, and deliberate over them. Through this process, we come to reject falsehood and embrace truth, and to cast off inferior opinions in favor of better ones.

Although Holmes gave us the most famous articulation of this theory, he did not originate it. John Milton's *Areopagitica* of 1644 and John Stuart Mill's *On Liberty* of 1859 had made essentially the same argument. Indeed, in later cases the Supreme Court cited both Milton and Mill in support of this conceptual construct.[8] Nevertheless, legal scholars have recognized the singular and canonical place of the *Abrams* dissent in First Amendment case law, contending that it "continues to influence our thinking about free speech more than any other document."[9]

Because of its confidence that the marketplace will (at least eventually) reject falsehood and bad ideas, this theory ends up protecting an extraordinarily broad range of expression. Thus, although we may find the speech at issue in *Snyder* to have no redeeming value whatsoever, the marketplace of ideas still allows it in. And why not? After all, the argument goes, sooner or later the competition among differing ideas will reveal worthless ones for what they are and will force them out of favor.

People sometimes argue that such worthless ideas contribute nothing to the marketplace and so should preemptively be excluded from it. On some occasions, the Supreme Court has allowed its own language to drift in this direction. For example, in explaining why the First Amendment does not protect some speech, the Supreme Court in *Chaplinsky* v. *New Hampshire*[10] declared that certain "utterances are no essential part of any exposition of ideas, and are of such slight social value as a step to truth that any benefit that may be derived from them is clearly outweighed by the social interest in order and morality."

This argument envisions ideas going through some sort of qualifying round before they can enter the competition. Only ideas deemed good enough get in. If objective criteria and omniscient decision makers existed to judge such a preliminary assessment, then perhaps that approach would make sense – although we will shortly encounter a theory that explains why it doesn't. But objective criteria are not available and subjectivity necessarily infects decisions about value. As the Supreme Court observed in *Cohen* v. *California*,[11] a case we consider at some length in Chapter 2, "one man's vulgarity is another man's lyric."

[8] *See* New York Times Co. v. Sullivan, 376 U.S. 254, 279 n. 19 (1964).
[9] Thomas Healy, The Great Dissent 7 (2013).
[10] Chaplinsky v. New Hampshire, 315 U.S. 568 (1942).
[11] Cohen v. California, 403 U.S. 15 (1971).

Indeed, one of the primary strengths of the marketplace of ideas theory lies in its rejection of authoritative selection, where the government chooses the ideas that are worthy of entertaining. The notion of a qualifying round, however, builds exactly that dynamic into the marketplace. Under such a model, we would be allowed to embrace whatever ideas we liked – as long as they appeared on the government's preapproved menu.

The marketplace of ideas theory has its weaknesses. This would not have come as news to Oliver Wendell Holmes. Holmes was not a dreamy-eyed idealist who failed to understand how imperfectly the world actually works. Nor was Holmes guilty of indulging in the exact state of mind he criticized at the beginning of his opinion – an unquestioning belief in the infallible rightness of his position. To the contrary, toward the end of his *Abrams* dissent he observed: "That, at any rate, is the theory of our Constitution. It is an experiment, as all life is an experiment."[12]

Opinions differ about how well the experiment has gone. Adherents claim that the marketplace of ideas theory remains our best justification for freedom of expression, despite the counterintuitive results we see in cases like *Snyder*. Critics have argued in turn that the theory incorporates a number of false assumptions and, as a result, has not yielded the results its architects envisioned.[13]

A comprehensive catalog of objections to the marketplace of ideas model lies beyond the scope of this book, but we can identify some of the principal criticisms. The theory assumes that all ideas have equal access to the marketplace; in fact, substantial barriers to entry can exist, particularly in the case of minority viewpoints. The theory assumes that participants in the marketplace want to find the truth; in fact, human beings often have other agendas. The theory assumes that those who *do* seek the truth have the intelligence and rational capacity to sort through the choices; in fact, good critical-thinking skills often seem in short supply in public discourse. The theory assumes that ideas and information arrive at a manageable pace and in manageable quantities; in fact, many people (particularly today) feel inundated with more inputs than they can process. And, finally, the theory assumes that these all-welcoming, truth-seeking, reason-applying, critical-thinking, deluge-managing individuals will act in a manner consistent with what the marketplace tells them; in fact, all too often they don't.

One of the difficulties in productively moving arguments forward regarding free speech now becomes evident. Advocates for free expression often invoke, whether knowingly or not, a marketplace of ideas ideology and framework. Skeptics can sensibly respond, however, that this theory doesn't align with their experience. At

[12] Holmes expressed a similarly reality-bound viewpoint on the very first page of his book THE COMMON LAW (1881), where he declared that "The life of the law has not been logic; it has been experience."

[13] *See, e.g.*, Leonard M. Niehoff and Devva Shah, *The Resilience of Noxious Doctrine: The 2016 Election, the Marketplace of Ideas, and the Obstinacy of Bias*, 22:2 MICH. J. RACE & L. 243 (2017) and authorities citied there.

Conversation about lack of education in rural America w/ Prof. Sullivan

one point in his *Areopagitica*, John Milton asks: Who has ever known truth to lose to falsehood when they have been put "in a free and open encounter?" Many of us would raise our hands and say: "I have."

Nevertheless, defenders of the marketplace of ideas theory have some fairly powerful rebuttals to critics. They point out that the alternative to a free marketplace is a restricted one, where the government decides which thoughts and facts people can share and receive. And, they contend, the evils of government regulation of speech are even greater and graver than those we encounter with the marketplace of ideas. This argument has powerful practical and moral force.

In his majority opinion in *West Virginia State Board of Education* v. *Barnette*,[14] a case we will cite and quote with some frequency, Supreme Court Justice Robert Jackson declared that "if there is any fixed star in our constitutional constellation, it is that no official, high or petty, can prescribe what shall be orthodox in politics, nationalism, religion, or other matters of opinion." The marketplace of ideas model may falter from time to time, but it at least keeps that star fixed in place. A statement often attributed to Winston Churchill (he was actually quoting someone else) holds that "democracy is the worst form of government except for all those other forms that have been tried"; we might say the same of the marketplace of ideas. If you do not like how it works, wait until you try totalitarianism and government censorship.

Over the years, additional instrumentalist theories have emerged that similarly support protecting an expansive range of speech, even speech that many people find offensive and meritless. First Amendment scholar Lee Bollinger sets forth one such theory in his book *The Tolerant Society*.[15] Because his theory offers a distinctive and helpful perspective, we explore it here.

As discussed above, one common rejoinder to the marketplace model contends that some ideas have little or no value but do real harm in the world. Their bad qualities plainly outweigh their good. Therefore, the argument goes, we should not allow such ideas the privilege of competing for our attention. This argument has some facial appeal, but, as noted earlier, it quickly raises important concerns about who gets to decide the relative worthiness of ideas and who gets to determine the criteria that will be applied.

Bollinger takes a different approach. He effectively assumes, for the sake of argument, that some speech exists that makes no meaningful contribution to the marketplace of ideas *and* that we can figure out which speech falls into that category. Perhaps neo-Nazis marching in a neighborhood of Holocaust survivors, an event that Bollinger considers at length in his book, provides an example. The provocative question he poses is whether such speech has value to us as a society even if it is ideologically bankrupt.

[14] West Virginia State Board of Education v. Barnette, 319 U.S. 624 (1943).

[15] Lee Bollinger, The Tolerant Society (1986).

Bollinger argues that it does. Under his theory, extreme speech is not just a useless irritant that we let into the marketplace because we can't come up with satisfactory protocols for keeping it out. Rather, extreme speech has value in how it can lead us to think and behave. Bollinger shifts attention from the value that lies in the speech itself to the value that lies in our learning how to manage our reactions to it. In his view, free speech helps us develop ways of thinking that push back against our natural intolerance and that carry with them substantial social benefits. Free speech – perhaps *particularly* speech at the extreme edges – makes ours a more tolerant, and therefore a better, society.

Other instrumentalist theories have taken a narrower approach, arguing for protection of particular forms of speech that advance specific values. One such theory contends that we must allow for free expression because of the indispensable role it plays in informed self-government. Just as the marketplace of ideas theory is inextricably linked with Oliver Wendell Holmes and *Abrams*, this self-governance theory is strongly associated with the philosopher and civil libertarian Alexander Meiklejohn and his book *Free Speech and Its Relation to Self-government*.[16]

In essence, the self-governance theory maintains that a right to free expression is a necessary part of a democracy. In a democratic system, the people ultimately exercise sovereign authority; government officials serve the electorate, not the other way around. The people need to share and receive as much information as possible so they can make informed decisions about which candidates to elect, which proposals to support, which reforms to advance, and so on.

Theories based on a narrower rationale than the marketplace of ideas or societal tolerance may have some appeal insofar as they make more modest claims about the speech the First Amendment protects. But the connection between the text of the First Amendment and the self-governance theory seems tenuous at best. On its face, the phrase "no law abridging the freedom of speech" sweeps much more broadly than does a model that protects only a discrete subcategory of expression that has political utility.

Furthermore, speech that furthers self-governance may turn out not to be much of a discrete subcategory after all. For the electorate to make informed decisions about taxation, environmental policy, armed conflict, and funding for the arts, it needs to know something about economics, science, military history, and the value of poetry and Impressionist painting. Trying to identify the point at which speech ceases to relate to self-governance poses substantial, maybe insurmountable, line-drawing problems.

Furthermore, the self-governance rationale does not dispose of many of the types of speech that we may feel most inclined to try to prohibit. People may find the speech of the Westboro Baptist Church at issue in *Snyder* worthless and morally obnoxious, but it clearly pertains to matters of public policy that the electorate must

[16] Alexander Meiklejohn, Free Speech and Its Relation to Self-government (1948).

decide. That's precisely why the Supreme Court held the speech protected. The same holds true with respect to the speech of neo-Nazis, white supremacists, and others whose political ideologies many people find odious but that remain political ideologies nevertheless.

Another narrower instrumentalist justification for free expression comes from First Amendment scholar Vincent Blasi. Blasi has written expansively on First Amendment theory, but one of his arguments focuses on a distinct power that the state has within our political system – the authority to use violence against human beings for a variety of ends, such as waging war and imposing capital punishment. In his view, free speech serves a critical "checking" function against the abuse of this dangerous monopoly.[17]

Blasi underscores the importance of having an assembly of well-financed, well-organized, and thoroughly independent watchdogs – the media – to serve this function. If Blasi's theory has merit, then the current state of journalism gives cause for grave concern. Today, some news outlets seem more like extensions of political parties than independent watchdogs, many media entities struggle to survive financially, and cuts to the staff necessary to support strong investigative journalism are common.

Many champions of free expression have declined to settle on only one justification, broad or narrow. Instead, they embrace multiple theories, some of which may have greater explanatory power than others in individual cases, depending on the speech and circumstances in question. This approach may lack the purity of one that clings to a single theory, but it allows us to draw on the rationale that best fits the situation at hand and it prevents us from making a fetish of any of them.

One of the most majestic of these expressions comes in Justice Louis Brandeis's concurring opinion in *Whitney* v. *California*,[18] which deserves quoting at some length:

> Those who won our independence believed that the final end of the State was to make men free to develop their faculties; and that in its government the deliberative forces should prevail over the arbitrary. They valued liberty both as an end and as a means. They believed liberty to be the secret of happiness and courage to be the secret of liberty. They believed that freedom to think as you will and to speak as you think are means indispensable to the discovery and spread of political truth; that without free speech and assembly discussion would be futile; that with them, discussion affords ordinarily adequate protection against the dissemination of noxious doctrine; that the greatest menace to freedom is an inert people; that public discussion is a political duty; and that this should be a fundamental principle of the American government. They recognized the risks to which all human institutions are subject. But they knew that order cannot be secured merely through fear of

[17] Vincent Blasi, *The Checking Value in the First Amendment*, 2:3 AM.B. FOUND. RES. J. 521 (1977).

[18] Whitney v. California, 274 U.S. 357 (1927).

> punishment for its infraction; that it is hazardous to discourage thought, hope and imagination; that fear breeds repression; that repression breeds hate; that hate menaces stable government; that the path of safety lies in the opportunity to discuss freely supposed grievances and proposed remedies; and that the fitting remedy for evil counsels is good ones. Believing in the power of reason as applied through public discussion, they eschewed silence coerced by law – the argument of force in its worst form. Recognizing the occasional tyrannies of governing majorities, they amended the Constitution so that free speech and assembly should be guaranteed.

Some of the arguments advanced here should sound familiar to you. In this passage, Brandeis touches on the themes of truth-finding and self-governance, as we have discussed.

But Brandeis offers a panoply of additional instrumentalist arguments in support of free expression as well. Freedom of speech, he contends, keeps us from becoming inert and ineffectual. It allows people to let off steam so they don't explode into violence out of the frustrations that come from repression. It empowers minority viewpoints against the "occasional tyrannies" of majorities. It gives us our most effective tool against the speech we hate: more speech.

Brandeis's opinion in *Whitney* is rich in ideas. And one could argue that it has grown in importance for another reason he probably would not have anticipated. That reason relates to his religious identity and the struggles he encountered as a result.

In contemporary conversations about free expression, particularly on college campuses, members of minority groups sometimes object that many pro-free-expression arguments come from a position of privilege. This is an important insight. After all, talk about how truth will eventually prevail in the marketplace of ideas sounds great if you're not one of the people who has to bear the burden of falsehood's interim reign. And celebrating the characteristics that are cultivated by a tolerance of offensive speech sounds terrific if hate doesn't have you in its crosshairs.

A passage from Meiklejohn demonstrates the point. In *Free Speech and Its Relation to Self-government*, he declares that "To be afraid of ideas, any idea, is to be unfit for self-government. Any such suppression of ideas about the common good, the First Amendment condemns with this absolute disapproval." Surely, this constitutes an extravagant overstatement that unfairly discounts the concerns of minority groups.

An individual of a particular color, religion, or gender can (and perhaps even should) experience rational fear in the face of racism, anti-Semitism, and misogyny. That sensible reaction hardly disqualifies them from engaging in thoughtful and productive decision making in the service of self-governance. Nor does it suggest that the individual will find themselves irresistibly drawn toward censorship. To fear extremist speech is one thing; to try to suppress that speech through law is something else altogether.

Brandeis fully understood that freedom of expression does not come without costs. To the contrary, it demands substantial courage, particularly from those on whom it makes the greatest demands. Indeed, his opinion in *Whitney* includes repeated references to fear and courage:

> Fear of serious injury cannot alone justify suppression of free speech and assembly. Men feared witches and burnt women. It is the function of speech to free men from the bondage of irrational fears . . . Those who won our independence by revolution were not cowards. They did not fear political change. They did not exalt order at the cost of liberty.

Importantly, these words did not come from the easy armchair of someone who sat above the fray. Brandeis experienced virulent anti-Semitism throughout his life: in law school, in practice, and on the Supreme Court. To take just one example, his high court colleague Justice James C. McReynolds harbored such strident anti-Semitic views that he refused to speak to his Jewish colleague – for three years.[19]

When Brandeis extolled the value of freedom of expression, he did so fully understanding the challenges that this approach poses for those who find themselves on the receiving end of hate. He also understood that silence enforced through laws adopted by the majority threaten even greater dangers to those who lack such political power. We might see a connection here between Bollinger and Brandeis, a joint recognition that free speech presses us to become better people, more tolerant ourselves and also braver in the face of the intolerance of others. It is a prescription not easily fulfilled.

The theories explored above help clarify why contemporary conversations about free expression so often stall. An absolutist advocates for an approach consistent with the marketplace ideas: everyone should be able to say what they want and the best ideas and truest narratives will prevail. A relativist responds that it doesn't always work out that way and, besides, some ideas do not deserve a chance to compete. The participants arrive at a stalemate because their discussion turns on whether the speech in question expresses an idea of sufficient value to get a turn in the marketplace.

To keep the conversation going – and to cultivate a more appropriately elaborate free speech theory and First Amendment doctrine – we need to introduce additional concepts. We must recognize the difficulties inherent in declaring some ideas worthy of expression and others not. We need to understand that placing those judgments in the hands of the majority (where a democracy would locate them if we did not have a constitutional provision like the First Amendment) would inescapably lead to dreadful abuses. Indeed, the First Amendment exists to protect minority viewpoints, and history includes numerous critical instances of it doing so, from the

[19] *See* Scott Jaschik, *Centre Removes Name of Bigot from Building*, Inside Higher Ed. (Feb. 7, 2017).

early labor marches to the civil rights protests of the 1960s to the more recent demonstrations of the #MeToo and Black Lives Matter movements. Majority speech, in contrast, does not need the First Amendment, because the majority will not exercise its political power to restrain its own expression.

And still *more* concepts and *deeper* thinking are needed to move the conversation forward. We have to acknowledge that the expression of ideas that have no merit in themselves may advance other values. Such speech allows people to let off the steam that might otherwise fuel violence. It fosters the skill of clear and critical analysis that is necessary to explain why an idea should be rejected. It cultivates the socially and individually essential qualities of tolerance and courage.

At the same time, however, we have to recognize the corrosive power of certain speech. We have to acknowledge that the burdens of free expression fall more heavily on some groups and individuals than on others. In the end, we may conclude that the contributions free expression makes to our political and personal lives warrant the costs that it exacts. But an absolutist who will not pause to think seriously about who suffers those costs, and what we need to do to help and support them and show solidarity with them, will have little chance of persuading a relativist of the rightness of their position. Anyone who makes the First Amendment into a heartless and soulless commandment will struggle to defend it.

In this chapter, we have addressed instrumentalist arguments for free expression – arguments that support the principle because of other values that it serves. Over the years, courts and scholars have advanced a different kind of argument as well: an argument that free expression has intrinsic value. We turn to that argument next.

2

Intrinsic Value Arguments for Free Speech

In Chapter 1, we cited the Supreme Court's decision in *Cohen* v. *California*[1] and quoted its famous admonition that "one man's vulgarity is another man's lyric." Reasonable people could question the lyricism of the speech at issue in *Cohen*, but it plainly qualified as vulgar. In that case, one Paul Robert Cohen expressed his opposition to the Vietnam War by wearing in a public courthouse a jacket that had the words "Fuck the Draft" emblazoned across its back.

Cohen was charged with violating a statute that prohibited anyone from "maliciously and willfully disturbing the peace" by engaging in "offensive conduct." The Supreme Court upheld Cohen's right to wear his jacket and to convey his message, his coarse choice of language notwithstanding. Ironically, Chief Justice Burger tried to keep the offending word from being uttered during oral argument in his own courthouse by telling the lawyers that they did not need to recite the facts of the case. Cohen's counsel nevertheless repeated the word while answering the first question put to him.[2]

In an opinion that was, perhaps surprisingly, written by the elderly and conservative Justice John Marshall Harlan, the Supreme Court recognized that Cohen's jacket conveyed an idea: his strenuous disapproval of the draft. And that idea related to a political issue of great public interest and concern, particularly in 1971: the wisdom of conscription during the conflict in Vietnam. The result in the case might, therefore, seem unremarkable under the marketplace of ideas theory. Cohen injected a political viewpoint into the public sphere that deserved a chance to compete with opposing perspectives.

Nevertheless, the fit between Cohen's speech and the marketplace of ideas theory seems imperfect. After all, whatever its merits, Cohen's idea did not come to its

[1] Cohen v. California, 403 U.S. 1971.

[2] *See* Thomas G. Krattenmaker, *Looking Back at Cohen* v. *California: A 40-Year Retrospective from Inside the Court,* 20 William & Mary Bill of Rights Journal 651, 654 n. 17 (2012).

audience as a well-developed argument. To the contrary, it consisted of just three words, one of which was an expletive. Nor would its audience likely have understood the speech as an invitation into calm and reasoned debate over military policy. The jacket seemed less like *The Federalist Papers* and more like a primal scream.

It is, therefore, worthwhile to ask whether better rationales exist for protecting Cohen's speech. We might, for example, argue that this speech provided a critical safety valve for feelings so powerful that they could lead to violence if repressed. In this spirit, the Supreme Court noted that Cohen's jacket conveyed not just an idea but an "otherwise inexpressible emotion."

Such an argument, however, protects Cohen's speech only because the alternative seems socially riskier. It rests on our fear of Cohen and of combustible people like him and of what they might do if they get frustrated, not our respect for their individual agency and dignity. It fails to capture the value inherent in Cohen having the right to express something that he believes very deeply and to do so in the strongest words he can muster.

To get at that value, we need to move from instrumentalist theories to theories that focus on speech's intrinsic worth. Theories in the latter category see free expression not just as a means to a good but as a good in itself. Of course, with respect to a particular example of speech, both instrumentalist and intrinsic value arguments may apply – they do not present mutually exclusive alternatives. But when the speech at hand does not align very well with instrumentalist theories, we need to consider whether free speech has intrinsic value *apart* from the good it may otherwise do in the world.

As a route into such arguments, it may help to highlight something about the text of the First Amendment that could otherwise escape our attention, particularly in the context of a discussion focused on free expression. It is this: the First Amendment addresses not just freedom of speech and of the press but a number of other rights as well. It recognizes an individual's right to exercise his or her religion, the related right to be free from a state-established faith, the right to assemble, and the right to petition the government for the redress of grievances. The Supreme Court has also inferred from this text, and from these expressed rights, an implicit right to freedom of association, even though the word "association" does not appear in the First Amendment.[3]

We have grown so accustomed to the fact that the First Amendment includes these various rights that we may fail to ask an important question: How, if at all, are they related to each other? The connection between them is less than obvious. Someone's right to share in communion at their church does not seem connected to their right to urge a state legislature to fund road repair. We can indeed, however, identify a fundamental relation between these principles.

3 *See* Leonard M. Niehoff, *Policing Hate Speech and Extremism: A Taxonomy of Arguments in Opposition*, 52 U. MICH. J. L. REF. 859, 864–865 (2019).

Perhaps the clearest and most developed expression of that relation comes to us in John Stuart Mill's book *On Liberty*, which we mentioned in Chapter 1. Mill saw the concept of liberty as concerning, first and foremost, an "inward domain of consciousness," that is, "liberty of conscience, in the most comprehensive sense." That inward domain includes "liberty of thought and feeling; absolute freedom of opinion and sentiment on all subjects, practical or speculative, scientific, moral or theological." In Mill's view, the state has no legitimate claim on controlling this territory. It must remain off limits from government interference.

In numerous opinions, the Supreme Court has followed this reasoning and has held human conscience inviolate. Indeed, throughout its history the Court has described only one freedom as absolute: freedom of conscience. "Freedom of conscience," the Court has declared, "*cannot* be restricted by law."[4] It has announced: "Courts, no more than Constitutions, can intrude into the consciences of men or compel them to believe contrary to their faith or think contrary to their convictions."[5]

Such a principle might, in theory, preclude certain extreme government practices, like psychological torture. But, to the extent that these noble sentiments offer protection against public officials regulating the internal thought processes of citizens, they do not seem to guarantee much. After all, "at the risk of stating the obvious, the government cannot control individual conscience in any event."[6] Or, as First Amendment scholar Harry Kalven put it, "when belief is silent, it would seem protected not by law, but by the sheer impracticability of policing it."[7]

For freedom of conscience to mean anything, we must therefore protect its expressions. We cannot imprison conscience in the metaphysical realm, ostensibly honored but practically mute and impotent. An approach that says "believe what you want, just don't say or do anything about it" drains conscience of its defining place in the identity, character, and dignity of individual human beings.

We can now see the connection between those various rights listed in the First Amendment: they all relate to the existential expression of human conscience. How do we put our conscience to work in the world? We speak – whether as individuals or as an institutional press. We worship – in the way that we think best, or not at all if that's what we prefer. We assemble – gathering with people who share our values and goals. We petition for change – making our voices heard to a government that, at least in theory, answers to its people. We associate – joining with others to speak, worship, assemble, and petition.

Of course, once conscience puts on its boots and goes out into the world to take action, the calculus changes. At that point, the state has the capacity to impose

4 Cantwell v. Connecticut, 310 U.S. 296, 303 (1940) (emphasis supplied).

5 Jones v. Opelika, 316 U.S. 584, 593–594 (1942).

6 Leonard M. Niehoff, *Policing Hate Speech and Extremism: A Taxonomy of Arguments in Opposition*, 52 U. Mich. J. L. Ref. 859, 894 (2019).

7 Harry Kalven, Jr., A Worthy Tradition: Freedom of Speech in America 332 (1988).

restrictions and may have valid reasons for doing so. As the Supreme Court has observed, the First Amendment "embraces two concepts – freedom to believe and freedom to act. The first is absolute but, in the nature of things, the second cannot be. Conduct remains subject to regulation for the protection of society."[8] Mill similarly recognized that, when someone acts upon their conscience, the possibility of harm to others arises and government intervention may be necessary and appropriate.

An example of this issue arose in 2020, when states began requiring individuals to wear masks to help prevent the spread of Covid-19. Some people refused, arguing that doing so went against their conscience and their freedom to make such choices for themselves. But, of course, that decision had an effect on the well-being of others, potentially imperiling their health.

First Amendment doctrine is so rich, complex, and interesting because it struggles with the immensely difficult questions that this tension presents. When should the government have the power to interfere with expressions of human conscience? If the government must leave conscience alone, when and why may it, nevertheless, restrict its manifestations, including speech? We spend the remainder of this book analyzing how courts and theorists have tried to answer those queries. Some answers prove better than others.

For purposes of this chapter, however, the important point is that we place such a high value on speech because of its indispensable role in bringing human conscience out of the abstract realm and into the real world. In turn, we hold conscience sacrosanct because it defines who we are, what we believe, how we want to live, which ideas we embrace or condemn, and so on. We cannot respect, honor, and protect someone's dignity as a human being if we do not preserve their ability to express their conscience. Free speech thus has intrinsic value because it empowers people to mobilize their conscience and to be fully and freely whoever they are – and aspire to become – regardless of any other good it may do.

A number of legal scholars have advanced arguments along these lines, most notably Thomas Emerson. Emerson proposed what he called an "Individual Self-Fulfillment Theory" of the First Amendment.[9] Although Emerson recognized the contributions of other free speech theories, including the marketplace of ideas, he gave self-fulfillment primacy of place.

Emerson rooted his self-fulfillment theory in two ideas. The first is the "widely accepted premise of Western thought that the proper end of [human beings] is the realization of [their individual] character and potential." Free expression, Emerson maintained, "is an integral part of the development of ideas, of mental exploration and the affirmation of the self." Our power to develop ourselves as human beings, he

8 Cantwell v. Connecticut, 310 U.S. 296, 304 (1940).

9 Thomas Emerson, *Toward a General Theory of the First Amendment*, 72 Yale L. J. 877 (1963).

charged, "begins at this point." Therefore, "suppression of belief, opinion or expression is an affront to [human] dignity."

This first premise does not offer a completely satisfactory theoretical justification for free expression. It is not intuitively obvious, for example, that we want everyone to achieve self-fulfillment. If the actions of Charles Manson, Jeffrey Dahmer, John Wayne Gacy, and Jeffrey Epstein reflect the full blossoming of their character and potential, then we can do without it. Repression has many attendant evils, but in some cases other things are worse. Emerson understood that his theory needed more support to be persuasive, so he added a second idea to shore it up.

His second idea is that human beings are social animals. We live in communities and we must be able to set common goals and to work toward achieving them productively and cooperatively. We cannot do so unless we have access to information, the opportunity to communicate our "needs, preferences, and judgments," and the chance to participate meaningfully in formulating the aims of society and the state. Through this process, we fulfill our role in the human collective.

There is some tension between the second idea and the first. The first paints an image of individuals as occupied with their own development – each of us fulfilling our potential as the "captain of our fate" and the "master of our soul," in the words of William Ernest Henley. It sounds like a fairly isolated and self-directed enterprise. The second idea, in contrast, locates the individual in community and imposes upon us an array of resulting responsibilities. This argument leads to some puzzles: one wonders, for example, what to make of individuals whose self-fulfillment lies in social isolation, like members of certain religious orders.

But the second idea is critical in advancing Emerson's argument. It clearly signals that limits on the first idea exist, as they must. Consider the following: sooner or later, all those self-fulfilling individuals will start bumping into each other. The second idea recognizes our obligation to try to live together peacefully and collaboratively – and to use our voices productively – when that happens.

Without the second idea, we might find the self-fulfillment theory solipsistic, encouraging individuals to think and to express themselves as if they were the sole occupants of a universe that revolved around them. Such an approach would have little to recommend it. Contemporary culture appears more than sufficiently self-absorbed without an argument that gives our natural inward focus the status of a constitutional right. Indeed, a model that does not account for the existence (and equal importance) of the dignity and agency of other human beings would have the effect of cultivating not a tolerant society but an intolerant and selfish one.

In any event, Emerson's theory focuses on two distinct activities: first, speaking to achieve fulfillment as an individual, and second, speaking to achieve fulfillment as a member of society. He maintained that both have intrinsic value, regardless of their results. Thus, he declared that "freedom of expression, while not the sole or sufficient end of society, is a good in itself, or at least an essential element in a good society."

Although courts and scholars generally associate a free speech theory based on notions of human dignity and self-fulfillment with Thomas Emerson, it neither began nor ended with him. Justice Brandeis's concurring opinion in *Whitney* included some references to the concept. For example, Justice Brandeis there observed that "[t]hose who won our independence believed that the final end of the State was to make men free to develop their faculties" and that "[t]hey valued liberty both as an end and as a means."

And the concept has continued to echo through Supreme Court decisions. In a concurring opinion in a 1974 case, Justice Thurgood Marshall declared that "[t]he First Amendment serves not only the needs of the polity but also those of the human spirit – a spirit that demands self-expression. Such expression is an integral part of the development of ideas and a sense of identity. To suppress expression is to reject the basic human desire for recognition and affront the individual's worth and dignity."[10]

A free speech theory based on concepts of dignity and self-fulfillment has powerful appeal. It aligns with our society's view of the centrality of the individual and the sanctity of the human spirit and mind. It lends itself to celebration through strong and rhapsodic language. It resists contradiction – after all, who wants to argue that human beings should live unfulfilled lives? The theory, therefore, makes frequent appearances in conversations about free expression, even if it is not expressed in the terms or detail that Emerson offered. Nevertheless, on closer analysis the theory runs into some problems.

Perhaps the most significant of them asks how we should think about other, competing dignity interests. After all, while free expression may advance human dignity, it is not the only thing that does so. Equality, privacy, and the protection of reputation help advance human dignity as well, but speech has the potential to injure them, even irreparably.

The Supreme Court has not ignored this issue. For example, in a leading case addressing the proper standard for defamation claims, the Court acknowledged the importance not just of speech but of reputation. The Court there observed that "the individual's right to protection of his own good name reflects no more than our basic concept of the essential dignity and worth of every human being – a concept at the root of any decent system of ordered liberty."[11]

The existence of multiple and fundamental dignity interests leaves us with a problem of priority and choice: when dignity interests collide with each other, which one prevails? All dignity interests might look equal, but perhaps (to borrow Orwell's memorable phrase) some are "more equal than others." If so, why is that the case? How should we rank these competing dignity interests? What is the source of, and authority for, that hierarchy?

[10] Procunier v. Martinez, 416 U.S. 396, 427–428 (1974) (Marshall, J., concurring).

[11] Gertz v. Robert Welch, Inc., 418 U.S. 323, 341 (1974) (internal quotation marks and citations omitted).

Emerson tried to answer this point, but reasonable people can disagree about whether he did so successfully. In his essay, he acknowledged that free expression does not necessarily advance other ends that a society might have, like virtue, justice, or equality. Indeed, these competing values sometimes appear to come into direct conflict: for example, one individual's interest in engaging in racist speech contravenes another individual's interest in being respected and treated as an equal.

In these contests, Emerson rather summarily declares free expression the winner. Certainly, he says, the state can attend to those other interests, but in general it must do so by means other than suppressing speech. It can, for instance, mobilize a program of counter-expression or regulate disruptive conduct that adjoins the offending speech. It cannot, however, advance another dignity interest through censorship and silencing.

Emerson is less than completely clear in explaining why this result follows from his theory. He appears to base this approach on the premise that, as among all dignity interests, free expression has a fundamental place in human liberty and is uniquely essential. He seems to think that, while in particular cases free expression may not always advance virtue, justice, or equality, it is in general a necessary precondition to their achievement and makes them possible. This theory has some empirical and historical support: for instance, the civil rights movement of the 1960s could not have occurred without free expression. This is perhaps most strongly confirmed by the fact that many southern efforts to defeat the movement consisted of efforts to suppress speech.

Some critics, nevertheless, have questioned the assumption that free expression has so strong a claim on primacy. An important example comes in the work of feminist scholar Catherine MacKinnon. In her book, *Only Words*,[12] MacKinnon argues that "the modern doctrine of speech dates from considerably after the entrenchment of equality in the Fourteenth Amendment, and still the First Amendment has been interpreted, with a few exceptions, as if it were not there." She suggests that First Amendment case law has evolved "as if the upheaval that produced the Reconstruction Amendments did not move the ground under the expressive freedom, setting new limits and mandating new extensions, perhaps even demanding reconstruction of the speech right itself." In short, she argues that theories like self-fulfillment have failed to account for the "collision course" that exists between the law of free speech and the law of equality.

MacKinnon's questioning of the primacy of free speech has drawn praise from some quarters and sharp dissent from others. Perhaps the most conspicuous example of the latter came from philosopher Ronald Dworkin, who critiqued *Only Words* in an article published in the *New York Review of Books*.[13] In that piece, Dworkin

[12] Catherine MacKinnon, Only Words (1993).

[13] Ronald Dworkin, *Women and Pornography*, New York Review of Books, October 21, 1993.

argued that the egalitarian argument advanced by MacKinnon is "much broader and more dangerous in its scope than might first appear."

Dworkin noted that, under MacKinnon's reasoning, the government could "forbid the graphic or visceral or emotionally charged expression of any opinion or conviction that might reasonably offend a disadvantaged group." Forbidden speech could include "performances of the *Merchant of Venice*, or films about professional women who neglect their children, or caricatures or parodies of homosexuals in nightclub routines." If liberty and equality really do conflict, Dworkin argued, then "we should have to choose liberty because the alternative would be the despotism of thought-police."

More fundamentally, though, Dworkin challenges MacKinnon's suggestion that liberty and equality actually collide in the way she describes. To the contrary, he argues, the First Amendment plays a critical role in political equality. The First Amendment "forbids censoring cranks or neo-Nazis," he contends, "not because anyone thinks that their contributions will prevent corruption or improve public debate, but just because equality demands that everyone, no matter how eccentric or despicable, have a chance to influence policies as well as elections."

In this view, the First Amendment becomes the ultimate egalitarian principle. Under it, Dworkin points out, "no one may be prevented from influencing [our society's] shared moral environment, through his own private choices, tastes, opinions, and example, just because these tastes or opinions disgust those who have the power to shut him up or lock him up." Dworkin sees the First Amendment as a bulwark against the preferences of those in power, and therefore as playing a central role in the promotion of equality.

Of course, the ruthless egalitarianism described by Dworkin does not appeal to everyone. Furthermore, a critic can object that while what he describes may be "equal," in the abstract it is not "equal" in its practical consequences. True, the individual who wants to say hateful things about Protestants, whites, and men has the same right to do so as the individual who wants to say hateful things about Jews, African Americans, and women. History and human experience tell us, however, that the latter is more common and carries with it dangers that the former does not. Still, anyone who disagrees with Dworkin faces the challenge of explaining why he is wrong in believing that government selection among ideas, even if well intentioned, leads inescapably to despotism and efforts at thought control.

Richard Delgado and Jean Stefancic offer a perspective similar to MacKinnon's in their book *Must We Defend Nazis?*[14] Among other arguments, they point out the disconnection between our theoretical justifications for freedom of expression and our lived human experience. They note, for instance, that no evidence supports the proposition that a white supremacist who lets off steam by using racial invective thereby becomes somehow less dangerous to society. Nor, they observe, do we think

[14] Richard Delgado and Jean Stefancic, Must We Defend Nazis? (2018).

that such individuals are typically subject to the influence of ideas that contradict their racist convictions.

So, to be evenhanded about this dispute, anyone who disagrees with MacKinnon, Delgado, and Stefancic faces a serious challenge as well. They need to explain why these theorists are wrong in believing that our failure to do something about hate speech strikes a terrible bargain: it places women, racial minorities, and other politically less powerful groups in grave and imminent peril, while placing speech that contributes nothing to the social good beyond regulation. As with Dworkin's argument, you may agree or disagree with this perspective, but it clearly deserves to be taken seriously.

The approach to free expression taken by the European Court of Human Rights is in some material respects similar to that advocated for by MacKinnon, Delgado, and Stefancic. European law tends to treat dignity interests as standing on equal or near-equal footing. This approach leads to an ad hoc balancing, in which courts weigh competing values and decide individual cases on their specific facts.

The notion of balancing conflicting values sounds reasonable and sensible, but it suffers from at least three serious shortcomings. First, describing such an approach as "balancing" may be misleading or even meaningless. After all, to work toward a balance is to work toward equipoise – in the end, the weight on one side of the scale must be the same as the weight on the other. If we seek to choose between alternatives, however, then an even balance does not help us do so.

To the contrary, an even balance puts us right back where we started, with one value (say, "speech") in one hand and another value (say, "equality") in the other. In order to decide which value prevails, we must achieve an *imbalance*. Something has to *tip* the scales one way or the other.

That "something" cannot come from the balancing process itself. Another concept must provide it. So, for example, we might achieve an imbalance by concluding that free expression has a weightier value than other things, or that equality does. But if we do not acknowledge this reality then balancing becomes a dodge: we say we are balancing, but in reality we are just choosing one value over another, based on some unexpressed preference determined by some unarticulated criterion.

A second problem with balancing is that it is very hard to predict how it will resolve specific cases. When balancing occurs, we know what the law means with respect to a given set of facts once the court tells us, but probably not a moment before. Balancing resists our efforts to forecast likely outcomes – we end up guessing at how the weighing process will probably go. As we discuss further in coming chapters, that unpredictability is deeply worrisome in the realm of free expression for a host of reasons. Among other concerns, laws of uncertain application may allow the powers in charge to punish speech simply because of its unpopularity or may cause individuals to self-censor out of concern that the restriction may encompass their speech.

A final problem with balancing is that it can end up focusing on the specific facts of a particular situation rather than on larger questions of values. We may find ourselves asking "On balance, who should prevail here?" rather than "On balance, which value has the stronger claim?" Such an emphasis on facts may have tremendous appeal in a given case, but it can result in a sacrifice of principles, and important values like freedom of expression can get lost in the existential mix.

The European experiment with a balancing approach confirms the validity of our concerns in this regard. Granted, that experiment has not fulfilled Dworkin's most dire predictions and resulted in continental bans on *The Merchant of Venice*. It has, however, resulted in a regrettably messy and unpredictable jurisprudence that makes it very difficult for people of good will to figure out what the law does, and does not, allow. We can almost imagine Paul Robert Cohen sitting at home, staring at his "Fuck the Draft" jacket, trying to figure out how some collection of judges he does not know will balance the interests if he is arrested for wearing it outside the house.

In Chapters 1 and 2, we have introduced arguments that locate both instrumentalist and intrinsic values in free expression. In Chapter 3, we explore connections between free expression and other values, including our commitment to due process. It turns out that we protect free expression not just because of the values it holds and promotes, but also because failing to protect it would implicate other values that our constitutional structure recognizes as highly important.

We believe that this insight has the potential to shape discussions about free speech in meaningful ways. It complicates those conversations, because it requires us to move away from a binary model and toward a more multidimensional one. In our view, however, that additional complexity is essential to a full and informed understanding of just how much is at stake when we debate free expression.

3

Free Expression and Due Process Values

In 1990, the city of St. Paul, Minnesota adopted a Bias-Motivated Crime Ordinance. That ordinance provided:

> Whoever places on public or private property a symbol, object, appellation, characterization or graffiti, including, but not limited to, a burning cross or Nazi swastika, which one knows or has reasonable grounds to know arouses anger, alarm or resentment in others on the basis of race, color, creed, religion or gender commits disorderly conduct and shall be guilty of a misdemeanor.[1]

It is not difficult to imagine the rational thoughts and good intentions that probably inspired this provision. It seems obvious that certain symbols (like Nazi swastikas and burning crosses) provoke anger, outrage, and fear among minority populations, at least in certain circumstances. And it seems equally obvious that the messages these symbols convey do not contribute any offsetting benefits to public discourse.

Cities and other local units of government often adopt ordinances to reflect the distinctive needs and values of their communities. An ordinance taking a strong stand against hate and some of its most pernicious symbols must have seemed like an excellent expression of the principles for which the city sought to stand. And, with respect to such an important issue, half measures would not do: the ordinance should be framed expansively in order to provide a comprehensive solution to the evils of this sort of speech.

On closer examination, however, we might wonder what this ordinance means and whether it encompasses certain conduct or expression. We might feel uncertain about whether the law prohibits us from doing something we are doing, have done, or plan to do. In short, the ordinance suffers from substantial vagueness: we may understand what the ordinance is getting at in the abstract but not understand how it will be applied, including to our own speech and actions.

[1] *See* R.A.V. v. City of St. Paul, 505 U.S. 377, 380 (1992).

Consider an example. Assume that Smith, a history buff, is currently working his way through Adolf Hitler's *Mein Kampf*. In between readings, he leaves the book on a coffee table in his living room. The book prominently features a large Nazi swastika on its cover.

Is Smith in violation of the ordinance? Maybe. The provision reaches private property and specifically prohibits the display of swastikas. Does Smith "know" or "have reasonable grounds to know" that the cover will cause "anger, alarm, or resentment" in someone who visits his home? Perhaps. The image horrifies lots of people, for good reasons. We can easily imagine the child of a Holocaust survivor who had come for dinner bristling at the sight of the book and asking Smith to put it away.

Do we get a different result if the swastika appears on the cover of William Shirer's historical tome *The Rise and Fall of the Third Reich*? On the cover of an Art Spiegelman *Maus* graphic novel? On the cover of a report by the Anti-Defamation League regarding neo-Nazi hate groups? Does the placement, the size, the intention behind the swastika make a difference? Given that swastikas have the inherent capacity to "arouse anger, alarm, or resentment," does the ordinance effectively mean that we can never make one visible in any setting? If the statute does not create an absolute prohibition, then when is the display of a swastika permitted?

Countless other examples come to mind. What if a local theater company dresses its performers in Nazi costumes or burns a cross as part of a performance? What if someone paints and displays an image of Mohammad, angering members of the Muslim community? What if a high school teacher writes the "N word" on a blackboard while teaching Huckleberry Finn, alarming the African American students in the room? What if the local car repair shop has on its wall a calendar with images that objectify women, prompting resentment among its female customers? Does the ordinance prohibit some or all of these?

Granted, we might think it unlikely that a prosecutor who became aware of any of the situations just described would feel inclined to pursue legal action against the "perpetrator." Surely, common sense would prevail and no one would face a misdemeanor prosecution for leaving a book on their table or staging a historic drama or putting a tasteless calendar on the wall. Indeed, if asked whether they intended the ordinance to reach these sorts of things, the city council probably would have responded with a resounding "of course not."

But that misses the point. The state should not tell people who are rationally uncertain about the scope of its law to console themselves with guesses about the probability of enforcement. Ill-advised laws, including unconstitutional ones, have a disquieting tendency to get enforced if they remain on the books. It takes only one poor exercise of judgment on the part of a police officer or prosecutor to move these scenarios from hypothetical to actual. And, even if someone feels fairly confident that an existing administration will not enforce such a law in an unreasonable way, they might wonder about future administrations made up of people they may not even know.

These concerns matter because, as we have discussed, contemporary conversations about free expression tend toward the binary: they pit the value of speech against the concerns that speech raises. Think about the St. Paul ordinance under discussion. A free speech enthusiast – what we have called an "absolutist" – might question the wisdom of such a law. They might argue that all ideas (even bad ones) should have a chance to compete in the marketplace or that the right to engage in self-expression (even when obnoxious to others) has value in and of itself.

But a skeptic – what we have called a "relativist" – may balk at such arguments. A burning cross, they would respond, doesn't have anything to do with finding the truth or achieving healthy self-fulfillment. The skeptic might say: "If those are the only arguments you have then you lose, because they don't persuade me that the St. Paul ordinance is a bad idea. The world would be a better place without swastikas and burning crosses." These arguments bring the absolutist and the relativist to a stalemate.

As the discussion above suggests, however, the St. Paul ordinance gives rise to an additional argument. It is an argument based not on speech freedoms but on the fundamental fairness values served by due process.[2] Later, we explore three doctrines (vagueness, overbreadth, and breathing space) that have a special place in First Amendment law and that bear a close relationship to these values. But in this chapter we focus on the principle of due process itself, which has applications well beyond free speech and the First Amendment.

Indeed, due process is a critical constitutional principle with respect to our laws generally. It applies regardless of the law's subject matter. And it protects an individual's autonomy and dignity from unreasonable government interference of many kinds.

In debates over free expression, framing the question as one of due process can sometimes break the stalemate described above. A free speech skeptic might think that *no one* should have the right to burn a cross or display a swastika. But that skeptic might simultaneously concede that *everyone* has a right to due process before the state may punish them. We, therefore, need to delve into this important constitutional doctrine to see how it might help conversations about speech make additional progress.

The concept of due process requires that a law – particularly a penal statute that puts someone's liberty, property, or life at risk – meet certain basic standards of clarity and specificity. Thus, in one early case the Supreme Court declared that a "statue must be sufficiently explicit to inform those who are subject to it what

[2] *See* E. Thomas Sullivan and Toni M. Massaro, The Arc of Due Process in American Constitutional Law (2013).

conduct on their part will render them liable to its penalties."[3] In contrast, a statute that "either forbids or requires the doing of an act in terms so vague that [people] of common intelligence must necessarily guess at its meaning and differ as to its application, violates the first essential of due process of law."[4]

The idea that a law must provide reasonable notice of what it does, and does not, permit is rooted in notions of fundamental fairness. It is simply unfair for the state to declare after the fact that a person's conduct was forbidden and punishable. A law must tell that person up front what they may and not do. Furthermore, the law's terms must be sufficiently clear and comprehensible that it does not leave its potential targets to resort to conjecture and legislative mind-reading.

Franz Kafka's novel *The Trial* famously put on display the evils of an absence of fair notice.[5] The book's protagonist, Joseph K., learns early on in the narrative that he has been charged with an unspecified offense. His efforts to determine the precise nature of the allegations against him, however, prove utterly unavailing. Indeed, the book largely consists of a detailed description of Joseph K.'s inability to get a straightforward answer to that question and his resulting helplessness in the face of the power of the state.

Fair notice also relates directly to the second component of basic due process: an opportunity to be heard.[6] Due process promises that we will have a chance to defend ourselves against any charge leveled at us. Of course, this defense might take many forms: an argument that we did not engage in the prohibited conduct at all; an argument that we have an excuse for doing so; an argument that we have no excuse but deserve mercy anyway; and so on. To identify and effectively raise such arguments, however, we must understand what the law means and what might count as a defense.

Again, Kafka's novel offers a chilling cautionary tale. Because Joseph K. cannot determine the precise nature of the charges against him, he cannot work productively to exonerate himself. Having no idea what kind of argument might make a difference to his case, he has no argument to make. The narrative presses inescapably toward his conviction and execution.

Kafka gives us a deeply unsettling portrayal of state power in *The Trial* and we might doubt that we will ever encounter anything quite so sinister in the real world. Those who have lived under authoritarian regimes quickly would disabuse us of such naïveté. But, putting aside the state's capacity for institutional wickedness, the more important point is that noble intentions do not solve due process problems. A deprivation of due process remains a deprivation, regardless of the merits of its goals and ends.

3 Conally v. General Constr. Co., 269 U.S. 385, 391 (1926).

4 *Id.*

5 FRANZ KAFKA, THE TRIAL (Willa and Edwin Muir trans. Schocken Books 1968) (1937).

6 Mullane v. Central Hanover Bank & Trust Co., 339 U.S. 306, 314 (1950).

An example demonstrates the point. Assume that a community's social fabric has frayed badly and people are routinely behaving cruelly toward each other. The elders of the community gather and decide that they must do something to interrupt the cycle of fragmentation. So they pass a law declaring that "anyone who behaves in a hateful manner toward anyone else shall be guilty of a felony."

Was the statute adopted in good faith? Yes. Does it reflect noble aspirations? Yes. Does it present massive due process problems? Absolutely. Such a law obviously fails to provide fair notice of what it prohibits and what it permits. People would disagree about what constitutes "hateful" behavior and would struggle to make day-to-day decisions confident that they had complied with the law. Joseph K., charged under such a statute, might be in no better shape than we find him in *The Trial*.

Due process does not require the government to achieve the impossible. Courts do not demand that legislatures express themselves with perfect clarity and through flawless statutory architecture. Some level of ambiguity will inevitably result from the natural indeterminacy of human language and the political give-and-take of legislative deal-making.

Furthermore, the courts may be able to provide clarity where the legislature has failed to do so. Say, for example, that the legislature passed a law five years ago that lent itself to multiple conflicting interpretations. Two years ago, however, the highest court in the state construed the statute to have a particular meaning that resolved the ambiguity. If someone now argues that the statute's literal language raises due process concerns, a defender of the law could point to that judicial decision as disposing of them.

Indeed, that is precisely what happened when a challenge to the St. Paul ordinance found its way to the United States Supreme Court. In *R.A.V. v. City of St. Paul*,[7] the Court decided it did not need to address the concerns raised by the ordinance's disturbingly broad and vague language because the Supreme Court of Minnesota had interpreted it in a way that resolved those issues. Specifically, the state's highest court had construed the ordinance to cover only "fighting words" – a legal term of art with a specific and relatively narrow meaning that we discuss in Chapter 11.

We do not now need to get into the details of the fighting words doctrine, or the reasons why the Supreme Court in *R.A.V.* found the statute unconstitutional despite this judicial narrowing. For present purposes, it suffices to note that poor legislative drafting can sometimes be solved by a clarifying judicial interpretation that saves the statute. Again, the due process doctrine does not demand the unachievable.

Having outlined the basics of the due process doctrine, we return to the idea that it can prove very helpful to discussions about free expression. It offers important insights and can break dialogical logjams. There are several reasons this is so.

7 R.A.V. v. City of St. Paul, 505 U.S. 377 (1992).

First, although due process problems can arise in a wide variety of contexts, they are extraordinarily common in laws that restrict and punish speech. As we discuss in Chapter 10, public bodies have a natural tendency to overlegislate when it comes to worrisome expression. Indeed, throughout this book we encounter statutes that fail judicial scrutiny because the legislature wrote them in hopelessly vague or overbroad terms.

Even a legislature that labors mightily to write a clear and narrow statute, though, may struggle to satisfy due process when drafting a law that targets speech. The infinite varieties of human expression make it a difficult subject for legislative definition, specification, and categorization. Someone who opposes "hate speech," for example, may imagine that it would be easy enough to write a statute that gives people reasonable notice of what they can and cannot do and that prohibits everything we want to prohibit and nothing we don't. Trying to draft such a law, however, can prove illuminating and humbling – as the authors of the St. Paul ordinance discovered.

Second, due process arguments often have appeal when free expression arguments do not. Due process has obvious instrumentalist and intrinsic values: it plays an indispensable role in achieving fair results and it signals our society's commitment to evenhanded justice by requiring proper notice and an opportunity to be heard. Carving out exceptions to due process may strike a skeptic as vastly more problematic than does carving out exceptions to free expression.

To take a concrete example, someone might believe that the government should have the authority to outlaw Holocaust denial. After all, such speech rests on a gross historical falsehood, contributes nothing useful to the marketplace of ideas, and feeds anti-Semitism, ignorance, and other social evils. Germany and France have adopted such a policy for just those reasons.

That same person, however, might demand that the government comply with due process in composing and imposing such a ban. For the law to satisfy fundamental notions of fairness, as due process requires, it must afford adequate notice through a sufficiently clear and specific law. A reader of the statute should be able to tell when they are engaging in the forbidden speech. They must be able to discern whether they are engaging in Holocaust denial if, for example, they express disagreement with certain historical accounts, or quarrel with the number of people executed, or challenge the generally accepted reasons for those executions. They must not be left to guess and take their chances.

Satisfying the demands of due process is tremendously important. Indeed, we would find ourselves in deeply paradoxical territory if we abandoned due process and adopted authoritarian methods to try to achieve anti-authoritarian goals. We do not want, in the service of the thing we value, to become the thing we hate.

Finally, introducing the concept of due process can help us understand the limitations of what the law can do. It may turn out that we agree that hate speech and Holocaust denial are terrible things, but also agree that drafting a due-process-compliant statute to punish them lies beyond our capacity. Such a realization may compel us to look toward other strategies to address the evils we confront. Law is one of the ways in which we build a better society, but it is not the only way. And sometimes it is neither the best way nor even a workable way.

Legal scholar Grant Gilmore maintained that a truly good society does not need much law. He remarked: "The better the society, the less law there will be. In Heaven there will be no law and the lion will lie down with the lamb." In contrast, "the worse the society, the more law there will be." "In Hell," he concluded, "there will be nothing *but* law."[8]

If, for one or more reasons, we cannot construct a law that fulfills our basic notion of fundamental fairness, then we are better off without it. We must look to other tools. Well-intentioned laws that violate due process do nothing for our aspirations toward a just society or for the dignity interests of individuals. To make matters worse, such laws often prove themselves durable and difficult to amend or discard. For political reasons, many legislators would hesitate to advocate for the repeal of an anti-hate-speech law, even if they had grave reservations about its constitutionality.

In the chapters so far, we have introduced the instrumentalist and intrinsic values of free expression and have noted how the values embedded in our doctrine of due process can usefully inform our thinking about free speech debates. Those chapters have something in common: they focus on protection of individual expression from suppression and punishment *by the government*. Up to this point, we have thought of the free speech principle as a shield against *government* meddling and oppression.

That approach aligns with the law of the First Amendment. As a general proposition, the First Amendment only provides a right from governmental infringement – not private interference. Whether your government employer can fire you for speaking out about a matter of public concern raises a First Amendment issue. Whether your private employer can do so does not. A public high school's decision to punish a student for engaging in a nondisruptive protest implicates First Amendment rights. A decision by that student's parents to discipline her for precisely the same speech does not. We may disapprove of the private employer and the parents in these cases, but their actions lie outside of the concerns of the First Amendment.

Nevertheless, current conversations about free expression often relate to restrictions that occur in the private sphere – the technical scope of the First Amendment notwithstanding. Indeed, in recent years many of the most heated controversies have concerned limitations imposed on speech by private actors rather than by governmental ones. Our society has argued vigorously over speech-restricting decisions by everyone from private universities to social media platforms to the National Football League (NFL). And those debates often continue to rage even after someone has

[8] Grant Gilmore, The Ages of American Law 110–111 (1977) (emphasis supplied).

pointed out that the First Amendment does not apply in the context under discussion.

Despite their legal imprecision, those discussions have important things to tell us about the values that free expression serves. These conversations treat the protection of free speech as a moral issue (not just a constitutional one) that applies broadly (not narrowly) and that deserves the attention of every member of our society (not just Supreme Court justices and law professors). In this book, we call this phenomenon the "Everyday First Amendment," and it is there that we turn next.

4

The Everyday First Amendment

On June 26 and June 27, 2019, some twenty contenders for the Democratic nomination for President of the United States participated in two evenings of political debate. The outsized group included Rep. Tulsi Gabbard of Hawaii, who was struggling to gain traction with voters. Shortly after the debate, while many viewers were conducting online searches to learn more about the candidates, Google temporarily suspended her campaign's advertising account.

Google claimed that the interruption occurred because an automated system flagged unusual activity on the account. But Gabbard did not accept this explanation; she believed that Google deliberately had tried to undermine her campaign in retaliation for statements she had made that were critical of the tech giant. As a result, in July of 2019 her presidential campaign organization sued Google, alleging that the company had violated her First Amendment rights. The lawsuit sought $50 million dollars in damages.[1]

Google filed a motion to dismiss the complaint, which the court granted in a terse three-page opinion.[2] A simple and fundamental principle drove the court's analysis: the First Amendment "prohibits the government – not a private party – from abridging speech" and "Google is not now, nor . . . has it ever been an arm of the United States government." The court concluded by declaring the complaint so legally baseless that a request for a further chance at pleading a viable claim would not even be entertained: "Because these facts could never give rise to a First Amendment claim, Plaintiff's complaint is dismissed with prejudice and without leave to amend."

[1] Complaint, Tulsi Now, Inc. v. Google, LLC, No. 2:19-cv-06444-SVW-RAO, 2020 U.S. Dist. LEXIS 41673 (C. D. Cal., filed July 25, 2019), https://www.courtlistener.com/recap/gov.uscourts.cacd.753634/gov.uscourts.cacd.753634.1.0.pdf.

[2] Tulsi Now, Inc. v. Google, LLC, No. 2:19-cv-06444-SVW-RAO, 2020 U.S. Dist. LEXIS 41673 (C.D. Cal. Mar. 3, 2020), https://www.courtlistener.com/recap/gov.uscourts.cacd.753634/gov.uscourts.cacd.753634.31.0.pdf.

Reactions to the litigation went beyond the realm of stiff criticism into that of eye-rolling sarcasm. The technology- and science-focused website *Ars Technica* published a piece called "Sorry, Tulsi Gabbard, Google Can't Violate the First Amendment."[3] And the cheeky legal website *Above the Law* expressed even greater exasperation over the misconceived lawsuit in the title of its article: "For the 847,329th Time, NO the First Amendment Does Not Apply to Businesses, Tulsi!"[4]

Indeed, a longstanding body of case law – and, for that matter, the very text of the First Amendment – made it easy to conclude that Gabbard had no legal claim against Google. As the judge who dismissed her lawsuit recognized, the First Amendment constrains only the government; it does not apply to private entities or persons. Some rare exceptions exist – for example, under the federal civil rights laws, a private organization or individual can violate the First Amendment by conspiring to do so with a public body, an issue to which we return shortly. But no such exception applied here.

It is more difficult, however, to conclude that Gabbard had no plausible *moral* objection to the company's conduct. If Google intentionally had obstructed access to information about Gabbard's campaign, and had done so as retribution for her demands for greater accountability by major technology corporations, then that might well offend our sense of right and wrong. Indeed, as the company's prompt and emphatic denial of the charge confirms, such actions would appear to violate the famous admonition of Google's founders: "Don't be evil." In sum, that Google did nothing wrong *legally* does not foreclose debate about whether it did anything wrong *ethically*.

Our society has these kinds of debates about nongovernmental restrictions on free expression all the time. Indeed, applications of free expression principles to situations where the law does not compel them are commonplace. And they occur even though everyone has been told, "for the 847,329th time," that the First Amendment does not limit the conduct of private actors. In this book we label that phenomenon "the Everyday First Amendment" – our society's impulse to extend First Amendment law to entities, persons, and circumstances beyond its technical reach.

Of course, to some extent this dynamic occurs because of public unfamiliarity with the details of legal doctrine. On this point, a 2019 study showed that 65 percent of those surveyed believe that the First Amendment applies to private social media

3 Timothy B. Lee, *Sorry, Tulsi Gabbard, Google Can't Violate the First Amendment*, Ars Technica (Mar. 5, 2020), https://arstechnica.com/tech-policy/2020/03/judge-smacks-down-tulsi-gabbards-free-speech-lawsuit-against-google/.

4 Elizabeth Dye, *For the 847,329th Time, NO the First Amendment Does Not Apply to Businesses, TULSI!*, Above the Law (Mar. 5, 2020), https://abovethelaw.com/2020/03/for-the-847329th-time-no-the-first-amendment-does-not-apply-to-businesses-tulsi/.

companies. Tulsi Gabbard's campaign organization thus had no monopoly on confusion over this issue.[5]

Still, ignorance of the law is not the only, or even the primary, explanation for the phenomenon. If it were, then public discussion of "rights" would end the moment someone pointed out the limited reach of the First Amendment. Instead, those arguments tend to continue unabated: "well, I'm not a lawyer, but it's a free country and I think X should have the right to say Y."

No, there must be some other explanation for our prevalent and persistent impulse to apply First Amendment principles to private actors. In this chapter, we explore some of the alternative possibilities. In any event, this much seems clear: regardless of whether the First Amendment formally dictates how Google *must* behave, people tend to think it says something meaningful about how Google *should* behave.

The fact that people want to provide greater protection for free expression than the First Amendment affords is, in one sense, surprising. In the same 2019 survey cited earlier, a substantial 29 percent of those asked indicated that they think the First Amendment goes "too far." And, as discussed in Chapters 1–3, free speech skeptics have compelling arguments that some of the expression current First Amendment doctrine shields from punishment has little, if any, value. It might seem logical that our society would want to cabin that already expansive doctrine so its influence does not creep outside the limited territory that the law assigns it.

In another way, however, the societal impulse toward the Everyday First Amendment makes perfect sense. After all, the values advanced by free expression discussed in Chapters 1–3 have considerable moral force. It seems perfectly sensible that people would want to extend them into as many corners of human existence as possible. The First Amendment comes up short in this respect, advancing those values only insofar as they are threatened by government action.

This structure leaves a significant void, given that private actors can frustrate those cherished values at least as effectively as public ones. Those values suffer whenever a private social media platform bans an individual, or a private employer gags its employees from making public statements about important subjects, or a private college imposes a draconian speech code on the members of its community, and so on. The First Amendment leaves a moral vacuum; the Everyday First Amendment rushes in to fill it. → Or at least attempts to

Cultural identity may also play a role. At a fundamental level, the members of our society view themselves as a people committed to free expression. That commitment therefore naturally extends beyond the boundaries of legal niceties. Of course, people take this position when the speech in question appeals to them but also

5 Fors Marsh Group, *The 2019 State of the First Amendment*, FREEDOM FORUM INSTITUTE, 5 (2019), https://www.freedomforuminstitute.org/first-amendment-center/state-of-the-first-amendment/.

when it doesn't. "I hate what he says, but he has the right to say it" is a common refrain in public discourse.

In any event, the Everyday First Amendment materializes in a wide variety of contexts. We focus here on three that we think demonstrate particularly well the moral force of the arguments in favor of free expression: employment, higher education, and online service providers and platforms. We begin with the first of these, using as our primary example a distinctive employment setting that helps cast our points in stark relief – professional sports.

EMPLOYMENT

In recent years, one of the most vigorous debates about whether employers should have the right to control the speech of employees has concerned professional athletes. This particular controversy began with NFL quarterback Colin Kaepernick, who launched his career in 2011 with the San Francisco 49ers as a backup player. In 2012, the first-string quarterback sustained an injury and Kaepernick stepped into the high-profile role.

Kaepernick had tremendous success, leading the 49ers to the Super Bowl and setting multiple records along the way. Although the 49ers narrowly lost the national championship, Kaepernick established himself as a star. In subsequent years, however, Kaepernick struggled: the 49ers went through a major coaching change; the team fared poorly; he sustained significant injuries; and he began publicly musing about being traded.

During the 2016 season, Kaepernick attracted attention for a different reason: he protested during the playing of the national anthem. Initially, he remained seated and refused to stand; later, he kneeled. He explained that, through these actions, he sought to express his concern over a series of fatal encounters between law enforcement and African Americans and his support for the "Black Lives Matter" movement. In short order, other NFL players and professional athletes began engaging in similar silent protests during the national anthem.

Public opinion divided swiftly and sharply. Some people saw the players as spoiled and unpatriotic and viewed their act of dissent as a stain on a distinctly American pastime. As the saying goes, they "voted with their feet" and walked away from the sport: the NFL experienced a decline in viewership that season.

Harsh criticism even came from unexpected sources – including liberal Supreme Court Justice Ruth Bader Ginsburg. In an interview promoting her recently published book, Ginsburg characterized Kaepernick's protest as "dumb and disrespectful."[6] She

6 Ariane de Vogue, *Ruth Bader Ginsburg on Kaepernick Protests: "I Think It's Dumb and Disrespectful"*, CNN.com (Oct. 12, 2016 4:21 PM), https://www.cnn.com/2016/10/10/politics/ruth-bader-ginsburg-colin-kaepernick/.

subsequently apologized, describing her comments as "inappropriately dismissive and harsh."[7]

Others, however, saw Kaepernick and his allies as heroes who were using their celebrity in support of an important cause. Various organizations gave Kaepernick awards for moral leadership. As support for Kaepernick grew, Nike released an ad that featured his image and the slogan: "Believe in something. Even if it means sacrificing everything." The company's endorsement of Kaepernick resulted in blowback from the opposing camp: some public officials pressed for boycotts of Nike by units of state and local government – ironically, policies that raised First Amendment concerns in their own right.[8]

In short order, however, a third perspective emerged: regardless of the merits of Kaepernick's viewpoint, he should have the freedom to express it. People taking that point of view generally adopted the rights-based language of the First Amendment. Interestingly, one of those people was a former constitutional law professor named Barack Obama.

In an interview in September of 2016, the President was asked for his opinion on Kaepernick's protest. He began by noting that honoring the national anthem is part of "what binds us together as a nation." But, he hastened to add, "what makes this country special is that we respect people's rights to have a different opinion." Invoking "freedom of speech" and the "importance of everybody listening to each other," President Obama opined that Kaepernick was simply "exercising his constitutional right."[9]

At the time he made these statements, President Obama had a point. No private entity had yet instructed Kaepernick to cease his protests. To the contrary, Roger Goodell, commissioner of the NFL, offered only the fairly tepid admonition: "I don't necessarily agree with what he's doing."[10] In the absence of any private restraints on his conduct, Kaepernick had a constitutional right to take a knee.

Over the next two years, however, pressure on Kaepernick increased from both the private and public spheres. In March of 2017, he opted out of his contract but no offers materialized. As other free agent quarterbacks found positions, rumors circulated that team owners had blackballed Kaepernick. Still, through most of 2017,

7 Ariane de Vogue, *Ruth Bader Ginsburg Apologizes to Colin Kaepernick After Criticizing Anthem Protest*, CNN.COM (Oct. 14, 2016 4:07 PM) https://www.cnn.com/2016/10/14/politics/ruth-bader-ginsburg-apologizes-colin-kaepernick/index.html.

8 Emerson Sykes, *The First Amendment Bars Officials from Targeting Nike because They Don't Like Colin Kaepernick*, AMERICAN CIVIL LIBERTIES UNION BLOG (Sept. 20, 2018 6:30 PM), https://www.aclu.org/blog/free-speech/first-amendment-bars-officials-targeting-nike-because-they-dont-colin-kaepernick.

9 Daniela Diaz, *Obama Defends Kaepernick's Anthem Protest*, CNN.COM (Sept. 29, 2016 4:50 PM), https://www.cnn.com/2016/09/28/politics/obama-colin-kaepernick-nfl-national-anthem-presidential-town-hall-cnn/index.html.

10 Victor Mather, *A Timeline of Colin Kaepernick vs. the N.F.L.*, N.Y. TIMES (Feb. 15, 2019), https://www.nytimes.com/2019/02/15/sports/nfl-colin-kaepernick-protests-timeline.html.

Goodell remained publicly respectful of players who wished to protest and he continued to use the language of the First Amendment: "The national anthem is [a point of pride, but] we also have to understand the other side that people do have rights and we want to respect those."[11]

In late 2017, however, presidential candidate Donald Trump entered the fray. In a series of characteristically fiery tweets, he condemned the protesting athletes and advocated for their immediate termination. With political pressure mounting, in May of 2018 the NFL team owners adopted a policy that players who kneeled during the national anthem would be subject to discipline. Various players and the union challenged the policy through grievances, which were settled on confidential terms in early 2019.[12]

The Kaepernick controversy provides a number of important insights into the Everyday First Amendment. As an initial matter, it demonstrates how quickly our societal dialogues move toward arguments favoring free expression – even when the law clearly does not dictate it. In this respect, it is useful to bear in mind that, at least in the early going, nothing about Kaepernick's case even remotely suggested the presence of government censorship. He engaged in his protest while in uniform, on the field, at work, employed by a private entity that operates under rules set by another private entity. Private employers generally believe that under the law they have expansive control over what their employees say under these sorts of circumstances, and they are right.

Second, the controversy demonstrates the formidable size of the gap that the First Amendment leaves by virtue of its limited application. When he launched his protest campaign, Colin Kaepernick was a leading sports celebrity and public figure. His stature made him a potential role model for countless young people, particularly those of color. His protest concerned a subject of major interest, concern, and discussion. And, yet, to the extent that his employer wished to silence him while on the job, the Constitution offered him almost no protection. The Everyday First Amendment sought to correct for this counterintuitive result.

Third, and intriguingly, as events unfolded it appeared that maybe the First Amendment *did* apply to Kaepernick's case after all. As noted above, private actors may render themselves subject to the First Amendment by colluding with public actors to violate rights that the law protects. An argument emerged that the NFL owners and President Trump may have done just that: after all, the President urged the owners to take adverse action against the protestors and appeared to have offered incentives for them to do so.[13] Kaepernick's inability to land a position, despite his record and his formidable talent, suggested that the owners might have given in and

[11] *Id.*

[12] *Id.*

[13] Leah Litman, *State Action Doctrine under an Autocrat*, TAKE CARE BLOG (Sept. 26, 2017), https://takecareblog.com/blog/state-action-doctrine-under-an-autocrat.

struck a deal with President Trump. For better or worse, the settlement of the grievances avoided a full and public exploration of the facts, which prevented this paradigmatic example of the Everyday First Amendment from becoming a case about the *actual* First Amendment.

With respect to the employment field more broadly, our society has sometimes filled the vacuum left by the First Amendment by adopting other laws. Thus, federal labor laws protect certain speech, even when it occurs in the context of private employment, as "concerted activity" among employees to address terms and conditions of employment. Similarly, whistleblower statutes prevent both government and private employers from retaliating against specified employee speech that serves the public interest. Private employers retain substantial control over the speech of their employees, but the moral force of the Everyday First Amendment may dissuade them from taking punitive measures and other laws may prohibit them from doing so.

COLLEGES AND UNIVERSITIES

Another context in which the Everyday First Amendment has a significant influence is higher education. Indeed, perhaps no institutions in our country struggle with free expression as commonly, as vigorously, or (sometimes) as divisively as do our colleges and universities. In Chapters 14 and 15, we take a closer look at First Amendment issues on campus. Here, we focus primarily on the fact that many private institutions of higher education embrace free speech principles even though the law does not require it. The Everyday First Amendment has a major role in the culture and environment of private campuses around the country – literally, "every day."

Of course, the First Amendment applies to public universities because they qualify as government actors. A state university can no more adopt a rule or regulation that violates the First Amendment than can a state legislature. And speech codes provide a conspicuous and widely discussed example of how public institutions of higher education can get themselves quickly into trouble.

A seminal decision addressing such a code came in the 1989 case *Doe v. University of Michigan*.[14] In *Doe*, a federal district court held that the speech policy adopted by the University of Michigan ran afoul of the First Amendment. A number of public university policies around the country subsequently have fallen for similar reasons.

Doe arose from facts that might make us feel sympathetic to what the university was trying to accomplish. In the late 1980s, a number of racist incidents occurred on

[14] Doe v. University of Michigan, 721 F. Supp. 852 (E.D. Mich. 1989). For a fuller analysis of the case, *see* Len Niehoff, *Doe v. University of Michigan: Free Speech on Campus 25 Years Later*, 71:2 U. MIAMI L. REV. 365 (2017).

campus and rocked the school's community. Someone distributed an anonymous flier around campus that used deeply offensive racial epithets and declared "open season" on Blacks. A student disc jockey allowed racist jokes to be broadcast on a campus radio station. When protests against these events occurred, someone suspended a Ku Klux Klan uniform from a dormitory window.

Although the university's president issued a formal statement condemning these incidents, pressure quickly increased for the school to do more. A subcommittee of the Michigan Legislature conducted hearings and threatened to hold up appropriations to the university. A campus anti-discrimination group announced plans to sue the institution. A national civil rights leader weighed in on the controversy. As a result, the university came forward with a multi-point plan to address concerns about racism on campus, which included a commitment to adopt an "anti-harassment" policy.

After more than a year of considering various drafts, the university finally adopted a policy that was elaborate in structure and broad in application. It controlled a wide array of campus spaces, including classrooms, libraries, laboratories, and recreation and study centers. In these areas, people could be disciplined on a number of grounds, including for engaging in speech that "stigmatized" or "victimized" someone based on a characteristic like race, ethnicity, gender, or sexual orientation. Sanctions depended on the gravity of the offense and could be severe.

The university also issued an "interpretive guide" that, among other things, offered examples of speech that it deemed discriminatory or harassing. Unfortunately, the guide managed to render the policy more, rather than less, problematic. Some of the examples offered involved speech that appeared to be protected under the First Amendment, like making a negative comment about someone else's "religious beliefs." This plainly overreached: it could, for instance, include a good faith disagreement about the respective merits of the Old and New Testaments, a debate over the connections between radical Islam and terrorism, or a discussion of the ways in which religion historically has been used as a tool of oppression.

The guide also made clear that the policy proscribed speech that seemed to have nothing to do with discrimination or harassment – supposedly the code's animating concerns. For example, the policy prohibited any negative statement about someone else's "physical appearance." Taken literally, this would allow for disciplinary measures against a student for making a good-natured joke about his roommate's shaggy beard, wrinkled shirt, or dubious fashion sense.

At the time of the policy's adoption, "John Doe" served as a psychology graduate student at the university. Doe taught courses that explored theories that he thought some students might view as "sexist" – for example, holding that because of certain biological differences men generally may be better than women at certain tasks. Doe brought a lawsuit asking that the policy be declared unconstitutional.

After an extended and thorough analysis, the court concluded that the policy violated the First Amendment on two bases. First, it was overbroad; it extended to speech that the First Amendment protects. Second, it was vague; a reasonable person could not tell what the policy prohibited, particularly given its use of ambiguous terms like "stigmatize" and "victimize." The *Doe* decision made fairly clear what a public university *could not* do in its regulation of speech on campus.

Doe provided significantly less clarity, however, about what a public university *could* do. As a result, institutions of higher education continued to experiment with a wide array of policies, some more defensible than others. Again, we further explore issues of free speech on campus in Chapters 14 and 15. For now, it suffices to note that arguments around college speech codes continue. Indeed, an organization called the Foundation for Individual Rights in Education has, as one of its central missions, the monitoring and assessment of such campus policies.

As a technical and legal matter, neither the First Amendment nor the reasoning of cases like *Doe* have any application to private institutions. The Constitution does not bar private colleges and universities from censoring vast swaths of speech on their campuses. One could sensibly even argue that, under the First Amendment, private institutions have the *right* to do so. We return to that seeming paradox later, when in Chapter 15 we discuss the doctrine of academic freedom.

Some private institutions of higher education have taken advantage of that prerogative and have chosen to impose relatively strict limits on campus speech. Schools making this choice overwhelmingly consist of colleges and universities with strong religious sensibilities and missions. For example, the student honor code of Liberty University, an evangelical Christian institution, prohibits "vulgar comments" and the viewing of "media and entertainment" that are "lewd" or include "anti-Christian" messages.[15] Such a policy at a public institution would violate not just the speech but also the religion clauses of the First Amendment.

Very few private institutions, however, have chosen to go in this speech-restrictive direction. Instead, the vast majority of private schools have adopted policies that are fairly – sometimes even highly – protective of free expression. They have not just embraced the Everyday First Amendment as a value; they have enshrined it in a binding and enforced statement of institutional norms. They behave as if the reasoning of *Doe* applies to them, when it plainly doesn't.

The leading example of such an approach almost certainly comes in the University of Chicago. In July of 2014, as many campuses struggled with free speech issues, Chicago President Robert Zimmer created a Committee on Freedom of Expression and tasked it with "articulating the University's overarching commitment to free, robust, and uninhibited debate and deliberation among all members of the

[15] Division of Student Affairs, Liberty University, The Liberty Way: Student Honor Code, 10–11 (2019), https://www.liberty.edu/students/wp-content/uploads/sites/89/2020/01/2019_11_06_LW_Final.pdf.

University community." The committee, chaired by distinguished First Amendment scholar Geoffrey Stone, issued its report in January of 2015; the position expressed there has come to be known as the Chicago Principles.[16]

The law of the First Amendment does not technically apply to the University of Chicago, which is private. Also, in light of the fact that faith-based institutions tend to be those most inclined to restrain speech, Chicago's religious history and affiliations might seem to make it an unlikely home for robust free expression. Indeed, the university was founded under the direction of the American Baptist Church and houses one of the nation's leading divinity schools. Nevertheless, the Chicago Principles align very closely with the law of the First Amendment and enthusiastically endorse the importance of free speech on higher education campuses.

Of course, the Chicago Principles do not stake out an uncompromisingly absolutist position. They recognize that some narrow categories of expression may be restricted, such as speech that violates the law (for example, extortion or blackmail), that defames someone or invades their privacy, or that rises to the level of a true threat. Furthermore, the Chicago Principles acknowledge that the university can impose content-neutral time, place, and manner restrictions on speech. But these limitations are largely consistent with those acknowledged by First Amendment doctrine.

Indeed, the Chicago Principles generally track the very strong protections for speech provided by the First Amendment. For example, they clearly reject the notion that individual or community sensitivities can serve as a justification to censor speech, banish ideas, or disinvite controversial speakers. The principles declare that the university will not suppress speech simply because some (or even most) people find it "offensive, unwise, immoral, or wrong-headed."[17] They insist that speakers be permitted to convey their messages, even when others find those messages loathsome. As with First Amendment doctrine, the Chicago Principles trust the marketplace of ideas to sort the good from the bad.

We might expect that the Chicago Principles would represent an outlier position that very few private schools would choose to follow given their range of options. To the contrary, they have proven highly influential. Indeed, as of the writing of this book, more than seventy colleges and universities (many private) have adopted them.[18]

The distance between the policies of Liberty University and the University of Chicago leaves lots of territory and many private schools have landed in that middle space. Take, for example, Colby College, a small but highly ranked private liberal

[16] Geoffrey R. Stone et al., Report of the Committee on Freedom of Expression, 1 (2014), https://provost.uchicago.edu/sites/default/files/documents/reports/FOECommitteeReport.pdf.

[17] *Id.* at 2.

[18] *Chicago Statement: University and Faculty Body Support*, theFIRE.org (Feb. 6, 2020), https://www.thefire.org/chicago-statement-university-and-faculty-body-support/.

arts school located in Maine. Colby's student handbook expressly declares that free speech "is essential in an academic community and will be vigorously upheld." Its list of sanctionable misconduct, however, includes such things as "bias-motivated" behavior, "hate and/or bias incidents," and "verbal abuse."[19] Without substantial definitional narrowing, all of those terms would suffer from serious overbreadth and vagueness problems under traditional First Amendment analysis.

It makes sense that many private institutions have adopted policies in between the extremes of Liberty and Chicago. On one hand, they feel the tug of the Everyday First Amendment toward broad protection for free expression – a particularly powerful pull in this context, given our society's sense that institutions of higher education should serve as enclaves of free enquiry, debate, and speech. As the Supreme Court declared in an often-quoted statement, the university "classroom is peculiarly the marketplace of ideas."[20]

On the other hand, those schools also empathize with the concerns expressed by members of their campus community about speech that marginalizes them, provokes anxiety or anger, or otherwise interferes with the educational process. Those schools want their students, faculty, and others to feel welcomed, included, and valued. And they do not want to sacrifice those important goals on the altar of expression that makes no apparent contribution to the marketplace of ideas or the enterprise of learning.

Granted, such a middling approach may appear intellectually incoherent or even disingenuous. It seems Janus faced to make strident declarations about the importance of free expression – but then to carve from that principle multiple exceptions of indeterminate scope and meaning. What these policies give in one section, they frequently take away in others.

Realistically, however, it is not surprising that private schools sometimes exercise the latitude that the law leaves them. To the contrary, it would be hopelessly naïve to expect *every* such school to reject *all* of the luxurious leeway that its private status affords. Rather, the remarkable fact is that so many colleges and universities forgo so much of that freedom by voluntarily subjecting themselves to a collection of norms that the law does not mandate. That they do so speaks volumes about the moral force of the values that free expression advances, particularly in the higher education context.

INTERNET PLATFORMS

When in 1967 the Supreme Court singled out college classrooms as "peculiarly" the marketplace of ideas, the internet did not exist. And one might reasonably wonder

[19] Colby College, Colby College Student Handbook, 20–21 (2015), http://www.colby.edu/deanofstudents/wp-content/uploads/sites/40/2016/02/Colby-College-Student-Handbook-2-16.pdf.

[20] Keyishian v. Board of Regents, 385 U.S. 589, 603 (1967).

whether online forums have supplanted universities and public squares as the places within our society where that marketplace operates in its freest, least regulated, quintessential form. In that spirit, half a century later the Supreme Court flatly declared: "While in the past there may have been difficulty in identifying the most important places (in a spatial sense) for the exchange of views, today the answer is clear. It is cyberspace . . . and social media in particular."[21]

Because of the special importance of these platforms in the exchange of views, public discussions about them tend to recreate the same debates that characterize conversations about the First Amendment – even though they are private entities and not arms of government. Free speech enthusiasts therefore argue that these platforms should allow for the unimpeded flow of information and ideas, should not manipulate the search for truth, and should remain neutral in those exchanges – just as the government must. Tulsi Gabbard's ill-conceived lawsuit against Google reflects such a point of view.

Social media skeptics, however, argue that these platforms have a responsibility to exorcise certain speech (and speakers) from their online environments. Consistent with that demand, those platforms adopt terms and conditions of usage, purge specified content, and banish offending users. Some restrictions mirror First Amendment doctrine – for example, prohibitions on true threats and obscenity. Other regulations clearly would not pass muster under the First Amendment if it were applicable. Public pressure for still greater constraints on these "marketplaces" continues unabated.[22]

The situation is rendered more complex by the fact that an increasing number of government actors and entities now use these platforms for official purposes. The paradigmatic example is President Trump, who so extensively deployed his Twitter account for government business that the National Archives treats his tweets as presidential records. When President Trump blocked certain individuals from his Twitter account based on their viewpoint, a federal court ruled that he had violated the First Amendment because he had transformed his part of this private platform into a public forum that required open access.[23] We have more to say about this "public forum" doctrine in Chapter 7.

What do these developments signify with respect to internet platforms? They mean that, in a practical sense, we may be engaged in the process of revising the latitude afforded to speech in this country – without actually rewriting the First Amendment. Consider: the Supreme Court is almost certainly correct when it says that cyberspace has become the most important place in our society for the exchange of ideas and that this holds true of social media in particular. But that

[21] Packingham v. North Carolina, 137 S. Ct. 1730, 1735 (2017).

[22] Daphne Keller, *Facebook Restricts Speech by Popular Demand*, The Atlantic (Sept. 22, 2019), https://www.theatlantic.com/ideas/archive/2019/09/facebook-restricts-free-speech-popular-demand/598462/.

[23] Knight First Amendment Inst. at Columbia Univ. v. Trump, 928 F.3d 226, 237 (2d Cir. 2019).

"marketplace" is private and therefore subject to popular pressure. If enough users object to the use of profanity on a platform, then its owners can bow to the pressure and prohibit such language (and, presumably, exile anyone who uses it). If enough users think a particular ideology too offensive to get any airtime on a platform, then its owners can fall in line and forbid its expression (and, presumably, excommunicate anyone who dares to think that way).

First Amendment doctrine does not endorse the so-called heckler's veto, where those who dislike speech have the power to silence it by loudly objecting. In the circumstances just described, however, the "heckler's veto" prevails. Censorship wins. Unpopular speech loses, precisely because it is unpopular. The majority gets to decide whose voices may be heard and whose stifled.

But, of course, the whole point of the First Amendment is to place such matters *beyond* majority control. As previously noted, the majority does not need the First Amendment, because the majority will not vote for self-censorship and impose limitations on the speech it favors. The First Amendment exists in order to protect those ideas that do not have the majority's support – including ideas that might even provoke the majority's strenuous opposition.

When a public official or entity uses a privately owned online platform for official government purposes (as in President Trump's Twitter account), First Amendment doctrine may apply. But, putting those extraordinary cases aside, what happens on those platforms largely will be left to the Everyday First Amendment – which is nothing more than a social norm that consists of whatever most of us think it should. In this sense, some of the most important developments for free expression in our time are coming not from the law of the First Amendment but from the conventions of the Everyday First Amendment – conventions that are still under construction, with great uncertainty about who gets to serve as architect.

In Part II, we undertake a historical consideration of First Amendment doctrine as expressed through the opinions of the Supreme Court of the United States. We there provide a series of necessarily brief overviews of three periods: prior to 1919, from 1919 to 1964, and from 1964 to the present. The values we have just discussed will inform the development and evolution of free speech doctrine across those eras. But we start with a period during which the Court largely addressed the First Amendment by ignoring it.

PART II

History

Example of speaker
@ Middlebury College

5

The First Amendment Prior to 1919

Two common features characterize the Court's First Amendment decisions prior to 1919. First, there were relatively few of them. This is, in part, attributable to the fact that it was not clear until 1925 that the First Amendment applies to the *states*.

The First Amendment declares that "*Congress* shall make no law abridging the freedom of speech." In its 1925 decision in *Gitlow* v. *New York*,[1] however, the Supreme Court held that the Fourteenth Amendment extends the First Amendment to reach abridgements of speech imposed by *state* government. This ruling had the effect of dramatically expanding the scope of the First Amendment and, accordingly, the number and range of free speech issues for the Court to decide.

Furthermore, as historian Michael Kammen notes, during this period neither the Constitution nor the Bill of Rights had the place in American consciousness and culture that they hold today.[2] As Kammen observes, the physical handling of the original copy of the Constitution tells the story symbolically. Today, we proudly display that document at the National Archives, where it is a tourist attraction. But this was not always the case.

To the contrary, until 1921 the Constitution was kept in storage at various locations, including at the Washington Orphan Asylum. And, even after the Constitution was moved to the Library of Congress so members of the general public could view it, the Bill of Rights remained in a cellar for years – tucked away in a green cabinet that included such other curios as six ancient Japanese swords and the sword of a Haitian emperor. As Kammen observes, this document was "out of sight, and almost out of mind." In short, prior to 1919 the Bill of Rights, including

[1] Gitlow v. New York, 268 U.S. 652 (1925).

[2] Michael Kammen, A Machine that Would Go of Itself: The Constitution in American Culture (1986).

the First Amendment, was not the centerpiece of American thought that it has become.

The second feature of the Court's pre-1919 decisions is that free speech fared very poorly in them. The Court generally took an extremely narrow view of First Amendment protections. In contrast, it took a strikingly expansive view of the authority of the government to limit speech, particularly in contexts involving supposed threats to public safety, order, morality, or national unity. The government invoked its inherent "police powers" to regulate speech, and the Court construed those powers broadly.

This period was marked by an unrelenting, and largely unchecked, attack by the legislative and executive branches on expression that was critical of the government and that therefore allegedly threatened national security. The Sedition Act of 1798 essentially criminalized statements disloyal to the federal government. During the Civil War in the 1860s, the writ of habeas corpus was suspended by President Lincoln, in part to limit speech directed toward the federal government. And the Espionage Act of 1917 and the Sedition Act of 1918 were intended to blunt opposition to the draft during World War I.[3]

Today, we often think of the courts as a bulwark against overreaching by the other branches of government. We count on the independence of judges to constrain the politicized whims and excesses of legislators and officials. During this period, however, the Supreme Court's performance of this role was anemic at best.

The Court's restrictive view of constitutional protections was not limited to the First Amendment. To the contrary, it took a similar approach to the Bill of Rights generally. The Court often observed in the early cases that the Bill of Rights was not intended to lay down new or novel principles of government but rather simply to incorporate "guaranties and immunities" inherited from well-recognized English principles, which were subject to recognized exceptions.[4]

Still, the frailty of First Amendment protections during this period seems particularly conspicuous. During World War I, the Court upheld a number of government regulations on speech that allegedly posed a clear and present danger to wartime efforts, such as undermining military recruitment or public morale. The Court reasoned that freedom of speech did not provide a blanket immunity from government oversight, but rather could be limited whenever reasonable or necessary, especially given the exigent circumstances of a nation at war.

In one of the most important cases of this era, *Schenck* v. *United States*,[5] the defendants had been convicted under the Espionage Act of 1917 for distributing leaflets decrying the draft and urging the public to disobey it – but only peacefully.

[3] For an excellent study of speech freedoms in the time of war, see GEOFFREY R. STONE, PERILOUS TIMES: FREE SPEECH IN WARTIME 12, 16–78, 80–134, 136–191 (2004).

[4] Robertson v. Baldwin, 165 U.S. 275 (1897). *See also* Patterson v. Colorado, 205 U.S. 454 (1907) (Harlan, J., dissenting).

[5] Schenck v. United States, 249 U.S. 47 (1919).

The Act made it illegal to attempt to cause insubordination in the military and to obstruct recruitment, and the defendants were found to have violated this ban. They appealed their conviction to the Supreme Court, arguing that the Act violated their First Amendment rights.

In an opinion written by Justice Oliver Wendell Holmes, the Court disagreed. The Court held that the leaflets were not protected speech because they created a "clear and present danger" of causing others to engage in criminal activity. As we have discussed, Holmes would shortly thereafter change his view of the First Amendment and would become one of the greatest champions of free speech in the history of the Court, but there is scant evidence of this mindset in *Schenck*.

The narrow view of free speech protection taken in *Schenck* is representative of the period. The Supreme Court cases up to and through World War I uniformly showed substantial deference to government claims that the censured speech was dangerous to national security or infringed upon wartime efforts.[6] Indeed, prior to 1919, the Supreme Court did not extend First Amendment speech protections to a single petitioner in such cases. And, even into 1919, the Court persisted in upholding restraints on speech, including under the Espionage Act.

The Court's forgiving approach to government regulation was not, however, limited to cases involving national security and war efforts. For example, the Supreme Court confronted two cases in the 1800s that challenged laws criminalizing the distribution of lottery advertisements through the United States Postal Service – speech that was hardly likely to pose an existential threat to the republic. In both of these cases, *In re Rapier*,[7] and *Horner* v. *United States*,[8] the Court upheld the laws, recognizing the government's authority to regulate speech that offends public morals. The Court declined to second-guess legislative judgments that such advertisements did so.

Across many different kinds of cases, the Court during this period minimized First Amendment protection and validated government limitations. Thus, in *United States Ex rel. Turner* v. *Williams*,[9] the Court upheld the Alien Immigration Act, a law that allowed Congress to deport noncitizens with supposed anarchist leanings. Even the formidable trial lawyer Clarence Darrow, who represented Turner, was unable to persuade the Court otherwise.

And in *Patterson* v. *Colorado*,[10] an opinion written by Justice Holmes, the Court affirmed a judicial order holding a newspaper publisher in contempt for printing cartoons and articles that criticized the state supreme court. In essence, Justice Holmes reasoned that even if the First Amendment applied to the states, its primary

6 *See* Debs v. United States, 249 U.S. 211 (1919); Abrams v. United States, 25 U.S. 616 (1919); Frohwerk v. United States, 249 U.S. 204 (1919); Gilbert v. Minnesota, 254 U.S. 325 (1920).

7 In re Rapier, 143 U.S. 110 (1891).

8 Horner v. United States, 143 U.S. 207 (1892).

9 United States Ex rel. Turner v. Williams, 194 U.S. 279 (1904).

10 Patterson v. Colorado, 205 U.S. 454 (1907).

purpose was to prevent "prior restraints" on publication, not subsequent punishments of harmful speech. As we will see, the Court has continued to view licensing schemes and other prior restraints as among the clearest violations of the First Amendment, but it has resoundingly rejected the notion that they are the *only* violations.

During this era, the Court even took a fairly forgiving view of at least some prior restraints. For example, in both *Mutual Film Corporation* v. *Industrial Commission of Ohio*[11] and *Mutual Film Corporation* v. *Hodges*,[12] the Court found no constitutional obstacle to laws that required films to be approved by government officials prior to their exhibition – a textbook example of a prior restraint on speech. In one memorable passage, the Court justified this result by reasoning that films were simply another business subject to state regulation, much like circuses and other spectacles. It may say a great deal about the Court's eagerness to uphold restrictions on speech that it resorted to an argument that equated celluloid with trained elephants.

We do not need to belabor the point. Prior to 1919, the Court saw freedom of speech as a right of extremely limited scope and strength. And the Court was highly deferential to legislative judgments about which kinds of speech did more harm than good and should be restricted or even criminalized. It would not be an overstatement to say that there was *no* free speech doctrine before 1919; rather, there was a doctrine of government authority *over* speech.

Absolutists see the pre-1919 cases as a chilling cautionary tale. These are the sorts of results you get, they argue, if you think of the right to free expression as just one of many considerations, if you view competing interests as at least co-equal in stature, and if you defer to government judgments about what those other interests are and how much weight to give them. The absolutists have a point: the outcomes in these cases are deeply worrisome to anyone who cares about individual liberty within a democratic society. But you should not necessarily conclude from this that the absolutists have the better part of the argument. As we see over the course of the book, the relativists have cautionary tales of their own.

The trajectory of First Amendment doctrine begins to change in 1919. That year commences an era in the Court's jurisprudence that scholars Lee Bollinger and Geoffrey Stone have aptly called "The Free Speech Century."[13] Ironically, the chief architect of this shift was the same Justice Holmes who authored *Schenck*, *Patterson*, and other decisions that had embraced the narrow view of the First Amendment. We turn to that period next, looking at developments from 1919 to 1963.

[11] Mutual Film Corporation v. Industrial Commission of Ohio, 236 U.S. 230 (1915).

[12] Mutual Film Corporation v. Hodges, 236 U.S. 248 (1915).

[13] Lee C. Bollinger and Geoffrey R. Stone, The Free Speech Century (2018).

6

The First Amendment from 1919 to 1963

As we saw in Chapter 5, prior to 1919 the Supreme Court narrowly interpreted the First Amendment and broadly construed the government's authority to restrict worrisome speech – and did so with remarkable uniformity. Of course, so entrenched a paradigm does not change overnight. And, certainly, 1919 does not signal a sudden and complete reversal in the Court's approach to free speech doctrine.

To the contrary, even following the end of World War I, the Court continued to recognize broad limitations on free speech, including with respect to "utterances inimical to public welfare" and statements "tending to incite to crime, disturb the public peace, or endanger the foundation of organized government."[1] The period between 1919 and 1963 marks an important evolutionary phase, but not an instantaneous 180-degree turn. Indeed, many decisions issued during this era are wholly inconsistent with our current understanding of the First Amendment.

Nevertheless, it seems clear that 1919 marks the beginning of a significant change in the Court's approach to free expression. As we discussed at length in Chapter 1, this is the year in which Justice Holmes issued his powerful dissent in the *Abrams* case, articulating the marketplace of ideas theory of free expression. After that dissent, and doubtless because of it, the Court started to move in a new direction – one much more attentive to the *value* of speech than to its potential *hazards*.

But that general movement toward greater protection for free speech began haltingly. Following World War I, the Court encountered numerous challenges to the constitutionality of the Espionage Act, which punished efforts to "obstruct the recruiting or enlistment service," and its application to various war dissenters.[2] Convinced that the First Amendment was not "intended to give immunity for every

[1] Gitlow v. New York, 268 U.S. 652 (1925).

[2] *See* 50 U.S.C. § 33 (1917) and United States v. Schenck, 249 U.S. 47, 53 (1919).

possible use of language,"[3] the Court declined to extend protection to speech that was thought to present a "clear and present danger" to American military defense.[4] The clear and present danger test became the standard for measuring the government's ability to regulate and criminalize speech, and in applying it during this era the Court consistently denied First Amendment protection to language perceived to threaten the nation's war efforts.[5]

Throughout the early 1920s, the Supreme Court continued to defer to the government under this standard and protection for speech was extremely limited and fragile.[6] In 1927, however, the Court ended its unwavering streak of upholding government restrictions and began extending First Amendment protection to various forms of speech, including political and religious speech.[7] A seismic shift in the Court's thinking was underway.

Over time, a distinction emerged between promoting specific destructive action, on the one hand, and engaging in mere debate, on the other. The Court continued to allow restrictions on speech that *knowingly* and *willfully* advocated violence or forcefully overthrowing the government.[8] But it started to extend substantial

[3] Frohwerk v. United States, 249 U.S. 204, 206 (1919).

[4] *Schenck*, 249 U.S. at 52. *See also* Abrams v. United States, 250 U.S. 616 (1919) (denying First Amendment protection to leaflets that were alleged to hinder the country's war efforts); Debs v. United States, 249 U.S. 211 (1919) (upholding the convictions under the Espionage Act for advocating refusal of draft and military duty); Gilbert v. Minnesota, 254 U.S. 325, 333 (1920) (upholding a law that punished any person who, in a meeting of five or more people or in any public space, advocated or taught men not to enlist in the army).

[5] *Schenck*, 249 U.S. at 52.

[6] *Schenck*, 249 U.S. 47 at 53; *see* Gitlow v. New York, 268 U.S. 652, 669 (1925) (finding a law that punished teaching, writing, and advocating anarchy constitutional, because the states can determine under their police powers which language poses a threat to the welfare of its citizens: "A single revolutionary spark may kindle a fire that, smoldering for a time, may burst into a sweeping and destructive conflagration"); Whitney v. California, 274 U.S. 357, 371 (1927) (finding a law punishing members of groups that teach, advocate, or aid criminal syndicalism constitutional, as states were free to limit "utterances inimical to the public welfare, tending to incite to crime, disturb the public peace, or endanger the foundations of organized government and threaten its overthrow by unlawful means").

[7] *See* Fiske v. Kansas, 274 U.S. 380 (1927) (striking down charges against the Industrial Workers of the World for violating Kansas's Criminal Syndicalism Act where there was no evidence that the organization posed a threat of crime, violence, or other unlawful acts or methods); De Jonge v. Oregon, 299 U.S. 353 (1937) (holding that charges under Oregon's Criminal Syndicalism Act were unconstitutional where the defendant was merely accused of presiding over a peaceful assembly of the Communist Party); Cantwell v. Connecticut, 310 U.S. 296 (1940) (holding that the state violated defendants' rights by convicting them for breach of the peace on the basis of their publicly playing a record that attacked the Catholic religion as part of an attempt to recruit bystanders to Jehovah's Witness, because defendants' conduct, while possibly offensive to many, raised no "clear and present menace to public peace and order"); Bridges v. California, 314 U.S. 252 (1941) (holding that California could not constitutionally punish petitioners for publishing their views on cases pending in the court, because the speech did not present a "clear and present danger" to justify the restrictions).

[8] Dennis v. United States, 341 U.S. 494 (1951).

constitutional protection to beliefs and opinions about national and world affairs, even when expressed in strong and provocative terms.[9]

In applying the clear and present danger standard, the Court came to focus on the concept of imminence, which afforded a bit more protection to speech. Thus, the Court held that a public speech posed a clear and present danger, and was therefore punishable, when it was offensive and put the safety of the speaker or others at risk because of the presence of an angry crowd.[10] But the Court also held that mere criticisms of the government and its officials did not give rise to a clear and present danger to public order because such statements created no imminent threat of disruption. For example, the Court held that negative remarks about judicial decisions failed to meet this standard because they did not interfere with a judge's ability to rule or imminently threaten the fair administration of justice.[11]

Although the *Abrams* dissent had a significant effect on the Court's thinking, it can be argued that contemporary free speech doctrine did not really begin to emerge until the 1940s. A signal moment came in 1943, with the Court's decision in *West Virginia State Board of Education* v. *Barnette*,[12] which we mentioned in Chapter 1. In order to understand the importance of *Barnette*, it is important to consider a case that the Court had decided just a few years earlier, *Minersville School District* v. *Gobitis*.[13]

In *Gobitis*, the Court had upheld in an eight-to-one decision a public school district's policy requiring students to salute the flag as part of a daily exercise. The children of the Gobitis family objected that the compelled salute forced them to engage in speech that violated their religious principles as Jehovah's Witnesses. The Court rejected their claim, finding more important the school district's professed interest in cultivating national unity through the mandatory practice.

Barnette, which came along just three years later, presented essentially identical facts. In that case, the West Virginia Board of Education required teachers and students to participate in a mandatory flag salute as part of their school day. When the children of some Jehovah's Witnesses refused, the school sent them home and threatened them and their parents with further action. Reversing course from its

[9] *See* Taylor v. Mississippi, 319 U.S. 583, 589 (1943) (holding that laws that criminalized the teaching, preaching, or disseminating of materials designed to encourage violence, sabotage or disloyalty to the federal or state government, advocate the cause of US enemies, or create distrust or an attitude of refusal to honor the flag of the federal or state government were unconstitutional).

[10] *See* Feiner v. New York, 340 U.S. 315 (1951) (upholding the arrest of a speaker who had continued to deliver a highly offensive address in spite of both the angry crowd forming around him and a police officer's continuing requests that he stop speaking). The Court would later reject this reasoning as allowing for a "heckler's veto" that empowers an angry group to silence an individual speaker who has unpopular ideas.

[11] *See* Pennekamp v. Florida, 328 U.S. 331 (1946); Craig v. Harney, 331 U.S. 367 (1947); Wood v. Georgia, 370 U.S. 375 (1962).

[12] West Virginia State Board of Education v. Barnette, 319 U.S. 624 (1943).

[13] Minersville School District v. Gobitis, 310 U.S. 586 (1940).

Court reversed course in almost identical cases over just 3 years

decision in *Gobitis*, the Court rejected the state's authority to prescribe political or ideological orthodoxy through a compulsory salute of the flag.

By itself, the fact that the Court so swiftly changed its mind and reversed an eight-to-one precedent makes *Barnette* a remarkable moment in Supreme Court history. But the case is all the more intriguing because of its full-throated endorsement of individualism and the "freedom to differ," even as to issues that go to core societal values. In an often-quoted passage from an opinion by Justice Robert Jackson, the Court declared:

> We can have intellectual individualism and the rich cultural diversities that we owe to exceptional minds only at the price of occasional eccentricity and abnormal attitudes. When they are so harmless to others or to the State as those we deal with here, the price is not too great. But freedom to differ is not limited to things that do not matter much. That would be a mere shadow of freedom. The test of its substance is the right to differ as to things that touch the heart of the existing order.[14]

In a sense, *Barnette* reflects not just a change in doctrine but a change in the role of the Court.

Barnette suggested that the Court would no longer sit by and passively serve as a rubber stamp to government decisions. This differed substantially from the approach taken in *Gobitis*, where the Court had declared that it did not want to serve as "the school board for the country." Instead, the Court now would actively ensure protection for the expression of diverse individual perspectives, even unpopular ones at which people took great offense.

Relatedly, the *Barnette* Court stridently rejected the notion that the government has the authority to tell people what to think and say. In another memorable and often-quoted passage, to which we have previously alluded, the Court declared: "If there is any fixed star in our constitutional constellation, it is that no official, high or petty, can prescribe what shall be orthodox in politics, nationalism, religion, or other matters of opinion or force citizens to confess by word or act their faith therein."[15] The language in *Barnette* marked the Court's embrace of peaceful intellectual individualism that did not tolerate government infringements on personal opinion.[16] And it cemented the Court's rejection of the alternative to the marketplace of ideas: a system in which government officials authoritatively select among ideas and information and dictate a prescribed orthodoxy of belief and understanding.

During the 1940s, the Court also came to recognize that even public disturbance would not necessarily suffice to remove constitutional protection from the speech that caused it. Thus, in 1949 the Court held that free speech "may indeed best serve

[14] *Barnette* at 641–642.

[15] *Barnette* at 642.

[16] *See also* Taylor v. Mississippi, 319 U.S. 583 (1943); Schneiderman v. United States, 320 U.S. 118 (1943); Murdock v. Pennsylvania, 319 U.S. 105 (1943) (overruling Jones v. Opelika, 316 U.S. 584 (1942)); Jamison v. Texas, 318 U.S. 413 (1943); and Thomas v. Collins, 323 U.S. 516 (1945).

its high purpose when it includes a condition of unrest, creates dissatisfaction with conditions as they are or even stirs people to anger."[17] The Court held that laws punishing controversial speech must be narrowly tailored to criminalize only expression fitting into a carefully defined category, such as that which creates a clear and present danger to public safety.[18]

The expansion of free speech rights in the 1940s also highlighted the need to recognize, define, and clarify exceptions. Toward that end, in its 1942 decision in *Chaplinsky* v. *New Hampshire* the Court offered a list of exceptions that had historically been acknowledged:[19]

> There are certain well-defined and narrowly limited classes of speech, the prevention and punishment of which have never been thought to raise any Constitutional problem. These include the lewd and obscene, the profane, the libelous, and the insulting or fighting words – those that by their very utterance inflict injury or tend to incite an immediate breach of the peace. It has been well observed that such utterances are no essential part of any exposition of ideas, and are of such slight social value as a step to truth that any benefit that may be derived from them is clearly outweighed by the social interest in order and morality.[20]

The Court's language here advanced three important ideas.

The first is that, even in a regime of robust protection for free expression, some speech will lie outside of the scope of the First Amendment and the government can therefore restrict and punish it. The second is that we can divide those exceptions into categories based on the content of the speech. As we will see in Chapter 7, the notion that First Amendment doctrine fragments into distinctive analytic categories based on the content of the speech or other factors (such as where it takes place) would become heavily influential in the Court's thinking, and remains so to this day. The third concept is that the categories of speech that fall outside of First Amendment protection must be well defined and narrowly limited.

We will see the Court struggle with the project of cabining these exceptions so they do not unduly limit free expression. As free speech doctrine evolves, the Court will conclude that some of *Chaplinsky*'s categories – like the profane – actually receive a very *high* level of First Amendment protection. Indeed, in today's jurisprudence it probably is not appropriate to think of some of these as true "exceptions" at all.

One of the categories of unprotected speech flagged by *Chaplinsky* was the "lewd and obscene," and during this era the problem of obscenity – and how to define it – began to bedevil the Court. In previous decades, both the states and the federal government had created a variety of laws intended to limit the availability and

[17] Terminiello v. Chicago, 337 U.S. 1, 4 (1949).
[18] *Id.*
[19] Chaplinsky v. New Hampshire, 315 U.S. 568 (1942).
[20] *Id.* at 571–572.

distribution of pornography and other materials deemed immoral. Private citizens challenged these laws, claiming they threatened their First Amendment rights to free speech and expression.

Several of these cases reached the Supreme Court, which then faced the troublesome task of defining obscenity and explicating the boundaries of government regulation of such speech. Although the Court consistently recognized the right of the government to regulate materials "injurious to public morals,"[21] it struck down many of these laws on the grounds of overbreadth or vagueness, indicating that regulations of speech must be specific and provide adequate warning and must not reach too far.[22] But the definitional problem remained, and it was substantial.

The Court struggled to come up with a satisfactory test for determining when materials qualified as "obscene." In *Roth* v. *United States*,[23] Justice Brennan declared that "implicit in the history of the First Amendment is the rejection of obscenity as utterly without redeeming social importance."[24] For years, that "utterly without redeeming social importance" standard guided the Court in its decisions to permit government regulation of obscene speech because of its purportedly base, immoral character.[25] As we will see in Chapter 11, however, over time the Court grew dissatisfied with this test.

Chaplinsky did not purport to list *every* category of speech that the First Amendment might not protect. For example, it did not identify demonstrating or picketing as unprotected expression, perhaps because it thought such activities did not qualify as speech at all. As a form of conduct, the Court may have thought these things simply stood outside of the concerns of the First Amendment.

[21] Winters v. New York, 333 U.S. 507, 515 (1948).

[22] *See Winters*, 333 U.S. at 518 (finding a law that made it a misdemeanor to print, sell, or distribute books comprised principally of "criminal news or stories of deeds of bloodshed, lust or crime" unconstitutional on the grounds that it was too vague); Joseph Burstyn v. Wilson, 343 U.S. 495 (1952) (finding the New York law permitting a censor to ban films for being sacrilegious unconstitutional, as it created an unlawful opportunity for a censor to arbitrarily regulate limit speech through an unclear standard); Smith v. California, 361 U.S. 147 (1959) (holding that a law criminalizing possession of obscene literature in any business where books were sold was unconstitutionally vague, because it did not provide adequate warning to retailers which of their books would be considered obscene); Marcus v. Search Warrant of Property, 367 U.S. 717 (1961) (finding that application of Missouri's search and seizure law in issuing a warrant to seize magazines believed to be obscene abridged the First Amendment, as the materials seized were not specified or confined to certain criteria, giving the police full discretion to determine which materials were lewd or obscene); Bantam Books, Inc. v. Sullivan, 372 U.S. 58, 59 (1963) (striking down an obscenity law created by the Rhode Island Commission to Encourage Morality in Youth on the grounds that it sought to censor or suppress materials without providing procedures that protect against the suppression of protected speech).

[23] Roth v. United States, 354 U.S. 476 (1957).

[24] *Id.* at 484 (upholding the constitutionality of the Federal Obscenity Statute, which punished anyone who attempted to distribute lewd or obscene materials through the United States Postal Service).

[25] *See* Kingsley v. Regents of the Univ. of New York, 360 U.S. 684 (1959).

But in the 1940s the Court confronted directly the question of whether such activities – especially picketing – receive First Amendment protection. In the face of the growth of organized labor, states had adopted a variety of measures to limit picketing. Unions and others began to challenge the constitutionality of those laws. Through a series of cases over the course of the decade, the Court defended the right to assemble and picket, so long as the speech was unconnected to violent or illegal activities.[26] And protestors could exercise this right, the Court held, even in the absence of a contemporaneous labor dispute.[27]

Still, during this era the Court did not hold peaceful protests completely immune from regulation, particularly if they became closely "enmeshed with contemporaneously violent conduct."[28] Similarly, the Court determined that states could enjoin picketing when the speech was intertwined with illegal activity[29] or when it perpetrated unlawful coercion of employers.[30] Finally, the Court held that states retain the power to confine the location of peaceful protests. Thus, in *Carpenters & Joiners Union* v. *Ritter's Café*,[31] the Court upheld a state's authority to limit protesting only to those locations "directly related to the dispute."[32]

Other issues regarding speech and organized labor arose as well. During this period, the Court addressed the first of many cases involving union dues. The Court held that employers could not require employees to pay dues that would later be used to fund political campaigns.[33] Such use of compulsory dues is unconstitutional, the Court reasoned, because it forces employees to support candidates with whom they did not agree – a form of compelled speech like that struck down in *Barnette*.[34] As we see in Chapter 7, this decision would not be the Court's last word on union dues.

The general expansion of First Amendment rights, of the right to dissent, and of the right to pursue union organization met with some setbacks during this era, especially in periods when concerns about Communism were at their height. The widespread fear of Communism, both domestically and abroad, shaped the landscape of American politics between 1919 and 1963, and states enacted laws and procedures designed specifically to identify and penalize members of the Communist Party. These policies presented the courts with the task of determining the extent to which free speech protected communists, and those believed to be communists, from government inquiries and regulations.

[26] *See* Thornhill v. Alabama, 310 U.S. 88 (1940).

[27] American Federation of Labor v. Swing, 312 U.S. 321, 323 (1941). *See also* Bakery & Pastry Drivers & Helpers Local. v. Wohl, 315 U.S. 769, 774 (1942).

[28] Milk Wagon Drivers Union v. Meadowmoor Dairies, 312 U.S. 287, 292 (1941).

[29] Giboney v. Empire Storage & Ice Co., 336 U.S. 490 (1949).

[30] Building Services Employees International Union v. Gazzam, 339 U.S. 532 (1950).

[31] Carpenters & Joiners Union v. Ritter's Café, 315 U.S. 722 (1942).

[32] *Id.* at 727–728.

[33] International Association of Machinists v. Street, 367 U.S. 740 (1961).

[34] *Id.*

In addressing laws targeting communist speech and association, the Court typically relied on the clear and present danger standard.[35] Early in the first third of the century, the Court defended the right to peacefully associate and express communist or anarchist viewpoints.[36] As the Red Scare intensified in the 1950s, however, the Court began to permit more and more state restraints on personal liberties, upholding government-mandated loyalty oaths or anti-communist vows.

The Court's increasing antipathy toward Communism is exemplified in the *Douds* case of 1950, where it declared that the government could withhold National Labor Relations Board benefits until union officers filed an affidavit declaring they were not communists or affiliated with Communism.[37] The Court ruled that this law did not abridge First Amendment rights to free speech or association, because it furthered Congress's interest in protecting interstate commerce from the threat of Communism.[38] Similarly, the Court held in 1952 that public schools could fire teachers for refusing to answer questions regarding their affiliation to parties or groups that advocated the overthrow of the United States government by violent or unlawful means.[39] Such a policy, the Court reasoned, protected the state's vested interest in thoroughly vetting their workforce.[40]

While the Court generally held that oath requirements were permissible, it did acknowledge that the procedures connected with them needed to comply with constitutional standards of due process and fairness.[41] This concession offered only limited consolation to those who were pressured to take loyalty oaths and answer questions about their beliefs and affiliations. After all, compelled speech does not become voluntary simply because due process is fulfilled.

During this era, the Court generally withheld First Amendment protection from those facing investigations into their communist affiliations, apparently accepting the claim that the national interest in fighting Communism outweighed private interests against compelled speech. In this spirit, the Court upheld the authority of

[35] *See* Dennis v. United States, 341 U.S. 494 (1951) (upholding the conviction of two members of the Communist Party under the Smith Act, a law that penalized knowingly and willfully advocating or teaching the propriety of overthrowing the government by force or violence, on the basis that such speech presented a clear and present danger).

[36] Stromberg v. California, 283 U.S. 359 (1931) (striking down a law that criminalized the displaying of any red flag or symbol that either opposed organized government or stimulated anarchistic action).

[37] American Communications Association v. Douds, 339 U.S. 382 (1950).

[38] *Id.*

[39] Adler v. Board of Education, 342 U.S. 485 (1952).

[40] *Id. See also* Beilan v. Board of Education, 357 U.S. 399 (1958) (upholding dismissal of employees for refusing to answer questions about Communist affiliations).

[41] Speiser v. Randall, 357 U.S. 513 (1958). Here, receipt of benefits from the Veteran's Property Tax Exemption was contingent upon applicants taking an oath not to advocate the overthrow of the US government or support foreign countries that wish to. *Id.* at 516. The Court took issue with procedures and structure of this law, citing that it unlawfully placed the burden of proof on the applicant instead of the government. *Id.* at 529.

the Congressional Committee on Un-American Activities to inquire into past or current membership in the Communist Party and to compel witnesses to answer questions on the subject.[42] Similarly, the Court upheld charges for refusing to cooperate, reasoning that the investigation of Communist Party members by Congress served the national interest.[43] The fear of Communism was so great that the Court allowed Congress to make membership in certain political groups a felony where it could be shown that the member knowingly supported the goal of overthrowing the government.[44]

Even the legal profession, which one might hope would be a bastion of liberty and free expression, joined in the anti-communist fervor. Bar application procedures were adopted to probe membership in the Communist Party. Twice the Court issued decisions allowing state bar associations to inquire into the potential communist affiliations of applicants and to deny admission if an applicant refused to answer.[45] In each case, the Court held that such questions were relevant to determining good moral character and that refusal to answer these questions provided the associations sufficient reason to deny admission.[46]

The era of the communist witch hunt marked a dark period in the evolution of free expression. In the 1940s, the Court in *Barnette* had offered lofty assurances about freedom of thought and conscience. But, during the Red Scare, clouds of paranoia and suspicion obscured the "one fixed star in our constitutional constellation" and "officials high [and] petty" were empowered to trample civil liberties.

By the mid-1950s, the anti-communist fever began to abate. In 1954, the Senate voted to censure Senator Joseph McCarthy, one of the leading figures in the movement. The frantic policing of communist speech and association gradually transformed from a cause to an embarrassment. The Court followed suit, ending its pattern of narrowing speech protections when allegations of Communism were involved and instead striking down laws that gave the government the ability to compel disclosure and inquire into people's affiliations. In so doing, the Court relied on both due process and First Amendment principles.[47]

During this era, the Court also began to develop a body of jurisprudence based not on the *content* of speech but on *where it takes place*. The Court decided a number of cases addressing speech on public property, setting the stage for the fuller

[42] Barenblatt v. United States, 360 U.S. 109 (1959). *See also* Braden v. United States, 365 U.S. 431 (1961) and Wilkinson v. United States, 365 U.S. 399 (1961).

[43] Braden v. United States, 365 U.S. 431 (1961). *See also* Communist Party of the United States v. Subversive Activities Control Board, 367 U.S. 1 (1961) (similarly finding that the Subversive Activities Control Act, which required all Communists to register, was constitutional).

[44] Scales v. United States, 367 U.S. 203 (1961) (upholding the Smith Act and reasoning that advocating the overthrow of the government is not protected speech).

[45] *See* Konigsberg v. California, 366 U.S. 36 (1961) and In Re Anastaplo, 366 U.S. 82 (1961).

[46] *See Konigsberg*, 366 U.S. at 56; *In Re Anastaplo*, 366 U.S. at 97.

[47] *See, e.g.*, Cramp v. Board of Public Instruction, 368 U.S. 278 (1961) and Gibson v. Florida Legislative Investigation Committee, 372 U.S. 539 (1963).

development of the "public forum doctrine" that we discuss in Chapter 7. In this line of authority, the Court generally upheld the individual right to disseminate information in such spaces as city streets, parks, and sidewalks, finding them to be "natural and proper places for the dissemination of information and opinion."[48]

The Court viewed the distributing of handbills and pamphlets in such areas to be an important means of circulating information and ideas.[49] Indeed, the image of the lone pamphleteer distributing printed materials in the public square has become something of a First Amendment trope. We revisit that image in Chapter 16 when we consider how social media has come to play a similar role.

Even in these public spaces, however, the Court allowed some limitations on speech.[50] For example, the Court held that states could regulate the mechanisms used in exercising free speech rights.[51] The Court therefore declared that regulations banning the use of loud-speakers on public streets or in public places were permissible, because the noise emitted from these devices is a nuisance and because they create a captive audience by forcing people to listen to the messages conveyed.[52] Such a restriction, the Court reasoned, was an example of constitutional restriction on the time, place, and manner of speech.[53] Importantly, because such a restriction has nothing to do with the content of the speech, it equally affects all ideas and viewpoints and discriminates against none.

In a related body of case law during this era, parties challenged a variety of permit and licensing schemes. Again, the Court recognized that states and cities have the authority to regulate the exercise of speech by specifying its "time, place and manner so as to conserve the public convenience." But the Court held that this authority did

48 Schneider v. State, 308 U.S. 147, 163 (1939).

49 *See* Schneider v. State, 308 U.S. 147 (1939) (striking down a law that prohibited the distribution of any circular, flier, pamphlet, or similar material on public streets, sidewalks or parks, streetcars, or placing these materials on cars); Jamison v. Texas, 318 U.S. 413 (1943) (finding that charges against a Jehovah's Witness for violating a law that forbade the distribution of handbills on public streets violated the First Amendment, as citizens have the right to profess their beliefs in an orderly fashion in public places); Marsh v. Alabama, 326 U.S. 501 (1946) (striking down a law prohibiting the distribution of religious materials on city sidewalks in a corporate-owned town, because the sidewalks were technically still public spaces and the town was not allowed to create laws that punish the distribution of information in these areas); and Talley v. California, 362 U.S. 60 (1960) (striking down a city ordinance on the grounds of overbreadth, reasoning that banning all handbills that failed to name authors and distributers overly and unnecessarily limited the circulation of anonymous publications, which are important tools in the dissemination of ideas).

50 *See* Kovacs v. Cooper, 336 U.S. 77 (1949).

51 *Id.* at 78.

52 *Id.*

53 *Id.* at 86. *C.f.* Public Utilities Commission v. Pollak, 343 U.S. 451 (1952), where the Court determined that a railway company could not be precluded from playing radio programs on its loudspeakers for passengers. *Id.* at 454. Although passengers are technically a captive audience, the Court reasoned that individuals relinquish certain personal liberties when they ride on public transit. *Id.* at 464. Furthermore, since the music was neither offensive nor propaganda, it did not preclude passengers from engaging in conversations. *Id.* at 463.

not endow the government with the power to restrict speech based on its content or the viewpoint it advances.[54]

Justice Owen Roberts, writing for the majority in an often-quoted case from 1939, reasoned:

> Wherever the title of streets and parks may rest, they have immemorially been held in trust for the use of the public and, time out of mind, have been used for purposes of assembly, communicating thoughts between citizens, and discussing public questions. Such use of the streets and public places has, from ancient times, been a part of the privileges, immunities, rights, and liberties of citizens. The privilege of a citizen of the United States to use the streets and parks for communication of views on national questions may be regulated in the interest of all; it is not absolute, but relative, and must be exercised in subordination to the general comfort and convenience, and in consonance with peace and good order; but it must not, in the guise of regulation, be abridged or denied.[55]

In short, the government may have legitimate reasons to exercise some control over the time, place, and manner of speech, and licensing schemes may embody those judgments; but that authority cannot serve as a basis for suppressing particular opinions, ideas, and information.

Even a licensing scheme that on its face does not disfavor any particular content or viewpoint may pose serious risks to free speech if it can be enforced in a discriminatory way. Recognizing this threat, the Court was highly suspicious of any permitting requirement that allowed state officials to apply arbitrary or subjective standards or gave them unbounded or content-based discretion. The Court declared that licensing schemes had to be limited to specific time, place, and manner restrictions, and could not employ broad or vague standards that allowed officials to make decisions based on subjective criteria, the content of the speech, or the character of the speech.[56]

While the Court recognized an expansive right to speak on public property, it struggled with the question of how to think about speech rights on the private

[54] Cox v. New Hampshire, 312 U.S. 569, 576–577 (1941).

[55] Hague v. Committee For Industrial Organization, 307 U.S. 496, 515–516 (1939).

[56] *See* Saia v. New York, 334 U.S. 558 (1948) (holding that an ordinance requiring the chief of police's permission to use sound amplifiers violated the First Amendment, as it provided the chief of police too much discretion in distributing licenses, creating a prior restraint on speech); Hague v. Committee For Industrial Organization, 307 U.S. 496, 501 (1939) (striking down a law requiring permits to lease public halls for meetings "at which a speaker shall advocate obstruction of the government"); Niemotko v. Maryland, 340 U.S. 268, 273 (1951) ("It thus becomes apparent that the lack of standards in the license-issuing 'practice' renders that 'practice' a prior restraint in contravention of the Fourteenth Amendment, and that the completely arbitrary and discriminatory refusal to grant the permits was a denial of equal protection"); Staub v. City of Baxley, 355 U.S. 313, 325 (1958) (striking down a law that required anyone recruiting members to a union or dues-paying organization to obtain a permit from the mayor prior to soliciting memberships because it "makes enjoyment of speech contingent upon the will of the Mayor and Council of the City").

property of others. Door-to-door solicitation required the Court to balance the privacy concerns of homeowners against the right to speak and share information. In a 1943 decision, the Court held that such activities could not be penalized because the importance of the free circulation of ideas outweighed the relatively minor nuisance caused by door-to-door solicitation.[57]

Eight years later, however, the Court reversed course and upheld a law that made door-to-door sales and solicitation a misdemeanor.[58] This time, the Court found that the right to peace and privacy of homeowners outweighed the rights of solicitors to sell door to door.[59] "Freedom of speech or press does not mean that one can talk or distribute where, when and how one chooses," the Court declared.[60] If a community finds door-to-door solicitation obnoxious, the Court ruled, it may regulate this activity.[61]

During this period, the Court also began to engage with issues around the solicitation of legal services, which is a form of speech but also an activity within a regulated profession. In *National Association for the Advancement of Colored People (NAACP)* v. *Button*,[62] the Court confronted a challenge to a Virginia law that prohibited "the improper solicitation of any legal or professional business."[63] The law severely limited the ability of the NAACP, a civil rights organization, to engage in litigation that challenged segregation and to gather the information necessary to pursue that litigation.[64] The Court struck down the law, reasoning that "abstract discussion is not the only species of communication which the Constitution protects; the First Amendment also protects vigorous advocacy, certainly of lawful ends, against governmental intrusion."[65]

This era also brought before the Court the related question of whether the First Amendment affords less protection to commercial speech, that is, speech that proposes a commercial transaction, like an advertisement for a product or service. It is easy to understand why the question might arise: after all, the government

57 Martin v. Struthers, 319 U.S. 141 (1943).
58 Breard v. Alexandria, 341 US 622 (1951).
59 *Id.*
60 *Id.* at 642.
61 *Id.* at 644–645.
62 NAACP v. Button, 371 U.S. 415 (1963).
63 *Id.* at 423–426.
64 *Id.*
65 *Id.* at 429. Justice Brennan explained: "The NAACP is not a conventional political party; but the litigation it assists, while serving to vindicate the legal rights of members of the American Negro community, at the same time and perhaps more importantly, makes possible the distinctive contribution of a minority group to the ideas and beliefs of our society. For such a group, association for litigation may be the most effective form of political association." *Id.* at 431. In 1988, the Court in Shapero v. Kentucky Bar Ass'n, 486 U.S. 466 (1988) further held that the First Amendment precludes states from prohibiting attorneys from attempting to solicit business by sending "truthful and nondeceptive letters to potential clients known to face particular legal problems." *Id.* at 468.

regulates many kinds of commercial activity and a promotion for a soft drink or appliance seems to have little to do with the marketplace of ideas or the informed participation in the democratic process. The Court struggled with the concept of commercial speech, resulting in uncertainty and confusion that will follow us into Chapter 7.

The Court's difficulties with commercial speech started early. During this period, the Court initially viewed commercial speech as unprotected. In a 1942 case, for example, it held that laws requiring revocable licenses to engage in economic activity, such as selling books, were constitutional because they restricted a commercial act, not the freedom to disseminate information.[66] Just one year later, however, the Court backed away from its wholesale exemption of commercial speech from the protection of the First Amendment.

The shift came in *Murdock* v. *Pennsylvania*,[67] which involved a challenge to a city ordinance that required anyone soliciting or delivering "goods, paintings, pictures, wares, or merchandise of any kind" to pay for a license to do so.[68] The city applied the law to Jehovah's Witnesses who had gone door to door in the city seeking small "donations" in exchange for certain religious books and pamphlets.[69] Although on its face the law targeted commercial activity, and although the Jehovah's Witnesses were in a sense selling their publications, the Court found that the law unconstitutionally abridged the free expression of religious beliefs.[70]

Still, the constitutional status of commercial speech remained unclear. After all, *Murdock* involved religious speech and therefore did not settle the question of how much protection the First Amendment affords to simple commercial speech, like a billboard promoting a used car dealership. As we see in Chapter 7, in the years that followed the Court would have numerous occasions to revisit that question and to craft its commercial speech doctrine; and, as we discuss, reasonable people can disagree about whether, to this day, the Court has gotten the doctrine right.

In this era, we also see an increased focus on the connection between due process and freedom of expression, an issue we explored in Chapter 3. During this period, the Court held that, even when a statute regulates only *unprotected* speech, the Due Process Clause still requires that it "give fair notice of what acts will be punished."[71] Of course, concerns about due process and vagueness apply to all criminal laws; but during this period the Court began to recognize their critical role in the context of restrictions on speech.[72]

66 Jones v. Opelika, 316 U.S. 584 (1942).
67 Murdock v. Pennsylvania, 319 U.S. 105 (1943).
68 *Id.* at 106.
69 *Id.* at 116.
70 *Id.* at 117.
71 Winters v. New York, 333 U.S. 507, 509 (1948).
72 Smith v. California, 361 U.S. 147, 151 (1959).

Due process also requires the presence of certain procedural safeguards. As Justice Brennan explained in *Marcus* v. *Search Warrant of Property*,[73] under the Fourteenth Amendment states may not regulate expression "without regard to the possible consequences for constitutionally protected speech."[74] The government must put in place procedures that "ensure against the curtailment of constitutionally protected expression."[75]

As we noted in Chapter 3, the ideas of due process and vagueness are closely related. During this era, the Court held that a law is unconstitutionally vague when men "of common intelligence must necessarily guess at its meaning" in determining which materials would be criminalized.[76] The danger with a vague law, the Court stressed, is that it will deter citizens from even lawful expression out of fear and confusion about what the law actually bans while encouraging prosecutors to engage in arbitrary and discriminatory enforcement.[77]

The Court declared that laws seeking to limit fundamental rights, like speech, must be explicit and specific in what they seek to regulate.[78] Vagueness can also be avoided through "objective measurement[s]" of the criminalized behavior.[79] As we observed in Chapter 3, the law does not require perfect clarity to avoid due process and vagueness problems; but, during this era, we see an increasing sensitivity to these issues on the part of the Court when laws limit speech.

In sum, the period from 1919 to 1963 signaled a paradigm shift in the Court's approach to free expression. Granted, some blemishes marked the Court's protection of speech, particularly during the Red Scare. Nevertheless, the march of First Amendment doctrine generally followed a pattern of expansion of free speech rights. Along the way, a number of essential themes emerged that persist in the development of free speech law: (1) a strong presumption against prior restraints; (2) a keen hostility toward viewpoint- and content-based restrictions; (3) a recognition that the government can impose content-neutral and reasonable time, place, and manner restrictions on speech in public spaces; (4) a rejection of laws that are vague or overly broad or leave too much discretion in the hands of public officials; and (5) a categorical approach to First Amendment doctrine, creating distinctive sets of rules to apply depending on such factors as the content of speech and where it occurs.

During this era, the Court also gradually abandoned the approach taken prior to 1919, when it substantially deferred to the judgments of government officials about which speech needed restricting and how to go about it. The modern approach to

73 Marcus v. Search Warrant of Property, 367 U.S. 717 (1961).
74 *Id.* at 730.
75 Bantam Books, Inc. v. Sullivan, 372 U.S. 58, 66 (1963).
76 *Winters*, 333 U.S. at 518.
77 *Id.* at 520.
78 *See also* Smith v. California, 361 U.S. 147, 151 (1959) (holding that the challenged law did not provide adequate warning to booksellers, as it was not clear which books would be considered obscene).
79 Cramp v. Board of Public Instruction, 368 U.S. 278, 286 (1961).

free expression began to materialize. Subject to a few interruptions, it did so steadily and aggressively.

As we will see, during the next era – from 1964 to the present – the results in the pre-1919 cases grew not just outdated but unimaginable. The vast protections that we currently associate with the First Amendment became a matter of settled precedent. Perhaps even more importantly, they acquired the status of a basic societal value and a key element of national identity. Our First Amendment doctrine took on the qualities of absolutism.

7

The First Amendment from 1964 to the Present

Free Speech Broadened and Compartmentalized

Chapters 5 and 6 describe the very different views that the Court held of the First Amendment prior to 1919 and then from 1919 to 1963. Before 1919, the Court certainly did not think the First Amendment meaningless. But, as we have seen, the Court did view the protections that the Constitution afforded as so narrow and fragile that they collapsed under the weight of almost any articulable government interest.

From 1919 to 1963, modern First Amendment doctrine began to emerge. As Chapter 6 explores, during this era the Court became more sympathetic to claims of free speech rights and more skeptical of claims of governmental interests and authority; it brought an increasingly nuanced approach to the exceptions to First Amendment protection; it recognized the unique evils of compelled speech; it singled out viewpoint- and content-based regulations for special hostility; and it recognized the problems caused by vague and overbroad laws and those that place unfettered discretion in the hands of government officials.

At some point, the robust protections currently associated with the First Amendment started to solidify and the current architecture of the doctrine fell into place. Reasonable people can disagree about the year that marks this transition. We have chosen 1964 for several reasons.

First, although the Court became increasingly sympathetic to free speech claims during the 1940s and 1950s, that era also featured serious departures from the overall trend toward protection. Among other examples, the Court's decisions during the Red Scare of the 1950s, limiting the rights of alleged communists, show that it had not yet arrived at an expansive and resilient-free speech doctrine. A great deal of work remained to be done.

Second, 1964 is the year the Court decided *New York Times* v. *Sullivan*,[1] often viewed as one of the high-water marks of free speech protection. We explore

1 376 U.S. 254 (1964).

Sullivan in greater depth in Chapter 11, when we consider defamation law as one of the so-called exceptions to the First Amendment. For present purposes, it suffices to note that *Sullivan* located speech on issues of public concern, and particularly speech critical of government officials, at the center of the First Amendment.

In addition, *Sullivan* included certain language that the Court has since used repeatedly in describing the role of speech in our democracy. For example, after quoting Justice Brandeis's opinion in *Whitney*, the *Sullivan* Court stated:

> Thus we consider this case against the background of a profound national commitment to the principle that debate on public issues should be uninhibited, robust, and wide-open, and that it may well include vehement, caustic, and sometimes unpleasantly sharp attacks on government and public officials.

The Court has cited and quoted this passage in a wide range of First Amendment cases, including many that have nothing to do with defamation. It is not too much to say that *Sullivan* gave the Court some of its most powerful and enduring First Amendment vocabulary.

There is another reason to take 1964 as signaling a critical pivot in First Amendment doctrine. The cases from 1964 onward tend to follow a more compartmentalized analytic approach than in previous eras. Certainly, in the period from 1919 to 1963 the Court had begun to think about the First Amendment by reference to categories of speech and forms of regulation – for example, recognizing that commercial speech and obscenity presented unique issues that required their own distinctive standards. But, after 1964, this modularity became a defining framework of First Amendment doctrine.

As the years passed, the Court spent less time talking about First Amendment values on a grand scale (although quotations from the rhetorical flourishes of *Abrams*, *Barnette*, and *Sullivan* remained common), and more time talking about the unique problems posed by commercial speech, obscenity, licensing schemes, public employee speech, defamation, and so on. This is unsurprising: as legal doctrine becomes more sophisticated and elaborate, it often gives up comprehensive pronouncements for narrower and more contextual ones. Still, such an approach can have the effect of unmooring legal principles from the foundational values that justify them, leaving people wondering why the law looks like it does. In our view, this phenomenon offers a partial explanation for our current predicament in discussing free speech issues.

In this chapter, we focus on some of the primary themes and categories of speech to occupy the Court from 1964 to the present. This will not exhaust the complexity of the project before us. In Chapter 11, we look more closely at the "exceptions" the Court has identified, refined, and generally narrowed. And in Chapter 8 we think about certain "hard cases" – recurring issues that have bedeviled the Court over the years and that have resisted straightforward answers.

As a result of all this complexity, a reader may conclude that the Supreme Court has not adopted a "First Amendment free speech doctrine" but a *collection* of assorted "First Amendment free speech doctrines." Indeed, that sense of things already may have occurred to you and for good reason: it has a large measure of truth to it.

This multiplication of doctrinal approaches complicates conversations about free expression, because nonspecialists sometimes apply ideas rooted in one area of doctrine to speech that calls for a different kind of analysis. Perhaps the leading example of this is the common invocation of the principle that "you can't cry 'fire' in a crowded theater." As we have discussed, this idea – from Justice Holmes's 1919 opinion in *Schenck* – arose in the context of the doctrine governing speech that incites people to engage in unlawful conduct. It only has limited utility even in that context, and the *Schenck* line of cases was later substantially modified by the Court's ruling in *Brandenburg*, as we discuss in the next section, "Political Dissent." Nevertheless, the phrase has become the most prominent cliché in our free speech conversations. People routinely apply it to any and every conceivable type of expression, including that which has nothing to do with incitement.

Furthermore, as we see in Chapter 8, the "hard cases" reveal yet another reason we struggle in our conversations about free expression. The cases that involve uniquely difficult problems are often the ones that attract public attention, capture its imagination, and invite debate and disagreement. But they also call for the most elaborate and specialized analytic models. Nonspecialist members of the general public usually have little or no familiarity with those more byzantine models or how to apply them.

To address all of these challenges, and to offer some clarity and cohesion, in Chapters 9–11 we identify a number of unifying themes that apply across all of these various categories and subcategories. We call these "basic principles" and believe that they can help conversations about free expression proceed productively, despite the extraordinarily high level of nuance within the formal doctrine. But, before we get to those hard cases and basic principles, we continue our historical overview and consider how First Amendment case law evolved from 1964 to the present.

POLITICAL DISSENT

The post-1963 era ushered in a time of substantial political unrest: protests over civil rights, women's rights, the war in Vietnam, and other controversies raised challenging questions about how much protection the First Amendment extends to speech that is harshly critical of the government, public officials, and the status quo. Beginning with this period, the Court granted significantly more constitutional shelter to such speech than it had previously enjoyed. The 1960s and 1970s were the age of dissent. The Supreme Court made clear that dissident voices do not fall outside of the First Amendment's scope.

As discussed at the beginning of this chapter, *Sullivan* provided a framing of the issues and a vocabulary that offered strong support for this shift. But another watershed moment came in the 1969 case of *Brandenberg* v. *Ohio*,[2] which overruled the Court's 1927 decision in *Whitney* v. *California*, discussed in Chapter 6. As you will recall, in *Whitney*, the Court had upheld a state's right to punish the advocacy of criminal syndicalism, broadly defined to include speech that endangered "the foundations of organized government."[3]

In *Brandenberg*, the Court distinguished between (1) advocacy that constitutes "[t]he mere abstract teaching ... of the moral propriety or even moral necessity for a resort to force and violence" and (2) speech that is actually "directed to inciting or producing imminent lawless action and is likely to incite or produce such action."[4] The Court held that while states have the power to regulate and restrict speech intended to incite imminent violence – and likely to succeed in doing so – the First Amendment protects everything short of that, including the "abstract teaching" of the moral urgency of force.[5]

Reflecting the change in the American political climate, only a handful of the political speech cases after 1963 related to restrictions on communist expression and association. And the few cases that did come before the Court led to very different rulings than those seen in the 1950s during the Red Scare. During this era the Court routinely struck down state laws and regulations that targeted communist speech and ideology.[6]

The bar examination cases offer a good example of this change. As we have discussed, during the preceding era the Court had upheld a state's right to inquire into an applicant's political affiliations and to deny access to those with communist leanings, based on the clear and present danger that communist ideology supposedly presented.[7] In 1971, however, the Court broke with this pattern and upheld the First

2 Brandenburg v. Ohio, 395 U.S. 444 (1969).

3 Whitney v. California, 274 U.S. 357, 371 (1927) (upholding law punishing members of groups that teach, advocate, or aid criminal syndicalism constitutional as "utterances inimical to the public welfare, tending to incite to crime, disturb the public peace, or endanger the foundations of organized government and threaten its overthrow by unlawful means").

4 *Brandenburg*, 395 U.S. at 447.

5 *Id.* at 448.

6 *See, e.g.*, Lamont v. Postmaster General, 381 U.S. 301, 307 (1965) (striking down a law that allowed the Postmaster General to detain any mail he determined to be "communist political propaganda," notify the sender of the detention, and require the sender to return an attached card in order to get the mail back); De Gregory v. Attorney General of New Hampshire, 383 U.S. 825, 830 (1966) (overturning a conviction for contempt imposed as a result of De Gregory's refusal to answer certain questions regarding his past political ideologies); and Keyishian v. Board of Regents, 385 U.S. 589 (1967) (finding that New York University's dismissal of professors for refusing to answer questions regarding Communist affiliations was an unconstitutional infringement on First Amendment rights).

7 *See* Konigsberg v. California, 366 U.S. 36 (1961). *See also* In Re Anastaplo, 366 U.S. 82 (1961).

Amendment rights of bar applicants to refuse to disclose their affiliations with such organizations.[8]

During this era, the Court further recognized that political dissent does not lose its constitutional protection simply because the speaker uses expletives to convey it. As we discussed in Chapter 6, in *Chaplinsky*, the Court had stated that the categories of unprotected speech included the "lewd" and the "profane." Consistent with this view, many states had adopted laws that criminalized the use of such language, particularly in the presence of women or children.[9]

In the post-1963 period, however, the Court afforded such expression a substantial measure of First Amendment protection. The Court held that states may not criminalize the mere display of expletives without particularized and compelling reasons that go beyond protecting unwilling members of the public from seeing these sorts of words. Thus, in *Cohen* v. *California*,[10] which we discussed in Chapter 2, the Court upheld the right of a protestor to wear a jacket in public with the phrase "Fuck the Draft" emblazoned across the back. The Court recognized that citizens have the freedom to convey their thoughts through powerful language, and that one person's vulgarity is another person's lyric.

EXPRESSIVE CONDUCT

The period in United States history after 1963 witnessed large-scale demonstrations and protests. First Amendment freedoms were exercised and challenged at every opportunity. As a result, the Supreme Court heard a plethora of cases regarding citizens' right to assemble and speak freely regarding issues of public importance.

Some of these cases involved the complex problems presented by "expressive conduct" – that is, conduct intended to convey a message. Conduct may give rise to safety and other concerns that pure speech does not, so the argument in favor of greater governmental power to regulate is stronger. At the same time, however, some of our most compelling and dramatic ways of communicating involve conduct, like burning a draft card or a flag. The Court faced the difficult question of how to weigh these competing considerations.

8 *See* Baird v. State Bar of Arizona, 401 U.S. 1 (1971). *See also* In Re Stolar, 401 U.S. 23, 27 (1971) (holding that the state of Ohio may not require an applicant for admission to the Bar to disclose whether they have been a "member of any organization which advocates the overthrow of the government of the United States by force"). *C.f.*, Law Students Civil Rights Research Council, Incorporated v. Wadmond, 401 U.S. 154 (1971) (upholding the New York State Bar's requirement that before admission applicants must undergo a character evaluation and take an oath that they will support both the New York and United States constitutions).

9 For a discussion of a state statute including such a prohibition and with roots dating to 1897, *see* People v. Boomer, 250 Mich. App. 534 (2002). The Michigan Court of Appeals held the statute unconstitutional.

10 Cohen v. California, 403 U.S. 15 (1971).

The issue came before the Court in 1968 in *United States* v. *O'Brien*,[11] which addressed a conscriptee's burning of his draft card as an act of protest against the Vietnam War. There, the Court adopted a test built around the assumption that sometimes the government will have a significant interest in regulating conduct that has nothing to do with that conduct's expressive quality. To take an obvious example, the government can legitimately prosecute someone for throwing a brick through their neighbor's window, even if the act was done to make a point.

The *O'Brien* Court summarized the resulting test this way:

> [W]e think it clear that a government regulation is sufficiently justified if it is within the constitutional power of the Government; if it furthers an important or substantial governmental interest; if the governmental interest is unrelated to the suppression of free expression; and if the incidental restriction on alleged First Amendment freedoms is no greater than is essential to the furtherance of that interest.[12]

There, the Court found that the government had a substantial interest in preserving the physical integrity of draft cards – specifically, to assist in the administration of the draft. It could, accordingly, prohibit their destruction, even if the draftee was burning his card for expressive purposes.[13]

Three decades later, however, the Court held that the same reasoning did not apply to a law that prohibited the burning of the American flag. In two earlier cases during this era, the Court had shown considerable skepticism regarding prosecutions for flag desecration.[14] But, in 1989, the Court finally had occasion to directly address the question.

In 1984, Gregory Lee Johnson burned an American flag in front of the Dallas City Hall in protest of the policies of the Reagan administration. He was tried and convicted under a Texas law that criminalized flag desecration, sentenced to a year in jail, and assessed a $2,000 fine. In its five-to-four decision in *Texas* v. *Johnson*,[15] the Court found flag-burning to be "sufficiently imbued with elements of communication" to fall within the scope of the First Amendment.[16] It further held that the state's purported interests in criminalizing flag-burning – keeping the peace and preserving a national symbol – did not override the foundational right to free and

[11] United States v. O'Brien, 391 U.S. 367 (1968).

[12] *Id.* at 377.

[13] It should be noted that *O'Brien* has been criticized and its continuing significance is unclear. At a minimum, on its specific facts and in connection with draft cards, technological advances would seem to call into question the government's interest in having someone preserve a piece of paper.

[14] *See, e.g.*, Street v. New York, 394 U.S. 576 (1969) and Smith v. Goguen, 415 U.S. 566, 568–569 (1974).

[15] Texas v. Johnson, 491 U.S. 397 (1989).

[16] *Id.* at 404.

public political expression.[17] Interestingly, the Court majority was made up of justices viewed as liberal (Brennan and Marshall), liberal-moderate (Blackmun), conservative-moderate (Kennedy), and conservative (Scalia).

In response to the *Johnson* ruling, in 1989 Congress swiftly passed the federal Flag Protection Act, making it a crime to destroy an American flag or a likeness of it. One Shawn Eichman, with equal promptness, set fire to such a flag on the steps of the United States Capitol. The same majority of the Court held the Act unconstitutional. The Court declared: "If there is a bedrock principle underlying the First Amendment, it is that the Government may not prohibit the expression of an idea simply because society finds the idea itself offensive or disagreeable."[18]

MARCHES AND DEMONSTRATIONS

Expressive conduct includes those circumstances when citizens take their speech to the streets to participate in marches, demonstrations, parades, sit-ins, and other forms of public protest. These activities obviously include "pure speech": the signs that people carry, the buttons they wear, the chants they recite, and the speeches they give. But they also entail conduct that has its own expressive significance. The very act of gathering with hundreds, or even thousands, of people says something that a lone voice does not and cannot.

Although such activities play a critical role in a democratic society and provide uniquely compelling ways to speak out, additional complications come with them. Crowds give rise to legitimate governmental concerns about safety and order. And even the most peaceful of large protests will disrupt things to some extent – indeed, that disruption can be part of the message as well. In the years following 1963, the Court had multiple occasions to consider these conflicting interests.

A number of these cases involved licensing ordinances, which states and local units of government used to prohibit or limit such activities. Those ordinances were often justified as restrictions on conduct like marching, assembling in a large crowd, holding a parade, and so on. But they also operated as prior restraints on speech – that is, as prohibitions against engaging in certain expression without the government's permission.

The Court struck down many of these laws as impermissible prior restraints on speech, particularly when they gave local officials "unfettered discretion" in the regulation of citizens' free speech rights.[19] In *Shuttlesworth* v. *Birmingham*,[20] Justice Stewart explained:

[17] *Id.* at 420.

[18] United States v. Eichman, 496 U.S. 310, 319 (1990).

[19] *See* Cox v. Louisiana, 379 U.S. 536, 558 (1965) (striking down the application of a Louisiana law that criminalized "(1) congregating with others 'with intent to provoke a breach of the peace, or under circumstances such that a breach of the peace may be occasioned,' and (2) a refusal to move on after having been ordered to do so by a law enforcement officer").

[20] Shuttlesworth v. Birmingham, 394 U.S. 147, 148 (1969). Petitioner had been convicted of violating a Birmingham ordinance that criminalized the participation in any "parade or procession or other public demonstration" without a permit from the City. *Id.* at 149. The

> Even when the use of its public streets and sidewalks is involved, therefore, a municipality may not empower its licensing officials to roam essentially at will, dispensing or withholding permission to speak, assemble, picket, or parade, according to their own opinions regarding the potential effect of the activity in question on the "welfare," "decency," or "morals" of the community.[21]

The Court recognized that granting officials this sort of unbridled discretion inevitably leads to the suppression of speech that is unpopular with those in power – exactly the type of abridgment of expression that the First Amendment exists to prevent.

FORUM ANALYSIS

Although protests and demonstrations tend to take place in public streets and parks, not all speech does so. Different settings call for different legal tests. During this era, the Court continued to solidify and clarify its conceptual model for dealing with this issue, usually called "forum analysis" or the "public forum doctrine."

Forum analysis divides the settings in which speech takes place into three different categories.[22] In a "traditional public forum," such as streets, sidewalks, and parks, the speech rights of citizens receive their highest levels of protection.[23] In this forum, the First Amendment prohibits a state from restricting "access to a single class of speakers, a single viewpoint, or a single subject."[24]

The government is not powerless to restrain speech in a traditional public forum, but its authority is highly circumscribed. The government may impose reasonable time, place, and manner restrictions on speech, provided that those limitations have nothing to do with the content of the speech, are narrowly tailored to serve a significant governmental interest, and leave open ample alternative channels for communication of the information.[25] A content-based restriction in such a forum will be subject to "strict scrutiny," which we define and discuss in the next section, "Content- and Viewpoint-Based Restrictions"; for present purposes, suffice it to say that very few content-based restrictions will be found constitutional under this highly demanding standard.

Ward v. *Rock Against Racism*[26] provides a good example of a permissible time, place, and manner restriction. There, the Court held that New York City's attempt

Court found that this granted too much discretion to authorities, allowing them to stifle citizens' First Amendment rights. *Id.* at 154.

21 *Id.* at 153.

22 The literature, and even the Court's opinions, reflect some differences in how to label these categories, particularly the last two. We have put aside the labels in favor of descriptions of how the Court thinks they differ.

23 Schneider v. State, 308 U.S. 147, 163 (1939).

24 Perry Education Association v. Perry Local Educators' Association, 460 U.S. 37 (1983).

25 Ward v. Rock against Racism, 491 U.S. 781, 791 (1989).

26 *Id.*

to control the noise from a concert by requiring performers to use city-provided sound technicians and equipment had been done through a properly tailored, content-neutral ordinance.[27] Notably, the city had not attempted to impose these restrictions on only those performances pertaining to a particular topic or advocating a particular viewpoint. The city had a concern about noise levels in an area that adjoined residential neighborhoods – regardless of what was being said and who was saying it – and had adopted a sensible and focused regulation designed to address that concern.

The second category of forum is space that the government has opened up to serve as a public forum, even though the space has not traditionally operated as such. These are often called "designated" public forums. Such a forum might be physical – for example, an auditorium in a public building. Or it might be virtual – for example, a municipality's Facebook page or Twitter feed. Or it might be economic – for example, a public university's fund to support student organizations. But the idea is the same: the government has made the forum available for speech, even though neither tradition nor necessity require it.

The third category of forum is a space that the government has *not* by tradition or designation opened up for public communication. Again, such a space could be physical, virtual, or economic. With respect to such a nonpublic forum, the government has much greater leeway. As with public forums, it can impose reasonable time, place, and manner restrictions. But, in the case of a nonpublic forum dedicated to a specific use, the government may also impose restrictions that preserve the forum's purpose.[28]

In a nonpublic forum, the government can therefore impose *subject matter-based* regulations that reasonably serve the forum's limited and specified goals. For example, a municipality could designate its Facebook page as a space restricted to speech relating to city business and could delete content that a local business posted to promote a commercial venture. Still, even in the case of a nonpublic forum, the government may not engage in *viewpoint-based* discrimination.[29] So, that same municipality could not limit its Facebook page to speech that favors Democrats and delete content that someone posted promoting Republicans. We will have more to say shortly about the content–viewpoint distinction and why it matters.

Forum analysis usually does not apply to private property. For the most part, private property owners can prohibit unwelcome speakers from coming onto their land or into their homes or businesses. Still, in some isolated and unusual cases, the Court has applied forum analysis to private property.

The leading example of such a case is *Amalgamated Food Employees Union v. Logan Valley Plaza*.[30] There, the Court held that banning picketing on land

27 *Id.*
28 Lamb's Chapel v. Center Moriches Union Free School District, 508 U.S. 384, 390 (1993).
29 Rosenberger v. Rector & Visitors of the Univ. of Va., 515 U.S. 819, 829 (1995).
30 Amalgamated Food Employees Union v. Logan Valley Plaza, 391 U.S. 308 (1968).

outside stores in a strip mall violated the First Amendment.[31] Even though the open areas surrounding shopping centers and strip malls were technically on private land, the Court reasoned that those areas were publicly accessible via sidewalks and roadways.[32] The Court held:

> Ownership does not always mean absolute dominion. The more an owner, for his advantage, opens up his property for use by the public in general, the more do his rights become circumscribed by the statutory and constitutional rights of those who use it. Logan Valley Mall is the functional equivalent of a 'business block' and for First Amendment purposes must be treated in substantially the same manner.[33]

CONTENT- AND VIEWPOINT-BASED RESTRICTIONS

As the preceding discussion makes clear, the public forum doctrine developed by the Court during this era takes a fairly sympathetic view of the government's need to impose reasonable time, place, and manner restrictions on speech but a conspicuously hostile view of the government's impulse to restrain speech based on its content or viewpoint. This makes sense, given the core values that underlie our protection of free expression: after all, content- and viewpoint-based regulations distort the "marketplace of ideas," effectively declaring the winners and losers in the competition. In this sense, such regulations impose the sort of prescribed orthodoxy against which Justice Jackson warned in *Barnette.*

We will have more to say about content- and viewpoint-based restrictions in Chapter 9. For now, it suffices to define a few terms and summarize the Court's approach. It is essential to understand this area of doctrine, because it explains our struggles with many complex issues we explore later, like hate speech in Chapter 12.

Let's start with "content-based" restrictions. A content-based restriction regulates speech based on its subject matter, prohibiting the discussion of some things while allowing the discussion of others. Content-based laws typically trigger strict scrutiny – the government must show that the law serves a compelling interest and does so in a narrowly tailored way. The Court has often held content-based laws unconstitutional.

A good example of such a restriction comes in *Police Dep't of Chicago* v. *Mosley.*[34] There, a Chicago ordinance prohibited picketing within 150 feet of a public school but provided an exception for "the peaceful picketing of any school involved in a labor dispute."[35] Mosley wanted to picket in front of the school with a sign that charged it with "black discrimination." Because this was a subject

[31] *Id.* at 309.
[32] *Id.* at 317.
[33] *Id.* at 325.
[34] Police Dep't of Chicago v. Mosley, 408 U.S. 92 (1972).
[35] *Id.*

disconnected from any ongoing labor dispute, the ordinance prohibited him from doing so. The Court had little difficulty concluding that the law amounted to unconstitutional content discrimination.[36]

This doctrine notwithstanding, it is important to recognize that the government can, and does, allow for the punishment of some speech because of its content. Indeed, we could hardly imagine a well-ordered society that did *not* do so. Criminal laws that punish blackmail, extortion, and threats do so because of their content. And the so-called exceptions we will examine in Chapter 11 – fighting words, obscenity, defamation, and so on – are given *less* First Amendment protection because of their content. Since 1964, the Court generally has proven extremely hesitant to approve content-based restrictions outside of these traditional categories.

Viewpoint discrimination is a subset of content discrimination. A viewpoint-based law targets the particular perspective of the speaker, not just the subject of their speech. If, for example, the ordinance at issue in *Mosley* had allowed only pro-employer picketing during a labor dispute, it would have been an instance not just of *content* discrimination ("you can only picket on the subject of labor disputes") but of *viewpoint* discrimination ("you must take the side of management").

The Court has declared that viewpoint discrimination is even more highly suspect than content discrimination. In the *Rosenberger* case,[37] Justice Kennedy explained:

> When the government targets not subject matter, but particular views taken by speakers on a subject, the violation of the First Amendment is all the more blatant. Viewpoint discrimination is thus an egregious form of content discrimination. The government must abstain from regulating speech when the specific motivating ideology or the opinion or perspective of the speaker is the rationale for the restriction.[38]

The distinction rests on a sensible proposition: the government may sometimes have very good reasons for punishing certain content; but it is hard to imagine any reason for the government to punish a particular viewpoint, beyond the fact that it likes some perspectives better than others.

The distinction between content and viewpoint discrimination therefore carries significant weight. It turns out, however, to be more challenging to apply than one might think. For example, a public university's regulation disadvantaging "religious" publications might seem to go to their *content*. But, in the *Rosenberger* case, the Court found that this constituted *viewpoint* discrimination, on the theory that religious discussion reflects "a specific premise, a perspective, a standpoint from

[36] *Id.* at 95. *See also Carey* v. *Brown*, 447 U.S. 455, 457 (1980) (holding that the state law prohibiting picketing in residential areas, but allowing "peaceful picketing of a place of employment involved in a labor dispute or the place of holding a meeting or assembly on premises commonly used to discuss subjects of general public interest," was an unlawful content-based restriction on free speech).

[37] Rosenberger v. Rector & Visitors of the University of Virginia, 515 U.S. 819 (1995).

[38] *Id.* at 828–829 (internal citations omitted).

which a variety of subjects may be discussed and considered." The Court also there acknowledged that the distinction between content- and viewpoint-based discrimination "is not a precise one."

In addition, the doctrine can lead to some highly nuanced, perhaps counter-intuitive, results. For example, the Court has held that the First Amendment allows the government to adopt a law that punishes certain threats, including threats communicated by cross-burning.[39] This is a content-based restriction, but a compelling government interest supports it. Still, the Court has also held that a law that punishes cross-burning that "arouses anger, alarm or resentment in others *on the basis of race, color, creed, religion or gender*" is an unconstitutional viewpoint-based restriction.[40]

As noted, we return to these ideas in Chapter 9. For now, the critical point is that during this most recent era the Court's doctrines regarding content- and viewpoint-based restrictions came to play a significant, often dispositive, role in First Amendment analysis. This marked a sharp departure from earlier eras, where the Court endorsed restrictions based not only on content but on viewpoint – for example, the anti-Communism laws at issue during the Red Scare.

The preceding discussion offers an overview of the general analytic landscape from 1964 to the present. During this period, we see the continuing refinement of doctrine, overwhelmingly characterized by greater protection for free expression. We turn next to some of the most difficult issues the Court has faced in this era.

39 Virginia v. Black, 538 U.S. 343, 359 (2003) (upholding law prohibiting cross-burnings with the "intent of intimidating any person or group of persons").

40 R.A.V. v. St. Paul, 505 U.S. 377 (1992) (holding a Bias-Motivated Crime Ordinance unconstitutional as a form of viewpoint discrimination). Emphasis added.

8

The First Amendment from 1964 to the Present

Hard Cases

The Court's increasingly categorical approach to First Amendment doctrine created a conceptual tool box: use this analysis for defamation, that one for obscenity; use this analysis for a content-based regulation, that one for a content-neutral time, place, and manner restriction; use this analysis for a traditional public forum, that one for a nonpublic forum; use this analysis for a prior restraint, that one for a subsequent punishment; and so on. In general, this approach yielded fairly clear guidance, although reasonable people can disagree about the merits of the results. Along the way, however, the Court encountered some hard cases that called for their own distinctive approaches.

COMMERCIAL SPEECH

As noted in Chapter 6, "commercial speech" is speech that proposes a commercial transaction, like an advertisement. The Court has struggled to settle on the correct approach to commercial speech, in part because this category encompasses such a wide range of communication. Commercial speech includes advertisements for legal services that are essential to the protection of constitutional rights, which would seem closely associated with the First Amendment's role in promoting democratic values. But it also includes advertisements for washing machines and antiperspirant, which would seem to have little to do with the vaunted marketplace of ideas.

As we discussed in Chapter 6, in some pre-1964 decisions the Court had held that the government could freely regulate purely commercial speech.[1] In the post-1963 era, however, the Court made clear that the First Amendment was not indifferent to

[1] Valentine v. Chrestensen, 316 U.S. 52, 55 (1942).

speech simply because it was commercial.[2] The challenge was to settle on a test for determining how much protection it received and when.

The turning point for commercial speech came in *Virginia State Board of Pharmacy* v. *Virginia Citizens Consumer Council*,[3] which involved a state law that prohibited pharmacists from advertising the prices of prescription drugs. The government argued that the law was necessary to preserve the professionalism of pharmacists and to prevent the decline in drug quality that could follow from intense price competition. The Court was not persuaded by either argument and struck the law down, holding that the First Amendment protects such speech so that consumers can receive the information they need.[4] Interestingly, the decision therefore rested not only on the right of pharmacists to *share* such information but on the right of consumers to *receive* it.

Throughout the 1970s, the Court decided a series of cases addressing a range of commercial speech issues without settling on a clear test.[5] Then, in its 1980 decision in *Central Hudson Gas & Electric Corporation* v. *Public Service Commission*,[6] the Court offered a streamlined analysis. In explaining the *Central Hudson* test, Justice Powell, speaking for the Court, wrote:

> For commercial speech to come within [the First Amendment], it at least must concern lawful activity and not be misleading. Next, we ask whether the asserted governmental interest is substantial. If both inquiries yield positive answers, we must determine whether the regulation directly advances the governmental interest asserted, and whether it is not more extensive than is necessary to serve that interest.

[2] Pittsburgh Press, 413 U.S. 376 (1973) (noting that "ordinary commercial speech" might serve a First Amendment interest in some cases, although it did not in this case where the advertised commercial activity was itself illegal) and Bigelow v. Virginia, 421 U.S. 809, 826 (1975) (holding that advertising is not "stripped of all First Amendment protection. The relationship of speech to the marketplace of products or of services does not make it valueless in the marketplace of ideas").

[3] Virginia State Board of Pharmacy v. Virginia Citizens Consumer Council, 425 U.S. 748 (1976).

[4] *Id.* at 765.

[5] *See* Carey v. Population Services International, 491 U.S. 678, 700 (1977) (holding, with respect to a law criminalizing the sale of contraceptives to minors under sixteen years old as well as any advertisement of these products, that the state cannot "completely suppress the dissemination of concededly truthful information about entirely lawful activity," even when that information could be categorized as "commercial speech"); Bates v. State Bar of Arizona, 433 U.S. 350 (1977) (holding that a law barring attorneys from advertising their services abridged the right to free speech); Ohralik v. Ohio State Bar Association, 436 U.S. 447, 449 (1978) (upholding a state law that subjected lawyers to disciplinary action "for soliciting clients in person, for pecuniary gain, under circumstances likely to pose dangers," because the state's interest in preventing attorneys from placing undue pressure and unfairly wielding influence over potential clients outweighed First Amendment concerns); and Friedman v. Rogers, 440 U.S. 1 (1979) (holding that the state interest in prohibiting practitioners of optometry from work under a trade name outweighed the right to free expression, particularly given that trade names can be used to conceal bad reputations and create false associations to higher quality optometry practices).

[6] Central Hudson Gas & Electric Corporation v. Public Service Commission, 447 U.S. 557, 566 (1980).

This test sends mixed signals about the amount of protection that commercial speech receives: clearly more than nothing, but definitely less than full. If the speech promotes a lawful activity and is neither false nor misleading, a state regulation of it will be subject to a kind of intermediate scrutiny, a more forgiving standard than the strict scrutiny we discussed earlier in the book and applicable in other First Amendment settings.

Posadas de Puerto Rico Associations v. *Tourism Company*[7] provides an example of the Court's validation of a commercial speech restriction under *Central Hudson*. There, the Court upheld a Puerto Rico statute restraining advertisements for gambling at casinos, even though gambling was legal in Puerto Rico.[8] The Court found the restrictions on such advertisements to be both connected to the valid interest of decreasing gambling as well as narrowly tailored to advance that goal.[9]

The relatively forgiving nature of the *Central Hudson* test was demonstrated in *Board of Trustees* v. *Fox*.[10] In that case, the Court declared that laws regulating commercial speech did not need to use the "least-restrictive" means possible, but instead only needed to be narrowly tailored and "no more extensive than reasonably necessary to further substantial interests."[11] In other words, the existence of a *less* restrictive means of regulation does not necessarily mean that a *more* restrictive policy is unconstitutional. This standard allows the government to regulate commercial speech in ways that would be constitutionally problematic if applied to other kinds of expression, like political speech.

Still, even under *Central Hudson* the Court has struck down many restrictions on commercial speech.[12] That may have less to do with the *Central Hudson* test being adequately protective of expression and more to do with a legislative tendency to overreach in its regulation of commercial speech. The Court has taken issue with laws that were overbroad, targeting both commercial and noncommercial speech.[13]

7 Posadas de Puerto Rico Associations v. Tourism Company, 478 U.S. 328 (1986).

8 *Id.* at 330.

9 *Id.* at 347. *See also* United States v. Edge Broadcasting Company, 509 U.S. 418, 421 (1993) (upholding a federal law prohibiting broadcasters from playing advertisements for lotteries in a state that prohibits lotteries).

10 *Board of Trustees* v. *Fox*, 492 U.S. 469 (1989).

11 *Id.* at 476–477.

12 *See* Edenfield v. Fane, 507 U.S. 761 (1993) (striking down a solicitation ban for certified public accountants, as the social interests advanced in a solicitation bans for lawyers are not advanced in a ban on certified public accountant in-person advertising); Greater New Orleans Broad. Association v. U.S., 527 U.S. 173 (1999) (holding that, because the state failed to demonstrate that their interests would be advanced, a law barring radio and television stations from running advertisements for private casinos violated the First Amendment); Lorillard Tobacco Company v. Reilly, 533 U.S. 525 (2001) (striking down sections of a statute that regulated the sale of cigarettes, including a section that forbade outside advertising).

13 *See* Metromedia Inc. v. City of San Diego, 453 U.S. 490 (1981) (striking down a law that prohibited posting advertisements or billboards and embracing both commercial and noncommercial speech). Although states have asserted various interests in regulating commercial speech, such as protecting confidentiality, Sorrell v. IMS Health Inc., 564 U.S. 552, 557 (2011),

And the Court has invalidated commercial speech regulations that compelled sellers to advertise,[14] dictated the information that could be included in an advertisement,[15] or precluded the dissemination of truthful, nondeceptive information.[16]

SPEECH RELATED TO ABORTION

Abortion is obviously among the most deeply divisive issues within our society. It is therefore not surprising that the state and federal governments have in various ways sought to regulate speech about it. The cases involving limitations on speech about abortion have tested the limits of First Amendment protection, for both sides of the debate.

The early cases related to state statutes that criminalized the publication of advertisements that facilitated or promoted the procuring of these medical services. In *Bigelow* v. *Virginia*,[17] the Supreme Court of Virginia upheld a state statute that included such a provision on the basis that such advertisements were commercial speech and were therefore outside the orbit of the First Amendment. Relying heavily on language from *New York Times* v. *Sullivan*, the United States Supreme Court reversed, holding that such advertisements include important information in the public interest and so constitute protected speech.

The Court took a different view of abortion-related speech, however, in *Rust* v. *Sullivan*,[18] when it addressed the constitutionality of a statute that provided funding for family-planning services. The law, and the regulations adopted under it, prohibited not just the providing but even the discussion of abortion as a method of family planning. The statute effectively defunded "all discussion about abortion as a lawful option – including counseling, referral, and the provision of neutral and accurate information about ending a pregnancy – while compelling the clinic or counselor to provide information that promotes continuing a pregnancy to

preventing the mailing of unsolicited advertisements, Bolger v. Youngs Drug Prods. Corp., 463 U.S. 60 (1983), deterring production of compound drugs, Thompson v. W. States Med. Ctr., 535 U.S. 357 (2002), or avoiding excessive competition in the beer industry, Rubin v. Coors Brewing Co., 514 U.S. 476 (1995), the Court held that free speech rights outweighed these interests.

14 *See* United States v. United Foods, 533 U.S. 405 (2001) (holding unconstitutional a law that required mushroom farmers to subsidize advertisements for mushrooms as a form of compelled speech).

15 *See* In re R.M.J, 455 U.S. 191 (1982) (holding unconstitutional a law dictating the information that lawyers could provide in their advertisements).

16 *See* Zauderer v. Office of Disciplinary Counsel of Supreme Court, 471 U.S. 626 (1985) (holding unconstitutional laws that allow states to punish attorneys for publishing truthful, nondeceptive advertisements) and Shapero v. Kentucky Bar Ass'n, 486 U.S. 466, 468 (1988) (holding that the First Amendment precludes states from prohibiting attorneys from attempting to solicit business by sending "truthful and nondeceptive letters to potential clients known to face particular legal problems").

17 Bigelow v. Virginia, 421 U.S. 809, 811 (1975).

18 Rust v. Sullivan, 500 U.S. 173 (1991).

term."[19] Physicians and grantees challenged the law as violative of their First Amendment rights.

The Court upheld the constitutionality of the statute. It reasoned that such a policy did not run afoul of the First Amendment because the government had the prerogative to decide which programs they thought were beneficial to the public and to fund those but not others.[20] The Court held that, because the government has the authority to allocate its funds, and because such choices always will result in the advancement of some goals at the expense of others, those decisions do not constitute forbidden viewpoint or content discrimination.[21]

A number of cases before the Court raised a different issue: protests outside abortion clinics. As the intensity of anti-abortion demonstrations escalated, clinics sought injunctions from courts to limit the activities of protestors. States adopted laws with similar goals.

These injunctions and laws varied in their details, resulting in a series of highly context-specific decisions from the Supreme Court. It is impossible to overstate the complexity of these cases, which pitted the exercise of a constitutionally protected privacy right against the exercise of a constitutionally protected speech right. Often, the Court upheld some aspects of the restriction while striking down others.

For example, *Madsen* v. *Women's Health Center*[22] involved a court order that created a thirty-six-foot "buffer zone" around the front of a clinic, created a similar zone along the back and side of the clinic, imposed noise limitations, restricted the use of images, barred protestors from approaching patients when they were within a 300-foot radius of the clinic, and prohibited all protesting within that same radius of clinic staff residences. The Court approved the buffer zone in front of the clinic and the noise limitation on the basis that they were content-neutral time, place, and manner restrictions that were necessary to facilitate ingress to, egress from, and use of the facility. But the Court struck down all of the other aspects of the injunction, either because they were not necessary to allow the clinic to function and for staff to peaceably occupy their homes or because they were otherwise overbroad.

Two years later, the Court considered an injunction that imposed somewhat different restrictions on protestors. Again, a mixed result followed. In *Schenck* v. *Pro-Choice Network of Western New York*,[23] the trial court entered an injunction that created "fixed buffer zones," which prohibited demonstrations within fifteen feet of clinic entrances, parking lots, and driveways, but also "floating buffer zones," which barred protestors from coming within fifteen feet of individuals seeking access to the clinic. The Supreme Court upheld the former part of the injunction because

19 Rust v. Sullivan, 500 U.S. 173, 192 (1991).
20 *Id.* at 193.
21 *Id.* at 194.
22 Madsen v. Women's Health Center, 512 U.S. 753 (1994).
23 Schenck v. Pro-Choice Network of W. N.Y., 519 U.S. 357, 364 (1997).

it advanced the government interest in public safety, but struck down the latter as overbroad and confusing to administer.

As abortion protests continued, states began adopting laws that imposed restrictions on demonstrators. In *Hill* v. *Colorado*,[24] 2000, the Court considered a Colorado statute that made it unlawful for any person within a hundred feet of a clinic entrance to knowingly approach within eight feet of another person, without that person's consent, "for the purpose of passing a leaflet or handbill to, displaying a sign to, or engaging in oral protest, education, or counseling with such other person." The Court upheld the law, reasoning that it was a content-neutral time, place, and manner restriction on speech. The Court found it important that the law did not restrict where protestors could stand; it just created a zone where they could not approach others without their consent.

Hill surprised some observers of the Court. The majority was made up of justices from across the ideological spectrum, including conservatives (like Chief Justice Rehnquist) and liberals (like Justice Ginsburg). And the decision seemed to allow greater restrictions on protestors than had been permitted in the past. Questions immediately arose as to whether the Court would in short order reverse course and overrule *Hill*.

The opportunity seemed to present itself in 2014 in *McCullen* v. *Coakley*.[25] In that case, a Massachusetts law created a buffer zone of a thirty-five-foot radius around the entrances, exits, and driveways of abortion clinics. A unanimous Court held the law unconstitutionally overbroad, in substantial part because it affected the rights of protestors to use the public streets and sidewalks, which are traditional public forums for speech.[26] The Court did not, however, overrule *Hill*.

Justice Scalia filed an intriguing opinion in *McCullen*, joining with the majority but offering different reasoning. In essence, Justice Scalia argued that the Massachusetts law was not really a content-neutral time, place, and manner restriction at all. To the contrary, he contended, the law regulated a space where – as a practical matter – only *one* type of political speech was likely to occur: the speech of those who oppose abortion. To restrict the space was, therefore, to restrict expression based on its content and viewpoint.

ELECTIONS AND POLLING PLACES

A fair and proper electoral process requires at least two different kinds of access: access to the ballot, so candidates can run for election, and access to polls, so people

[24] Hill v. Colorado, 530 U.S. 703, 707 (2000).
[25] McCullen v. Coakley, 573 U.S. 464, 497 (2014).
[26] *Id.* at 497. The Court rejected the law as overbroad, holding that "the Commonwealth has pursued those interests by the extreme step of closing a substantial portion of a traditional public forum to all speakers. It has done so without seriously addressing the problem through alternatives that leave the forum open for its time-honored purposes."

can vote. Both implicate the First Amendment. But, again, these issues present distinct challenges and require new doctrinal models. In order to maintain the integrity of elections and to prevent voter fraud and intimidation, the government must exercise some control over balloting and polling places; but it must do so without unduly infringing on free expression.

In this spirit, the Court has held that although states can regulate access to ballots – a critical concern for minor-party candidates – they must do so through statutory schemes that "do not operate to freeze the political status quo."[27] Regulations of elections must avoid favoring one party's access over another's.[28] The Court has explained: "The right to form a party for the advancement of political goals means little if a party can be kept off the election ballot and thus denied an equal opportunity to win votes."[29] Permissible election regulations must honor rights of speech and association by allowing multiple parties to access and fully participate in elections.[30]

Direct ballot referendums have also given rise to First Amendment concerns. In addition to candidates' names, many parties have vested interests in having their proposed laws and referendums placed on ballots during elections. In two cases in which the Court reviewed limits on this process, it struck down both laws because they substantially inhibited "communication with voters about proposed political change" and because they were not warranted by purported state interests in administrative efficiency, fraud detection, and informing voters.[31] The Court has, however, upheld laws compelling disclosure of the names of those who signed petitions, reasoning that "[p]ublic disclosure also promotes transparency and accountability in the electoral process to an extent other measures cannot."[32]

Polling places raise issues that are analogous to those presented in the abortion clinic cases that we just discussed. In cases involving those sites, the Court must reconcile the conflict that arises when one party has a constitutional right to engage in an activity and another party has a constitutional right to try to persuade them in their exercise of it. As with the abortion cases, the concept of "zones," where free speech rights are limited, emerged.

[27] Jenness v. Forston, 403 U.S. 431, 438 (1971).
[28] Williams v. Rhodes, 393 U.S. 23 (1968).
[29] *Id.* at 31.
[30] *Jenness*, 403 U.S. at 441–442. In that case, the Court upheld a Georgia law that required fringe candidates to have their name on the ballot by obtaining signatures from 5 percent of registered voters. Georgia, however, also allowed voters to write in names, candidates to run with no party affiliations, and voters to sign multiple petitions without promising to vote for any of the candidates.
[31] *See* Buckley v. American Constitutional Law Foundation, 525 U.S. 182, 192 (1999) and Meyer v. Grant, 464 U.S. 414 (1988).
[32] Doe v. Reed, 581 U.S. 186, 199 (2010).

The Court has recognized a state's compelling interest in protecting the right to "cast a ballot in an election free from the taint of intimidation and fraud."[33] As a result, it generally has upheld laws that create campaign-free zones outside polling stations as a constitutionally acceptable compromise.[34] Through a properly framed statute, a state may also be able to regulate the attire of voters at polling stations so that they do not, for example, wear hats or buttons promoting certain candidates or proposals.[35] Of course, while such a content-based restriction is permissible, any such regulation must be narrowly tailored and viewpoint-neutral.[36]

UNION PICKETING AND DUES

When union members picket outside the premises of the employer, many of the principles we already have encountered apply in straightforward ways. Picketing on streets and sidewalks receives a high level of protection because it constitutes speech in a traditional public forum. But, as we have seen, even there the state will be able to enforce content-neutral time, place, and manner restrictions – for example, laws that prohibit picketing that blocks ingress and egress from a facility.

The Court has faced more complicated questions in connection with "secondary picketing" of businesses. Secondary picketing does not target the responsible party but rather someone who does business with the responsible party. The objectives of secondary picketing can differ.

Secondary picketing may have *coercive* goals, putting pressure on the responsible party by putting pressure on someone with whom they have a commercial relationship. The Supreme Court has held that the government can prohibit at least some kinds of secondary picketing that have this purpose. For example, in *Electrical Workers* v. *Labor Board*,[37] a contractor used unionized carpenters but nonunion electricians. The members of an electrician's union picketed the construction site in an effort (which proved successful) to persuade the carpenters on the site to walk off the job, forcing the contractor to hire unionized electricians. The National Labor Relations Board found this an "unfair labor practice" under the National Labor Relations Act, and the union challenged this finding on constitutional grounds.

The Supreme Court tersely ruled that the First Amendment does not protect peaceful picketing where that speech has "unlawful" objectives. The secondary picketing at issue here, the Court declared, had as its goal a powerful form of

33 Burson v. Freeman, 504 U.S. 191, 212 (1992).

34 *Id.*

35 Minnesota Voters Alliance v. Mansky, 138 S.Ct. 1876, 1887 (2018). In this case, the Court struck down the law for its failure to define the term "political" but also held that there was no basis for rejecting Minnesota's determination that some forms of advocacy should be excluded from the polling place, to set it aside as "an island of calm in which voters can peacefully contemplate their choices."

36 *Id.* at 1888.

37 Electrical Workers v. Labor Board, 341 U.S. 694 (1951).

coercion, akin to extortion or blackmail. The Court held that, because of the "substantive evils" of the secondary picketing engaged in here, Congress and the states have the authority to prohibit it.

The Court has viewed secondary picketing differently, however, when its goal was not *coercive* but *communicative*. Thus, in *National Labor Relations Board* v. *Fruit and Vegetable Packers & Warehousemen*,[38] the Court held that the National Labor Relations Act's prohibition of "unfair labor practices" did not include the peaceful picketing and distribution of handbills by striking employees at markets that sold the employer's products. The Court reasoned that appeals to consumers do not bring with them the same concerns as coercive secondary picketing.[39] Because the statute did not prohibit such appeals, it was not constitutionally objectionable.

Another issue with which the Court has struggled relates to mandatory union dues imposed on public sector employees. Unions, historically, have collected and expended money to support politicians and causes that furthered their interests. But, when a public sector union shop imposes this requirement on employees, it raises questions of "compelled speech," analogous to the compelled flag salute at issue in the *Barnette* case.

In the 1977 case of *Abood* v. *Detroit Board of Education*,[40] public school teachers in Detroit objected to paying mandatory dues that, among other things, supported political activities of which they disapproved. The Court held that the union could collect fees from nonmembers related to the benefits of collective bargaining that they received. But, the Court held, the First Amendment requires that employees have the choice of whether to pay the fees that support the union's ideological activities. *Abood* sought to strike a balance: public employees did not have to pay for speech they did not like; but they could not be "free riders," enjoying the fruits of the union's collective bargaining activities but paying nothing for them.

In the 2018 case of *Janus* v. *AFSCME*,[41] the Court concluded that *Abood* had gotten the First Amendment analysis wrong. The Court ruled that it was unconstitutional to require nonunion employees to pay even a partial union fee for the union's nonpolitical efforts toward collective bargaining. In sum, the Court found that compelled speech is compelled speech – ideological or not.[42]

The *Janus* opinion, driven by the conservative majority of the Court, has proven highly controversial. Supporters of the Court's opinion argue that it signals a First Amendment victory for public employees, freeing them from the burden of supporting speech in which they do not believe. Critics argue that the decision amounts to

[38] 377 US 58 (1964).
[39] National Labor Relations Board v. Fruit and Vegetable Packers & Warehousemen, 377 U.S. 58, 71–72 (1964).
[40] 431 U.S. 209, 235 (1977).
[41] 138 S. Ct. 2448, 2460 (2018).
[42] *Id.*

nothing more than a thinly guised attack on organized labor, gutting their financial support and forcing them to work on behalf of nonmember employees.

ORGANIZATIONS AND CORPORATIONS

One of the implicit (and sometimes explicit) elements of the union cases is that they do not just involve the First Amendment rights of individual union members but of the unions themselves. Indeed, unions are just one example of the many different types of entities and organizations that people create specifically for expressive and advocacy purposes. The National Rifle Association, the American Civil Liberties Union, the Sierra Club, and the United Methodist Church are not people. But, surely, the First Amendment would not allow the government to prohibit their existence on the basis that it did not like their perspective or messages.

In this spirit, the Supreme Court has held that the First Amendment protects the free speech of corporations, stressing that the marketplace of diverse ideas benefits from all viewpoints, regardless of their origin.[43] In *Consol. Edison Co.* v. *Public Serv. Comm'n*,[44] for example, the Court struck down an order from a state agency that prohibited electric companies from including "inserts discussing controversial issues of public policy" in customers' bills.[45] This order, the Court held, was neither "a valid time, place, or manner restriction, nor a permissible subject-matter regulation, nor a narrowly drawn prohibition justified by a compelling state interest."[46]

The law was not content-neutral, because it based restrictions on the subject matter of the speech – namely, controversial political topics.[47] Furthermore, the purported state interest in preventing customers from being a captive audience to unwanted messages was insufficient. After all, customers were free to dispose of any papers they did not wish to read.[48]

In many respects, the Court did not have to work very hard to conclude that the First Amendment protects corporate speech; a contrary result would have been surprising and detrimental to free expression. But, it is worth noting that some of the instrumentalist and intrinsic value arguments offered in support of free speech (and discussed in Chapters 1 and 2) do not align particularly well with the corporate form. It would seem odd to talk about corporations engaging in "self-fulfillment," or needing a "safety valve" to let off steam, or expressing their "conscience" through speech.

43 First National Bank v. Bellotti, 435 U.S. 765, 777 (1978) (declaring that the "inherent worth of the speech in terms of its capacity for informing the public does not depend upon the identity of its source, whether corporation, association, union, or individual").

44 Consol. Edison Co. v. Public Serv. Comm'n, 447 U.S. 530 (1980).

45 *Id.* at 532.

46 *Id.* at 544.

47 *Id.* at 543.

48 *Id.* at 542.

For many years, those disconnections did not receive much attention. In 2010, however, they came to the fore when the Court issued its decision in *Citizens United* v. *Federal Election Commission*,[49] discussed in Chapter 13. That case prompted substantial public dialogue over the question of whether it made sense to think that corporations have a right to freedom of expression.

PUBLIC EMPLOYEE SPEECH

Since 1964, the Court has dealt with a number of important issues that are related to public employees and that go well beyond organized labor and union dues. Indeed, they go to the heart of what public employees can say and when they can say it. Restrictions on employee speech do not implicate the First Amendment when the employer is a private entity; but, when the employer is a governmental body, "state action" is involved and First Amendment rights are triggered.

As we have seen, during the Red Scare of the 1950s the Court rendered a series of decisions that approved government restrictions on public employees based on their political ideology, associations, and speech. After 1964, the Court viewed matters quite differently. For example, in *Pickering* v. *Board of Education*,[50] the Court addressed the dismissal of a teacher for negative remarks he made in a local newspaper regarding the school board. The board argued that the criticisms were inaccurate, that the teacher had a duty of loyalty to support his superiors, and that his termination was therefore proper.

This argument, if correct, would have left the teacher with fewer rights than other citizens enjoy to speak out on issues of public importance. After all, under the Court's decision in *New York Times* v. *Sullivan*, anyone *else* making such a criticism of an elected school board would have been protected by the "actual malice" standard, which requires proof of *knowing* falsity. The board essentially argued that Pickering had forfeited this constitutional protection because of his public employee status.

The Supreme Court rejected this argument. The Court held that when public employees speak out on matters of public concern they deserve the same protection that other citizens have. Thus, *Sullivan* applied to Pickering's speech just as it would to any other criticism of the school board.

In later years, however, the Court issued two decisions that weakened the protection afforded to public employee speech. In *Connick* v. *Myers*,[51] the Court continued to endorse the principle that First Amendment protection generally applies when the employee speaks on matters of public concern. The Court further held,

[49] Citizens United v. Federal Election Commission, 558 U.S. 310, 319 (2010).
[50] Pickering v. Board of Education, 391 U.S. 563 (1968).
[51] *See* Connick v. Myers, 461 U.S. 138 (1983).

however, that government agencies retain the power to dismiss employees for speech pertaining to office or private matters.

Justice White explained: "When employee expression cannot be fairly considered as relating to any matter of political, social, or other concern to the community, government officials should enjoy wide latitude in managing their offices, without intrusive oversight by the judiciary in the name of the First Amendment."[52] Furthermore, *Connick* indicated that – even where a public employee's speech related to a matter of public interest – the government could still take action against them if it could clearly show that the expression "substantially interfered" with their official responsibilities.[53] In sum, *Connick* recognized that, while a public employer is a state actor, it is also an employer, and so must have some authority to maintain an effective workplace.

The second major limitation on public employee speech came in *Garcetti v. Ceballos*.[54] There, the Court recognized that sometimes public employees speak on behalf of the government; indeed, doing so may make up an important part of their job responsibilities. Under these circumstances, the Court held, the speech belongs to the government, which can therefore exercise broad control over it. The *Garcetti* Court stressed that "[r]estricting speech that owes its existence to a public employee's professional responsibilities does not infringe any liberties the employee might have enjoyed as a private citizen." Instead, the Court held, "[i]t simply reflects the exercise of employer control over what the employer itself has commissioned or created."

These decisions notwithstanding, First Amendment protection for public employee speech has remained relatively strong, and certainly more robust than in the period before 1964. For example, in 2014 the Court declared in *Lane v. Franks*[55] that "public employees do not renounce their citizenship when they accept public employment, and ... public employers may not condition employment on the relinquishment of constitutional rights." The Court went on to emphasize the limited reach of the *Garcetti* doctrine.

Perhaps the most forceful reaffirmation of the speech rights of public employee, however, came in the 2016 case of *Heffernan v. City of Paterson*.[56] In that case, a sheriff's office demoted an employee based on a mistaken belief he had supported a particular mayoral candidate.[57] Although the employee did not even engage in the speech for which they were demoted, the Court held that he retained a cause of action under the First Amendment because "a discharge or demotion based upon an employer's belief that the employee has engaged in protected activity can cause the

52 *Id.* at 146 (1983).
53 *Id.* at 150.
54 Garcetti v. Ceballos, 547 U.S. 410 (2006).
55 Lane v. Franks, 134 S. Ct. 2369, 2377 (2014).
56 Heffernan v. City of Paterson, 136 S. Ct. 1412 (2016).
57 *Id.*

same kind, and degree, of constitutional harm whether that belief does or does not rest upon a factual mistake."[58]

It should be noted that the holding in *Garcetti* is really just a specific application of a broader principle: a limitation on *government* speech does not trigger constitutional concerns because the First Amendment exists to protect *private* speech from interference by the state – not to protect the state from itself. The executive, legislative, and judicial branches of our federal government, individual states, large cities, and small municipalities all engage in speech – and, as *Garcetti* recognizes, they commonly do so through the human beings who act on their behalf. But, because all of that communication is *government* speech, none of it falls within the ambit of the First Amendment.

The phenomenon of the Everyday First Amendment, which we discuss in Chapter 4, can result in confusion around this point. For example, sometimes a presidential administration will order revisions to an executive department website so as to delete references to climate change, or abortion, or disappointing economic data. Such actions are occasionally met with accusations that this sort of "censorship" violates free speech, but those charges are mistaken. These decisions may be bad policy and may deserve criticism. But they are instances of the government restraining its own speech, and so do not give rise to any First Amendment problems.

COMPELLED ASSOCIATION

As we have seen, in its 1943 decision in *Barnette* the Supreme Court recognized that the First Amendment includes not just the right to speak but also the right to refrain from doing so. And, in its 1958 decision in *NAACP* v. *Alabama*,[59] the Court also recognized that there is a First Amendment-based right to freedom of association. Although the text of the First Amendment does not include an explicit reference to association, the Court found the right "an inseparable aspect of the 'liberty' assured by the Due Process Clause of the Fourteenth Amendment, which embraces freedom of speech." This makes perfect sense: the right to speak necessarily entails the right to associate with others who wish to do so to achieve the same ends.

The next logical step, of course, was for the Court to recognize that freedom of association includes the right *not* to associate. This interpretive move is problematic, however, because it brings liberty rights into direct conflict with equality rights. After all, to refuse to associate with someone because of their gender, race, or sexual orientation is to discriminate against them, perhaps in violation of federal, state, or local law. Since 1964, the Court has faced a number of cases that have highlighted this doctrinal tension.

[58] *Id.* at 1419.
[59] NAACP v. Alabama, 357 U.S. 449 (1958).

The Court's first foray into these issues came in *Roberts* v. *United States Jaycees*.[60] In that case, two local chapters of the Jaycees (an organization of young business leaders) sued the national Jaycees for threatening to revoke their charters because they wished to admit women. The chapters argued that the national organization's policy of limiting membership to men violated state anti-discrimination law. The national Jaycees defended the policy on the basis that enforcing the law against it would violate the organization's right to freedom of association.

In an opinion written by Justice Brennan, the Supreme Court rejected the argument. The Court construed the right to freedom of association fairly narrowly, and concluded that the national Jaycees had offered no evidence that accepting women into its ranks would change the content or impact of the organization's speech. Indeed, the Court suggested, any argument to that effect would rest on gender stereotypes.

In time, however, the Court came to think differently about this tension. In 1995, the Court ruled in *Hurley* v. *Irish-American Gay, Lesbian, and Bisexual Group of Boston*[61] that parade organizers had a freedom-of-association-based right to exclude an LGB group from its event because they did not approve of its message, despite a state law prohibiting discrimination based on sexual orientation. And, in 2000, the Court held in *Boy Scouts of America* v. *Dale*[62] that the Boy Scouts had the right to revoke the membership of an assistant scoutmaster after he publicly announced that he was gay, despite an applicable state anti-discrimination law. In these cases, the Court did not wholly dismiss the state's interest in prohibiting discrimination; but it did find that this interest did not outweigh the constitutionally based right *not* to associate.

These cases received a great deal of public attention. This is unsurprising, because they are emblematic of an issue central to current discussions about the First Amendment – the tension that can arise between the robust protection of First Amendment rights and the protection of the equality rights of minorities. Consider: the Court's first freedom of association decision, in the *NAACP* case, protected the rights of minorities and those who had joined with them to promote their cause. But, in the later cases, the expansion of the right *not* to associate resulted in a diminution of protection for political minorities. First Amendment skeptics often point to these later cases in support of their concern that freedom of expression has increasingly been weaponized against minority voices – an issue we explored in Chapter 2 and return to again in connection with hate speech in Chapter 12.

PRISONS AND MILITARY BASES

As the discussion above indicates, even within the hard cases, the Court's decisions since 1964 generally trend toward the expansion of First Amendment rights. Still,

60 Roberts v. Jaycees, 468 U.S. 609 (1984).

61 Hurley v. Irish-American Gay, Lesbian, and Bisexual Group of Boston, 515 U.S. 557 (1995).

62 Boy Scouts of America v. Dale, 530 U.S. 640 (2000).

exceptions to this trend exist. Speech on prisons and military bases presents one of them.

Forum analysis holds that there are certain spaces like parks, streets, and sidewalks to which people have broad access to speak and exchange information. Other government spaces exist, however, where access and expression are by tradition – and arguably by necessity – significantly constrained. Those include prisons and military bases. Since 1964, the Court has confronted cases asking how the First Amendment applies in those contexts, if it applies at all.

With respect to prisons, the Court settled on a "reasonableness" test that gives correctional institutions broad regulatory authority.[63] This analysis involves several steps. First, the Court determines if the purpose of the prison rule is legitimate and neutral.[64] It also asks if the rule is rationally related to its purpose.[65] Next, the Court assesses the reasonableness of the rule based its scope, specifically inquiring into whether it leaves prisoners with alternative ways of exercising their rights.[66] Finally, the Court examines the impact "accommodation of the asserted constitutional right will have on others (guards and inmates) in the prison."[67]

Because these regulations are subject to forgiving "reasonableness" and "rational relation" tests, and because courts hesitate to second-guess the professional judgments of correctional personnel, the Court has upheld a number of prison restrictions on speech. These include policies that limit correspondence between inmates[68] and that allow prison officials to determine which reading materials inmates can receive.[69] Of course, many prison policies that violate even this forgiving standard will go untested because prisoners will not have the knowledge or resources necessary to challenge them.

As with prisons, the Court has afforded special considerations to speech on military bases and within the military more generally. Because of the military's unique role and responsibilities, the Court provided the government with considerable leeway for the restriction of rights.[70] For example, in one case the Court upheld the military's authority to punish its members for speaking out against the Vietnam War.[71] Furthermore, the Court has held that the military can bar civilians from distributing political materials on a base[72] and can require its members to "obtain

63 Turner v. Safley, 482 U.S. 78, 89 (1987).
64 Thornburgh v. Abbott, 490 U.S. 401, 414 (1989).
65 *Id.*
66 *Id.* at 418.
67 *Id.* at 419.
68 *Turner*, 482 U.S. at 100.
69 *Thornburgh*, 490 U.S. at 419. *See also* Beard v. Banks, 548 U.S. 521, 536 (2006).
70 Parker v. Levy, 417 U.S. 733, 758 (1974) (explaining that "the different character of the military community and of the military mission requires a different application" of First Amendment speech protections).
71 *Id.*
72 Greer v. Spock, 424 U.S. 828 (1976).

approval from their commanders before circulating petitions on Air Force bases."[73] Still, special considerations for military policy end in areas where the military has not restricted access.[74] Streets and sidewalks surrounding military bases, therefore, are subject to standard First Amendment principles.[75]

WHERE DOES THIS LEAVE US?

As First Amendment law has evolved, the Court has taken an increasingly nuanced approach, analyzing cases by reference to doctrinal categories and subcategories. We will see this trend again when we consider the exceptions. For example, within the category of "defamation," the Court has created different modes of analysis for defamation claims generally, for defamation claims based on statements on matters of public interest, and for defamation claims involving public official plaintiffs.

This elaborate doctrinal architecture makes it difficult for nonspecialists to think about and discuss some dimensions of free expression. As we have seen, in the hard cases even the Supreme Court has struggled to identify and apply the correct analysis. But, for the most part, intelligent and informed discussions of free speech do not require a detailed understanding of every corner of First Amendment doctrine; a solid grasp of certain basic principles suffices.

In that spirit, we offer in Chapters 9, 10, and 11 the essential principles that we think emerge from the body of case law that we have just discussed. We believe that focusing on those principles can help current debates over free speech proceed in more disciplined and productive ways. As we will see, they have important connections with the core values we discussed in Chapters 1, 2, and 3.

[73] Brown v. Glines, 444 U.S. 348 (1980).
[74] Flower v. United States, 407 U.S. 197, 198 (1972).
[75] *Id.*

PART III

Basic Principles

9

Content and Viewpoint Restrictions Are Disfavored

In the mid-1970s, a serial killer terrorized the New York boroughs of the Bronx, Queens, and Brooklyn, leaving six dead and many more wounded. In a letter left at one of the crime scenes, the killer identified himself as the "Son of Sam." The moniker stuck. As the shootings continued, public concern escalated and a widespread manhunt ensued. In August of 1977, police arrested one David Berkowitz, who quickly confessed and ultimately pled guilty to the crimes. He was sentenced to twenty-five-years-to-life for each murder, to be served sequentially. An oddity of New York law, however, made him technically eligible for parole every few years once he completed the first term.

The story of the search for the Son of Sam killer, his capture, and his swift admission of guilt made for compelling drama. And the theoretical possibility that Berkowitz might someday receive parole intensified public interest. The commercial value of rights to his story was not lost on the New York Legislature, which was concerned that he might profit from his criminal celebrity while his victims remained uncompensated. As a result, the legislature promptly passed a statute known as the "Son of Sam Law."

The law imposed certain responsibilities on entities (like publishers) who entered into contracts with criminals for the right to tell their story about their misdeeds. The statute required such an entity to provide a copy of the agreement to the state Crime Victims Board and to turn income generated by the project over to the board. The board would then deposit that income into an escrow fund, against which victims of the crime in question could make claims.

Such a law had tremendous popular appeal on simple fairness grounds. As state senator, Emanuel Gold, the author of the statute, declared: "It is abhorrent to one's sense of justice and decency that [a criminal] can expect to receive large sums of money for his story once he is captured," while the victims of his crimes are left injured or dead "as a result of his conduct."[1] Of course, as a practical matter, the law would apply exclusively to the very worst criminals. After all, only their stories would have sufficient commercial value for a publisher to have interest in entering into such an agreement. But those were precisely the types of cases most likely to provoke public outcries for victim compensation.

Indeed, the law saw little use after its passage and came into play only in connection with such relatively rare high-profile cases. It was, for example, invoked with respect to Jean Harris, who murdered the famous "Scarsdale Diet" Doctor Herman Tarnower; Mark David Chapman, who assassinated John Lennon; and R. Foster Winans, a former *Wall Street Journal* columnist convicted of insider trading.

Ironically, the statute was never applied to the Son of Sam himself. The court found Berkowitz incompetent to stand trial, and at that time the statute reached only contracts with convicted criminals. To compound the irony, Berkowitz voluntarily paid his share of the royalties from the book *Son of Sam*, published in 1981, to his victims or their estates.[2] A lawsuit over the constitutionality of the statute did not arise until later, when a colorful former gangster named Henry Hill decided to write a memoir.

In the course of his long criminal career, Henry Hill had done everything from committing extortion to selling narcotics to pulling off the largest cash robbery in American history. After his arrest, he struck an immunity deal with prosecutors, testified against his former organized crime colleagues, and took refuge in a witness relocation program. From the safety of that perch, Hill (along with a co-author) signed a contract with Simon & Schuster to write a book about his exploits.

The fruit of those efforts was an autobiographical tell-all called *Wiseguy*, which received favorable reviews and sold widely. Further commercial success followed when the book was made into a film called *Goodfellas* that did very well at the box office and received multiple awards. When the Crime Victims Board sought to enforce the Son of Sam Law against Simon & Schuster and Hill, demanding payment of the amounts due under the statute, the publisher sued.

This statute may have served the interests of fairness, prevented grotesque injustices, and seemed like sensible public policy, but the Supreme Court nevertheless had little difficulty concluding that it also violated the First Amendment. In doing so, the Court relied on a well-settled principle: a statute is presumptively unconstitutional if it places a burden on speech because of its *content*.[3] Indeed, the Court observed that this principle had become so "obvious" as to require no explanation – although the opinion went on to offer one anyway.

1 Simon & Schuster, Inc. v. Members of New York State Crime Victims Board, 502 U.S. 105, 108 (1991).
2 *Id.* at 111.
3 *Id.* at 115.

Reflecting on the values discussed in Chapters 1 and 2 shows why content-based regulations of speech are especially problematic. If the government skews the inputs, then the marketplace of ideas will not function fairly and properly. Such interference makes it impossible for people to assess the truth of a claim on its merits, for participants in a democracy to become fully and accurately informed, and for individuals to enjoy the benefits of self-expression. If the state burdens some speech and favors others based on the content of the ideas expressed, then it distorts and corrupts these processes. In numerous cases, the Court has stressed that the First Amendment seeks "to remove governmental restraints from the arena of public discussion, putting the decision as to what views shall be voiced largely into the hands of each of us ... in the belief that no other approach would comport with the premise of individual dignity and choice upon which our political system rests."[4]

In describing the evils of content-based restrictions, the Supreme Court has often invoked the language of discrimination. The Court has declared that, as a general proposition, the state may not discriminate against speech based on the substance of the ideas the speech conveys. In the *Simon & Schuster* case, for example, the Court observed that the First Amendment "presumptively places this sort of discrimination beyond the power of the government."[5]

The Supreme Court easily concluded that the Son of Sam Law discriminated against speech based on its content. As the Court pointed out, the statute singled out certain speech because of its subject matter; indeed, the law would not have applied if Hill had written a cookbook or a spy novel rather than a memoir of his criminal exploits. And, the statute placed a special financial burden on that speech: income from the book had to be surrendered to the Crime Victims Board for distribution to victims.

The board raised a number of arguments in defense of the statute, all of which the Supreme Court summarily rejected. For our purposes, the most interesting of them is that the legislature did not adopt the statute with the intent of suppressing certain ideas. This was probably true: indeed, if the law had the effect of suppressing the criminal's speech, then there would be no income to share with the victims. Regardless of its truth, however, the Court found the point irrelevant. Simon & Schuster did not need to show that the State of New York had an "improper censorial motive," the Court reasoned, in order to prove that the publisher had suffered a violation of its First Amendment rights.[6]

In some instances, the government discriminates against speech based not just on the *content* of the expression but, more specifically, on the *viewpoint* that the speech reflects – another idea explored in the cases we have discussed. In theory, distinguishing between content and viewpoint should not prove unduly difficult. For

4 *Id.* at 116.
5 *Id.*
6 *Id.* at 117.

example, the Son of Sam Law put a special burden on speech because of its content – that is, its subject matter. The law's requirements applied when criminals wrote about their crimes. But that law did *not* discriminate based on any particular viewpoint reflected in the speech. The Son of Sam Law applied regardless of whether the author argued that his crimes were morally reprehensible, morally defensible, or morally meaningless.

The distinction matters because, as we earlier noted, the Supreme Court has on a number of occasions declared that viewpoint discrimination is even worse than content discrimination. In *Rosenberger* v. *Rector and Visitors of the University of Virginia* (1995), for example, the Court observed that "When the government targets not subject matter, but particular views taken by a speaker on a subject, the violation of the First Amendment is all the more blatant." The Court added: "Viewpoint discrimination is an egregious form of content discrimination."[7]

A thought experiment may help us understand why viewpoint discrimination further escalates our already elevated concerns about content discrimination. Let's say that a public university finds itself in the throes of painful political divisiveness among its students. In an effort to provide a sanctuary from the incessant bitterness that infects the campus, the university commits a large but currently unused room in its student activities building to a new purpose: it will serve as a "politics free zone." As a matter of official university policy, students may not discuss any political subject matter while in this specially designated space. A student who does so is subject to discipline.

Such a policy would raise significant First Amendment concerns. For the reasons just discussed, allowing the state to impose any content-based prohibition skews the marketplace of ideas, limits the search for truth, and so on. Plus, this policy suffers from serious vagueness and due process problems. Reasonable people could easily disagree about what constitutes "political" speech. Is a conversation about the influences on Picasso's art "political"? The motivations behind Beethoven's *Eroica* symphony? The role of science fiction in popular culture? The policy does not put a student on fair and reasonable notice of what is, and is not, prohibited.

And, yet, for all those infirmities, this policy is less worrisome than one that discriminates based on viewpoint. Let's say, for example, that the university administration concludes that the divisiveness on campus has resulted from clashes between a vocal minority that strongly supports the President of the United States and a similarly outspoken majority that vehemently opposes him. The university reasons that, to ensure the minority have an opportunity to express their viewpoint, the specially created "zone" will be one where criticism of the President is forbidden.

Such a policy creates even greater distortions in the marketplace of ideas, the search for truth, and the dynamics of self-expression than does the content-based policy. After all, this policy does not just exclude a subject matter from discussion; it

[7] Rosenberger v. Rector and Visitors of the University of Virginia, 515 U.S. 819, 829 (1995).

declares a winner in the debate over which viewpoints deserve our attention. It ensures that the voice it prefers will continue to prevail by excluding all challengers from the competition. And, as noted in Chapter 7, it is hard to imagine a situation where the state will have a constitutionally legitimate reason to discriminate against speech based on its viewpoint.

In contrast, as we have previously observed, the Court has recognized a variety of circumstances where the government may indeed single speech out because of its content. First, as we explore more deeply in Chapter 11, the Court has recognized that certain categories of speech historically have been deemed outside of First Amendment protection. Thus, the Court has held that Congress may pass a law that criminalizes threats even though such a law obviously targets speech based on its content.[8] As the Court has recognized, the state has strong reasons to place threats outside of the First Amendment, such as "protecting individuals from the fear of violence, from the disruption that fear engenders, and from the possibility that the threatened violence will occur."[9]

We should note that the argument for allowing discrimination against such speech disappears if a law strays from the concerns that justify it. The Supreme Court offered this example: although Congress can constitutionally pass a law targeting threats against the President, it cannot pass one that targets threats against the President based on his policies regarding aid to inner cities.[10] After all, those policies have nothing to do with the justification for the law: to provide protection against fear, violence, and the like. Such a law simply chooses to place additional burdens on selected speech based on its content.

For the same reason, Congress could not pass a law targeting threats against the President for taking pro-life positions on the abortion issue. Again, the reasons for allowing the content-based prohibition have nothing to do with the viewpoint that the law singles out. Congress has powerful rationales for penalizing threats against the life of the President; but its only rationale for punishing this narrow class of threats is that Congress disfavors the viewpoint that those threats represent.

The Court has identified a second basis on which speech may, consistent with the First Amendment, receive less protection as a result of its content. The state may have compelling reasons to address the consequences and "secondary effects" of creating and distributing certain speech, even though that speech does not fall into a historically unprotected category. For example, early lists of unprotected speech do not include the category of child pornography. Nevertheless, the government obviously has special concerns about the creation and secondary effects of such speech – specifically, the abuse, exploitation, and ongoing humiliation of juveniles. Those factors justify laws prohibiting the creation, sale, and distribution of that

8 R.A.V. v. City of St. Paul, 505 U.S. 377, 388 (1992).
9 *Id.* at 388.
10 *Id.* at 388.

speech. In short, the government can discriminate against such speech; it can adopt a law that targets this specific type of content, even if it chooses not to prohibit other forms of obscenity.[11]

Finally, the Court has recognized that the government has the authority to use its own resources and property to promote speech based its content, even though doing so may adversely affect opposing content and contrary viewpoints. To use examples offered in a Supreme Court opinion, the government can fund a program that promotes recycling or that encourages vaccination without having also to dedicate resources to programs that discourage these practices.[12] Indeed, as the Court observed, "[w]ere the Free Speech Clause interpreted otherwise, government would not work."[13]

A relatively straightforward doctrinal framework seems to emerge from these principles. As a general proposition, the government cannot discriminate against speech based on the speech's *content*. The government can do so in some cases as we just discussed, but for the most part content-based discrimination against speech is prohibited. Furthermore, the government will very rarely, if ever, have an adequate justification for discriminating against speech based on the *viewpoint* expressed. These constitute basic principles of our free speech doctrine.

These fundamental and evidently straightforward principles do, however, give rise to some hard questions. For example, in some cases it may be difficult to tell whether the government restriction goes to *content* or *viewpoint*. Consider *Rosenberger* v. *University of Virginia*, quoted earlier in this chapter. That case involved a policy adopted by a public university regarding the permissible uses of its student activities fund. In pertinent part, the university's policy did not allow for the disbursement of funds for "religious activities" and defined such an activity as one that "primarily promotes or manifests a particular belief in or about a deity or an ultimate reality."[14]

In light of this prohibition, the university denied a request from student Ronald Rosenberger for funds to subsidize his publication of a Christian-oriented publication. One of the central questions in the case was how to think about this policy: Was it a constitutionally permissible decision by a public body not to fund certain content? Or was it a constitutionally impermissible act of viewpoint discrimination? The Supreme Court closely divided over the issue.

A majority of five justices concluded that the policy ran afoul of the First Amendment. They began with a familiar starting point: "the government may not regulate speech based on its substantive content or the message it conveys," and therefore any "discrimination against speech because of its message is presumed to

[11] *Id.* at 389.
[12] Walker v. Sons of Confederate Veterans, 135 S. Ct. 2239, 2246 (2015).
[13] *Id.* at 2246.
[14] Rosenberger v. University of Virginia, 515 U.S. 818, 825 (1995).

be unconstitutional."[15] The Court acknowledged that a state can create and fund a forum for specific purposes and limit discussion within it to certain topics – an idea we discussed in Chapter 7 in connection with public forum doctrine.[16] But, the Court observed, even under those circumstances the state may not discriminate based upon viewpoint.

The university argued that the policy's prohibition on funding religious activities was a permissible exercise of its control over institutional resources. Just as the state could decide to spend its money on a pro-vaccination campaign, rather than on an anti-gambling campaign, so the university could decide to spend its money on many different kinds of student activities but not on religious ones. Moreover, the school argued, a public university like Virginia had good reason to avoid entanglement with religious activities: doing so could run afoul of the Establishment Clause of the First Amendment, which requires separation of church and state. This certainly must have seemed like a proposition that the university's founder – Thomas Jefferson – would have endorsed.

A majority of the Court rejected these arguments. It recognized that the distinction between content and viewpoint discrimination "is not a precise one."[17] But it maintained that discrimination against religious perspectives was inherently discrimination against a viewpoint. "Religion may be a vast area of inquiry," the Court conceded, "but it also provides [a] premise [and] standpoint from which a variety of subjects may be discussed and considered."[18] The refusal to fund Rosenberger's project, the Court concluded, was not attributable to the content of the publication in some general sense. Instead, it related specifically to the publication's "prohibited perspective."[19]

Four justices dissented. The dissent primarily argued that analysis under the free speech clause of the First Amendment was wholly unnecessary. In the view of the dissent, for the university to fund a religious publication like Rosenberger's would indeed pose serious problems under the Establishment Clause. The dissent essentially argued that it made no sense to punish the university under the Speech Clause of the First Amendment for adopting a policy that was required by the Establishment Clause of the First Amendment.[20]

But the dissent thought that the majority erred in its analysis under the Speech Clause as well. The dissent acknowledged the special evil of viewpoint discrimination: it skews public debate by allowing the state to use its coercive power to declare a winner.[21] But the dissent thought that the policy in question did not amount to

[15] *Id.* at 828.
[16] *Id.*
[17] *Id.* at 831.
[18] *Id.*
[19] *Id.* 831.
[20] *Id.* at 892 (Souter, J., dissenting).
[21] *Id.* at 894–895 (Souter, J., dissenting).

viewpoint discrimination because it did not favor one religious perspective over another. The dissent pointed out that the funding prohibition applied with equal force to Christians, Muslims, Jews, and Buddhists. Indeed, because the policy reached activities promoting or manifesting a particular belief "about" a deity or ultimate reality, the policy even applied to agnostics and atheists. *Rosenberger* shows how close a call the distinction between a content regulation and a viewpoint regulation can be.

Another question that complicates our thinking about the prohibition against content and viewpoint discrimination goes to the identity of the speaker. As discussed in Chapter 4, the First Amendment protects *private* individuals and entities from government abridgment of *their* free speech rights. But, as we have noted, when the government itself does the speaking it has vast control over the content of the speech and the viewpoint it advances. Again, if the state wants to invest resources in an official pro-immunization campaign then it may do so, and it can decide what it wants to say and how it wants to say it.

This distinction seems even more straightforward than that between content and viewpoint discrimination. Surely, one would think, it is easy enough to tell when the government is speaking and when a private individual or entity is doing so. But it turns out not to be quite so simple, and some cases have seriously challenged the Supreme Court's capacity to articulate coherent First Amendment doctrine. To demonstrate the point, we will look at two cases that concern one of the most mundane of communicative platforms: license plates.

The Court's first excursion into this perhaps unexpectedly messy terrain came in *Wooley* v. *Maynard*.[22] That case involved New Hampshire's license plates, which were proudly embossed with the state motto "Live Free or Die." A statute made it a misdemeanor for someone to obscure any letters on a license plate, and the state's highest court had interpreted that prohibition to include the motto.

George and Maxine Maynard – practicing Jehovah's Witnesses – objected to displaying this slogan on their vehicle on moral, religious, and political grounds. Mr. Maynard therefore covered the motto on the plate, which put him on the receiving end of multiple citations and prosecutions. Finally, he'd had enough and sued, arguing that the statute violated his First Amendment rights. The trial court agreed and issued an injunction against further enforcement of the law against the Maynards. The case made its way to the Supreme Court, which affirmed.

The Court began with the proposition that the First Amendment protects both the right to speak and the right to *refrain* from speaking. The New Hampshire statute, the Court reasoned, effectively required the Maynards to "use their private property as a 'mobile billboard' for the State's ideological message."[23] It thus compelled them to become "an instrument for fostering public adherence to an

[22] Wooley v. Maynard, 430 U.S. 705 (1977).

[23] *Id.* at 715.

ideological point of view [they found] unacceptable," thereby invading the "sphere of intellect and spirit" that the First Amendment protects.[24]

The state contended that the presence of the motto made it easier for law enforcement officials to determine whether vehicles had the proper plates. The Court found this argument unpersuasive, given that other features of New Hampshire plates made them easily identifiable. The state further maintained that the motto helped advance an appreciation of such values as history and New Hampshire pride. The Court found this argument *worse* than unpersuasive, noting that it was the ideological nature of the message that gave rise to the problem.[25]

Wooley is a deeply interesting case for two reasons. First, it entailed a complicated relationship between the speech in question and the various parties. In essence, the Court viewed the government as the *source* of the speech but the Maynards as the *speaker*, forced to promote the state's message over their keen objections. Second, it involved a government regulation that compelled, rather than restricted, speech based on its content. This seems like a particularly grave intrusion on the individual conscience: it is one thing to limit an individual's self-expression; it is something else to force someone, on pain of criminal punishment, to declare publicly something that they find repugnant.

More than thirty years later, the Court returned to these issues in a case involving a different kind of license plate. *Walker* v. *Sons of Confederate Veterans*[26] concerned a Texas program that allowed automobile owners to order "specialty" plates featuring a customized design, slogan, or both. An organization – the Texas Division of the Sons of Confederate Veterans – proposed a plate that displayed a Confederate battle flag. The Motor Vehicles Board, which reviewed all proposed designs, rejected it. The organization sued, the lower appellate court ruled in its favor, and the Supreme Court agreed to review the case.

One might expect the Court to have thought about the case the following way. In *Wooley*, the words in question were displayed on a private party's vehicle but came from the State. We treated that speech as if it were made by the individual. Here, the words are displayed on a private party's vehicle *and* come from that private party. These facts present an even stronger case, then, for concluding that the speech belongs to the individual, and not to the State.

A majority of the Court, however, reasoned through these issues very differently. The Court concluded that the statements on the specialty plates qualified as government speech – even though the words and images came from private parties. The Sons of Confederate Veterans therefore had no First Amendment claim; as the Court noted, "[w]hen government speaks, it is not barred by the Free Speech Clause

[24] *Id.* at 716.
[25] *Id.* at 717.
[26] Walker v. Sons of Confederate Veterans, 135 S. Ct. 2239 (2015).

from determining the content of what it says."[27] The Court relied on a number of arguments in support of its conclusion.

First, the Court noted that, as a historical matter, to the extent license plates have gone beyond simple letters and numbers to convey a message, that message typically has been one sponsored by the state. Indeed, prior to the development of vanity plates, slogans and the like that appeared on license plates were uniformly and unilaterally put there by the government. The "Live Free or Die" plate at issue in *Wooley* provides an example.

Second, the Court posited that members of the general public strongly associate Texas license plates with the state. The Court noted that these plates are "essentially, government IDs."[28] Therefore, the Court reasoned, someone who places a special message on a plate "intends to convey to the public that the state has endorsed that message" and observers will understand the significance of the plate that way.[29]

Third, and finally, the Court pointed out that "Texas maintain[ed] direct control over the messages conveyed on its specialty plates."[30] Under Texas law, the state exercised final decision-making authority over such matters as the design, typeface, and color of all plates. And the Court noted that the state did not simply rubber stamp every proposed specialty plate; to the contrary, it had in the past rejected at least a dozen designs.

Four justices vigorously dissented, testing the majority's reasoning against common sense and experience. The dissent posed this hypothetical. Suppose you sat by the side of a Texas highway, studying the license plates on the passing vehicles.[31] You would see plates that honor colleges, universities, high schools, fraternities, sororities, the Masons, the Knights of Columbus, the Daughters of the American Revolution, a realty company, a soft drink, a hamburger restaurant, a NASCAR driver, the citrus industry, and the sentiment "I'd rather be golfing." Would you *really* think that these plates represent the official positions of the State of Texas – as opposed to those of the owners of the cars?

As the dissent saw things, these specialty plates actually consisted of speech from *two* sources by *two* parties. Yes, some of the speech that appeared on the plate came from the state: the number and the Texas designation, for example. But the customized message came from the vehicle owner, who wished to offer a show of support for an organization, school, activity, product, or person. The majority opinion, the dissent argued, erred by giving the State of Texas viewpoint-based control not only over its *own* speech but over the *vehicle owner's* speech as well.

As the Court did in *Wooley*, the dissent considered these facts through the lens of a "mobile billboard" analogy. The State of Texas had converted part of every

[27] *Id.* at 2245.
[28] *Id.* at 2249.
[29] *Id.* at 2249.
[30] *Id.*
[31] *Id.* at 2255 (Alito, J., dissenting).

specialty license plate into "little mobile billboards on which motorists [could] display their own messages."[32] If the state could pick and choose among the viewpoints represented on those "billboards," then it could do so with respect to any others.

The dissent asked: What if a public university had a billboard, campus bulletin board, or dorm list serve that worked the same way – with space for institutional speech but also for private speech?[33] Surely, it would offend the First Amendment for the university to favor some viewpoints over others in the private portion. Why, the dissent asked, should we have a different outcome here?

The dissent acknowledged the controversy that surrounds the Confederate battle flag and the differing perspectives on its symbolism. The Texas Sons of Confederate Veterans argued that for them the flag evoked the memory of their ancestors and other soldiers who fought for the South in the Civil War; for others, the dissent conceded, it unambiguously stands for "slavery, segregation, and hatred."[34] But, the dissent observed, the state does not have the authority to reject speech simply because some people object to it. The dissent concluded that when the board rejected the plate design because it thought many Texans would find the symbol offensive, that "was pure viewpoint discrimination."[35]

Like *Wooley*, this case shows the complexities that can arise in trying to determine whether speech belongs to the government or to a private individual. Indeed, reasonable people can disagree about whether the majority or the dissent have the better part of the argument here. On one hand, the dissent has a point: the state here is undoubtedly preferring some viewpoints over others. On the other hand, the majority makes a strong case that the state has controlled the contents of its license plates, the messages on them therefore constitute government speech, and the risk exists that people will think the state approves of whatever words or images appear there.

In sum, as often holds true with respect to the law of free expression, the doctrinal hostility toward content and viewpoint discrimination proves easier to proclaim than to apply. And the sorts of complications just described have implications far beyond college student publications and license plates. Federal, state, and local governments elect to fund (or *not* fund) countless activities that involve some element of speech and perspective. Uncertainty about when something counts as viewpoint discrimination and when something counts as government speech leaves us with a deeply unsatisfying and worrisome lack of clarity.

Whatever its ambiguities, however, the doctrinal hostility toward content and viewpoint discrimination does yield one point of clarity: when the government

32 *Id.* at 2256 (Alito, J., dissenting).

33 *Id.*

34 *Id.* at 2262 (Alito, J., dissenting).

35 *Id.*

restricts speech for some good reason *that has nothing to do with content or viewpoint*, it has considerably greater latitude to act. As we discussed in Chapter 7, the case law describes these as reasonable and content-neutral time, place, and manner restrictions.[36] They include, for example, a law that prohibits sound above a certain decibel level after midnight or assemblies that block vehicular traffic.

Even content- and viewpoint-neutral laws may, however, run into constitutional trouble. These difficulties typically arise because the state failed to draft the law in terms that are sufficiently clear or sufficiently narrow. Such infirmities implicate other basic principles in our doctrine: the special concerns raised by laws that restrict speech and that are vague or overly broad. We turn to those principles next.

[36] *See* Ward v. Rock Against Racism, 491 U.S. 781 (1989).

10

Vagueness and Overbreadth Are Special Concerns

In the fall of 1931, a nineteen-year-old African American named Angelo Herndon went to Atlanta to serve as an organizer for the Communist Party. Even at that young age, Angelo was already experienced in hard labor and in leftist politics. Five years earlier, he had left home to work in the mines of Kentucky and for the railroad in Alabama. He became an enthusiastic convert to Communism and his activities led to a few legal skirmishes with Alabama authorities.

Angelo's organizational skills came to the fore in the summer of 1932, when Georgia closed its unemployment relief stations, supposedly for lack of funds. Angelo led hundreds of protestors on a march to the Fulton County Courthouse in protest. The stratagem worked: within twenty-four hours, authorities announced that they had found additional money for immediate relief.[1]

Shortly thereafter, Angelo was arrested while he was engaged in the unremarkable act of retrieving mail from his post office box. He admitted to coming to Atlanta to organize Communist Party events and acknowledged that he had called three meetings. A search of his room revealed that he was in possession of a number of documents related in one way or another to the Communist Party, including miscellaneous receipts, membership forms, periodicals, pamphlets, books, and meeting transcripts. Angelo indicated that he had assembled only half a dozen or so members in Atlanta, although the receipts suggested that the number may have been greater.

Angelo was charged with attempted insurrection against the government of the State of Georgia. A jury found him guilty. The relevant law included no explicit requirement that he engage in any act of force or violence in order to be convicted. Instead, the statute proscribed actions that amounted to "combined resistance to the lawful authority of the State." But what did *that* mean?

[1] *See* John Hammond Moore, *The Angelo Herndon Case*, 1932–1937, 32:1 PHYLON 60 (1960).

As we discussed in Chapter 3, in some cases a court can issue an opinion that saves a statute from vagueness problems by interpreting it and explaining its terms. Here, the Supreme Court of Georgia rendered a ruling that purported to clarify the law. Borrowing language from a different provision of the penal code, the court concluded that an accused could only be convicted under the statute if he had contemplated that other people might resort to the use of force against the government as a result of his statements and activities. Still, the court added, the accused did not need to believe the force would occur immediately or even soon – he just needed to think that it might happen at some time in the future.

The Supreme Court of the United States reversed Herndon's conviction on multiple grounds.[2] In part, the prosecution's case suffered from massive failures of proof: the State had not even shown that Angelo had read or distributed the pro-communist publications that served as the basis for his conviction, let alone that he had done so with the required intent. In addition, much of the material in his possession related to such unobjectionable subjects as unemployment and emergency relief for those out of work.

But the Court also reversed because the statute – even as "clarified" by Georgia's highest tribunal – was unconscionably vague, failing to furnish "a sufficiently ascertainable standard of guilt."[3] The statute did not identify any specific "conduct or utterance" that would violate the statute. It did not require that the accused advocate for the use of force. Rather, the Court observed, the accused was guilty under the law if he could "prophesy" that at "some time in the indefinite future" someone who had found him persuasive would "resort to forcible resistance to government."[4]

So vague a statute yields a trifecta of serious problems. First, it fails to provide people who wish to advocate for social change with sufficient notice of what they can and cannot do. Assume, for example, that an activist declares to a gathered crowd, "We must achieve racial equality by any means necessary!" If this slogan might inspire someone in the audience to engage in a violent act at some imagined future time, can the speaker be prosecuted and convicted? What about a chant often heard during protests: "No justice, no peace!"? Same result?

Second, so vague a statute grants essentially unbridled discretion to authorities in making enforcement decisions. The law here left open to government officials "the widest conceivable inquiry, the scope of which no one can foresee and the result of which no one can foreshadow or adequately guard against."[5] The fact that the law provided so little guidance about when it applied gave the state license to enforce it

[2] Herndon v. Lowry, 301 U.S. 242 (1937).
[3] *Id.* at 261.
[4] *Id.* at 263.
[5] *Id.* at 263.

(or not) whenever it chose – including as a cudgel against speech or speakers that it did not like.

And, finally, a statute of such conspicuous vagueness gave juries room to punish unpopular ideas. Indeed, even a jury that was acting in good faith might be convinced that in convicting the accused it was simply applying the law. As the Court observed, "[t]he statue, as construed and applied, amounts merely to a dragnet which may enmesh anyone who agitates for a change of government if a jury can be persuaded that he ought to have foreseen his words would have some effect in the future conduct of others."[6]

In Chapter 3, we discussed the idea that basic notions of due process require that *all* laws provide reasonable notice of what they do, and do not, allow. To some extent, the concerns we have about vague laws that restrain free expression are the same concerns we have about *all* vague laws. Thus, in striking down an anti-picketing ordinance in *Grayned* v. *City of Rockford*,[7] the Supreme Court talked about the fair notice and enforcement problems raised by laws that are ambiguous.

In *Grayned*, the Court declared that "we insist that laws give the person of ordinary intelligence a reasonable opportunity to know what is prohibited so he may act accordingly"[8] and that "laws must provide explicit standards for those who apply them." Otherwise, those officials may execute those laws in "arbitrary and discriminatory" ways.[9] In a sense, there is nothing distinctive about free speech here. We would have these concerns whether a vague ordinance criminalized picketing or criminalized waste disposal.

But vague laws punishing speech raise additional concerns as well. One might think that an important difference lies in our level of certainty that the proscribed conduct actually does any harm. A vague arson statute may run the risk of violating due process. Still, we may think that risk worth taking: after all, arson unquestionably endangers life and property, and too specific and narrow a statute might leave some of this menacing conduct unpunished.

It could be argued that the same analysis does not apply to speech. Surely, the class of speech that poses a serious threat to physical safety, property, or the stability of the republic is extraordinarily small. We tend to shrug off most hurtful and offensive speech as "mere words" – in a way we would never dismiss an intentionally set fire as "mere arson." We all know the childhood rhyme: "Sticks and stones may break my bones, but words will never hurt me."

In some cases, the Supreme Court has resorted to this sort of reasoning. In essence, the Court has implied that the speech in question derives some of its protection from the fact that we don't take it seriously and therefore can't think it

6 *Id.* at 264.
7 Grayned v. City of Rockford, 408 U.S. 104 (1972).
8 *Id.* at 108.
9 *Id.* at 108.

dangerous. For example, in *Herndon* the Court variously described the speech at issue as "foolish," "pernicious," and "vague."[10] And Justice Holmes uses even more dismissive language in the midst of his otherwise rhapsodic defense of free speech in *Abrams*, referring to the "leaflets" before the Court as "poor and puny anonymities" that express a "creed" of "ignorance and immaturity."[11] In short, the Court has sometimes implied that we can and should be especially protective of speech because it's unlikely to hurt anyone.

For at least two reasons, however, it is perilous to use such an argument to explain why our concerns are elevated when vague laws target speech. First, as a factual matter, some categories of speech can indeed inflict great harm: a libel can ruin a reputation; a threat can destroy peace of mind; an incitement can spur violence; a pornographic film can victimize children or those enslaved by human trafficking. Second, as a theoretical matter, an argument that discounts the power and impact of speech leads us into a deep intellectual inconsistency. After all, if speech has so little influence on circumstances in the world then why bother to protect it so vigorously?[12]

No, vague laws punishing speech raise special concerns for other, different reasons than because of our possible uncertainties about the effects of the speech. The Supreme Court identified one such concern of central importance in the *Grayned* case. "Uncertain meanings," the Court observed there, "inevitably lead citizens to 'steer far wider of the unlawful zone' ... than if the boundaries of the forbidden areas were clearly marked."[13] Where the statute "abut[s] upon sensitive areas of basic First Amendment freedoms," this tendency will necessarily "inhibit the exercise of [those] freedoms."[14]

In this passage, the Court offers a compelling observation about human behavior. Vague laws leave people uncertain about what they can, and cannot, do. As a result, most people will behave cautiously in deciding how to proceed. For safety's sake, they will tend to "steer far wider" of the law's ambiguous borders. When the statute

[10] *Herndon*, 301 U.S. at 249–250.

[11] *Abrams*, 250 U.S. at 630.

[12] In some contexts, considering the negligible impact of a given instance of speech makes sense. Consider, for example, Pickering v. Board of Education, 391 U.S. 563 (1968). In that case, a teacher was dismissed from his employment for sending to a local newspaper a letter where he criticized the manner in which the school board and superintendent had addressed revenue issues. The board concluded that the teacher's conduct had been "detrimental" to the school and terminated him. The Supreme Court held that the dismissal violated the teacher's First Amendment rights. The Court noted that teachers do not lose their First Amendment right to speak about matters of public importance simply by virtue of their public employment. And the Court further observed that there was no reason to believe that the speech had in fact been detrimental to the school. "So far as the record reveals," the Court declared, the letter was greeted by everyone but the board with "massive apathy and total disbelief." *Id.* at 570.

[13] *Grayned*, 408 U.S. at 109.

[14] *Id.*

targets speech, this excessive wariness has the effect of artificially limiting First Amendment rights and constraining their full exercise.

We can imagine two objections to the Court's analysis. First, someone might question the behavioral assumptions embedded in this reasoning. These days, people do not seem hesitant about offering their thoughts and opinions – especially via social media platforms. We might wonder whether the existence of a vague law will really cow people from saying what they think.

This objection has some intuitive appeal but does not hold up well under close scrutiny. It may be true that in the United States today we see largely unfettered expression going on all around us. But that may not tell us anything about how those same speakers would respond if our First Amendment doctrine shifted and allowed for the enforcement of vague laws against controversial speech.

Furthermore, this objection does not take into account how human beings make decisions when they think their speech might run afoul of the law. As First Amendment scholar Geoffrey Stone has observed, free speech is relatively easily "chilled" because each of us tends to believe that "our individual act of expression is unlikely to make a difference."[15] It may seem unlikely that the absence of our particular voice will matter much, if at all – especially with regard to big issues over which we have no direct control, like public policy. As Professor Stone points out, however, "if many people are individually chilled, the overall impact on public discourse can be quite dramatic. This is why courts formulating First Amendment doctrine generally pay special attention to the dangers of chilling effect."[16]

The second objection to the Court's analysis goes not to the premise of the argument but to its conclusion. "Alright," someone might say, "vague laws may make people proceed more cautiously when they speak. But it is not clear that this is a bad thing. Perhaps it's for the best if our laws encourage people to act carefully and responsibly when they speak. After all, our laws generally try to direct people toward careful and responsible conduct."

This objection, too, fails on close analysis. It does not acknowledge a distinctive characteristic of speech – that it may have great social value even when incautious, indeed, especially when incautious. Speech may seem imprudent because it challenges the status quo, or speaks truth to power, or offends the majority, or leads to social upheaval. Nevertheless, such disruptive speech plays a critical role in advancing knowledge, promoting justice, and achieving political change. In many circumstances, and for many different reasons, we want people to be bold rather than timorous when they engage in speech.

The same does not hold true for most other activities that human beings engage in and that the law regulates. We don't want people to be bold when driving a car,

[15] Geoffrey R. Stone, *Chilling Effect*, HUFFPOST (Feb. 16, 2007), https://www.huffingtonpost.com/geoffrey-r-stone/chilling-effect_b_41430.html.

[16] *Id.*

handling a firearm, or discharging fireworks. We don't want people to be imprudent when manufacturing pharmaceuticals, flying airplanes, or performing surgery. In those contexts, our laws set protocols designed to lead people and entities to err on the side of caution, because their doing so serves a variety of social values. A similarly cautious approach to speech, however, would keep ideas out of the marketplace, discourage the sharing of important information, frustrate self-expression, stifle criticism, and inadvertently channel energy toward *more* dangerous outlets, like violence.

The Supreme Court has sometimes used the phrase "breathing space" to describe what we seek to achieve here. One example comes in the Court's landmark decision regarding defamation claims in *New York Times Co.* v. *Sullivan*,[17] which we discuss in Chapter 11 when we consider the "exceptions" to free speech. In *New York Times*, the Court addressed the standard applicable to defamation cases brought by plaintiffs who are public officials. The Court held that such plaintiffs must prove by clear and convincing evidence that the defendant acted with "actual malice" when making the allegedly defamatory statement. And the Court went on to define actual malice as knowledge of falsity or reckless disregard of the truth.[18]

The Court conceded that this standard makes it difficult for such plaintiffs to prevail. It therefore ends up protecting some speech that is false, even negligently false. But the Court declared that "erroneous statement is inevitable in free debate, and ... must be protected if the freedoms of expression are to have the 'breathing space' that they need to survive."[19] In other words, if we want to protect *all true* speech then we need to protect *some false* speech as well in order to leave a margin for error.

We see the same idea in the other so-called exceptions to free speech that the Court has recognized. True, the Court has held that some exceptions exist, like obscenity and fighting words. But, as we discuss further in Chapter 11, it turns out that those categories are narrow in scope, and that many things we might view as obscene or provocative do not fit the Court's carefully crafted definitions.

For example, someone might find Henry Miller's erotic novel *Opus Pistorum* obscene, but it does not fit the definition set forth in *Miller* v. *California* (1973).[20] And, someone might experience violent outrage over a newspaper editorial supporting protestors who burn the American flag, but such an article does not qualify as "fighting words" under existing doctrine. In addition, as we discuss in Chapter 11, the Court has shown absolutely no interest in creating additional unprotected categories to deal with new issues, even when presented with sympathetic cases – like

[17] New York Times Co. v. Sullivan, 376 U.S. 254 (1964).
[18] *Id.* at 280.
[19] *Id.* at 271–272.
[20] Miller v. California, 413 U.S. 15 (1973).

horrifically violent video games that find their way into the hands of minors or films of fetishistic animal torture.[21]

Of course, the goal of providing breathing space to speech has its limitations. With a properly crafted law, we can punish the knowing libel, the deliberate fraud, and true "fighting words." Giving speech room to work does not mean allowing it to prevail over all other interests in all cases. Still, preserving breathing space is essential to maintaining a robust principle of free expression.

Closely related to, but distinct from, the issue of vagueness is a problem addressed by the "overbreadth" doctrine. This doctrine comes into play when a law encompasses speech that the First Amendment does not protect – but also reaches speech that it does. For example, a law criminalizing the distribution of "visual depictions of naked minors" would punish child pornography, but it would also apply to a textbook on pediatric anatomy, a forensic documentary about how to identify the signs of child abuse, and a videotape shared among family members of a nude infant crawling around the living room floor.

The overbreadth doctrine has a critical role in addressing a common and worrisome dynamic in the drafting of statutes. In many instances, lawmakers tend to overlegislate, for understandable reasons. Think of it this way: any problem worthy of a legislative solution demands an adequate one, and the bigger the problem the more expansive the fix. Unfortunately, in the effort to be comprehensive, legislation often turns out to be excessive. One of the authors of this book has described this phenomenon by using a variation on one of Newton's principles of physics: "for every action, there is an unequal and opposite overreaction."[22]

Consider the example of the statute prohibiting the distribution of "visual depictions of naked minors" discussed above. Even though the hypothetical law reaches very broadly, we can understand why a legislature might arrive at so exhaustive a prohibition. If we want to punish all child pornography – and every sensible person will agree that we should – then we need a law that corresponds to the magnitude of the task and that leaves no omissions or loopholes. Real life examples of this abound: for instance, in the process of passing a law intended to punish sexually fetishistic animal torture, Congress inadvertently drafted a statute that arguably also criminalized travel films that showed bullfighting.[23]

Because the overbreadth doctrine plays an important role in the protection of speech, the Supreme Court has allowed its aggressive application. For example, the

[21] *See* Brown v. Entertainment Merchants Ass'n, 564 U.S. 786 (2011) (striking down a California law banning the sale of certain violent video games to children without parental permission) and United States v. Stevens, 559 U.S. 460 (2010) (striking down a federal law that criminalized certain depictions of cruelty to animals).

[22] Len Niehoff, *Doe v. University of Michigan: Free Speech on Campus 25 Years Later*, 71 U. Miami L. Rev. 365, 375–76 (2017).

[23] *See* United States v. Stevens, 559 U.S. 460 (2010) (striking down a federal law that criminalized certain depictions of cruelty to animals).

Court has allowed plaintiffs in First Amendment cases to attack overly broad statutes even though the plaintiffs' *own* conduct was "clearly unprotected and could be proscribed by a law drawn with the requisite specificity."[24] This reflects an exception to a generally applicable principle: in cases not implicating the First Amendment, plaintiffs typically do not have "standing" to challenge overly broad statutes if their own conduct was appropriately subject to punishment.

Still, the overbreadth doctrine also raises some concerns. The Court has recognized that holding a law unconstitutional on overbreadth grounds is "strong medicine" and so should be done only "with hesitation" and "as a last resort."[25] We can see why: a declaration of unconstitutional overbreadth usually invalidates the entire statute, taking down the *legitimate* exercise of legislative power right along with the *illegitimate*.

Think again about the "naked minor" statute discussed above. Application of the overbreadth doctrine brings down the senseless prohibition against pediatric anatomy texts – but also the socially critical prohibition against child pornography. As a result, the Court has limited the doctrine in various ways, for instance declining to apply it unless the overbreadth is substantial[26] or if the apparent overbreadth has been solved by a court's definitive interpretation.[27]

With these principles of vagueness, breathing room, and overbreadth before us, we can now see the substantial drafting challenges that public bodies face when they try to adopt laws that regulate problematic speech. It is easy enough to say that we want to prohibit hate speech, threats, or obscenity – but reasonable people have very different understandings of what those terms mean. Even putting aside all other constitutional objections, trying to draft such laws in terms that are specific, narrow, and leave adequate breathing space in close cases turns out to be a daunting task.

Take the seemingly simple project of drafting a law that prohibits "disorderly conduct," as the Chicago ordinance did in the early case of *Terminiello v. Chicago*,[28] which we discuss again in Chapter 12 on "hate speech." That case involved the prosecution of Father Arthur Terminiello, an outspoken and vitriolic Catholic priest who had been suspended by his bishop. Terminiello gave a ranting anti-Semitic speech to a large group while protestors picketed and grew increasingly angry outside.[29] He was arrested and charged under the disorderly conduct ordinance. The jury found him guilty. The case went to the Supreme Court of the United States, which reversed.

[24] New York v. Ferber, 458 U.S. 747, 769 (1982).
[25] *Id.* at 769.
[26] *Id.* at 770.
[27] *See* R.A.V. v. City of St. Paul, 505 U.S. 377 (1992).
[28] Terminiello v. Chicago, 337 U.S. 1 (1949).
[29] *Id.* at 14–15 (Jackson, J., dissenting).

Despite the inflammatory nature of Terminiello's speech, the Court held that his conviction under the ordinance violated the First Amendment.[30] The Court did not deny that the City of Chicago could adopt a disorderly conduct ordinance of some kind. But, here, the judge had instructed the jury that the phrase "breach of the peace" in the ordinance included speech that "stirs the public to anger, invites dispute, brings about a condition of unrest, or creates a disturbance."[31]

Many of these terms are impossibly vague. What does it mean for speech to "invite dispute?" Does criticizing an opposing political party qualify? What about angrily denouncing a public policy? How about expressing a position on the abortion debate? Does the phrase embrace a strident expression of opinion about the historically best team in all of major league baseball or the most authentic recipe for chicken curry?

Furthermore, the Supreme Court recognized that the ordinance (particularly as interpreted and applied) was overly broad. It reached speech that we have good reasons to protect. In this spirit, the Court declared that "a function of free speech under our system of government is to invite dispute. It may indeed best serve its high purpose when it induces a condition of unrest, creates dissatisfaction with conditions as they are, or even stirs people to anger."[32]

So, this ordinance would punish speech that the state may have the authority to restrict – like face-to-face fighting words intended and likely to result in immediate violence. But, because of its overbreadth, it would also punish speech that we value and that the First Amendment shields. Indeed, a statute that punishes speech simply because it makes people angry or agitated encompasses expression that we view not only as legitimate but as an essential catalyst to political change and progress.

The limitations of human language, when combined with the doctrines of vagueness, breathing space, and overbreadth, may render it practically impossible for us to punish some speech that we find troublesome, perhaps even deeply so. We may have the capacity to imagine a category of speech that we have good reasons to proscribe but not to describe that category with sufficient specificity and narrowness. Careful craftsmanship can solve some of our legislative drafting challenges but not all of them.

Consider, for example, the category of speech so "outrageous" that it results in emotional distress. We might intuitively believe that we should proscribe such speech: after all, people can express ideas and share information in ways that *don't* result in such injury; the qualities of the speech that cause such harm seem to have little or no social value; and, in other contexts, the law recognizes the importance of protecting the emotional well-being of individuals. On first blush, allowing a civil

30 *Id.* at 3, 5.

31 *Id.* at 4.

32 *Id.*

claim for infliction of emotional distress, particularly where the speaker clearly intended to inflict it, makes perfect sense.

But, when the Supreme Court considered this issue in *Snyder* v. *Phelps*,[33] it concluded that such a claim did not pass constitutional muster. We discussed *Snyder* in Chapter 1 and, as you will recall, it involved speech by the homophobic Westboro Baptist Church that most of us would unhesitatingly label as outrageous and emotionally harmful. And yet the Court had no difficulty concluding that the First Amendment barred a claim based upon it.

In reversing the jury verdict below, the Supreme Court expressed particular concern over the state law standard applied to civil claims for intentional infliction of emotional distress: "outrageousness."[34] Here, the trial court had instructed the jury that if it found Westboro had engaged in "outrageous" behavior then it should find for the plaintiff. Again, most of us would agree that the label clearly applied to Westboro's hateful speech.

The Court noted, however, that the "highly malleable standard" of "outrageousness" has "an inherent subjectiveness about it."[35] And, indeed, the standard's intrinsic mushiness triggers all of the concerns discussed in this chapter. The standard is vague: it does not provide adequate notice of what is, and is not, allowed.

The standard is also overly broad. It may encompass some speech that the First Amendment does not protect, such as a direct threat against someone's physical safety. But it also reaches speech that the First Amendment does protect, like an over-the-top parody of an elected official.

Furthermore, precisely because the borders of the standard are imprecise and excessively expansive, it does not afford adequate "breathing space" to speech. All the dangers we have previously discussed follow from these infirmities, including, as the Court noted, that it allows "a jury to impose liability on the basis of the jurors' tastes or views."[36] The First Amendment exists in order to shield controversial speech from just such condemnations.

These doctrines admittedly do not leave us in a place that everyone will always find satisfactory. As a result of their application, our laws will not be able to rectify some injustices, right some wrongs, and remedy some harms. As we discuss in Chapter 12, these doctrines substantially complicate the project of trying to draft an anti-hate-speech law. They yield results that we do not like.

The lawsuit brought by Matthew Snyder's father is a compelling case in point. The Supreme Court reversed the verdict he secured there, even while acknowledging that the protestors' conduct had undoubtedly added still more anguish to the

[33] Snyder v. Phelps, 562 U.S. 443 (2011).
[34] *Id.* at 458.
[35] *Id.*
[36] *Id.*

plaintiff's "already incalculable grief."[37] Still, First Amendment jurisprudence holds that this uncomfortable balance makes doctrinal sense, in large measure because it has more to recommend it than the alternatives.

In Chapter 11, we turn back to an issue we explored in this one – the necessity of exceptions. We will see the Supreme Court grapple there with many of the problems we have just discussed. After all, a judicially recognized exception, like a statute, must also have the virtues of clarity and narrowness. And that is easier said than done.

[37] *Id.* at 456. *See also Id.* at 460–461 (noting that the church's speech "is certainly hurtful" and "inflict[ed] great pain").

11

Exceptions Must Be Limited and Narrowly Crafted

As we have seen, the Supreme Court repeatedly has given primacy to freedom of speech, recognizing our "profound national commitment to the principle that debate on public issues should be uninhibited, robust, and wide-open."[1] And it has done so across a wide range of content and forms of expression. The Court has protected a citizen's right to burn American flags,[2] to display expletives on their clothing,[3] and to criticize government officials.[4]

Still, the Supreme Court has long recognized that free speech must be subject to some exceptions. Commonly cited examples include defamation, obscenity, speech incident to a crime (like blackmail), and "fighting words" likely to incite immanent lawless action. We have in passing mentioned all of these earlier in the book, and we now look at some of them in greater detail.

The early grounds for these exceptions were laid out in *Chaplinsky* v. *New Hampshire*.[5] Writing for the Court, Justice Murphy stated:

> Allowing the broadest scope to the language and purpose of the Fourteenth Amendment, it is well understood that the right of free speech is not absolute at all times and under all circumstances. There are certain well-defined and narrowly limited classes of speech, the prevention and punishment of which have never been thought to raise any Constitutional problem. These include the lewd and obscene, the profane, the libelous, and the insulting or "fighting" words – those which by their very utterance inflict injury or tend to incite an immediate breach of the peace. It has been well observed that such utterances are no essential part of any exposition of ideas, and are of such slight social value as a step to truth that any

1 New York Times Co. v. Sullivan, 376 U.S. 254, 282 (1964).
2 Texas v. Johnson, 491 U.S. 397 (1989).
3 Cohen v. California, 403 U.S. 15, 26 (1971).
4 *New York Times Co.*, 376 U.S. at 270.
5 Chaplinsky v. New Hampshire, 315 U.S. 568 (1942).

> benefit that may be derived from them is clearly outweighed by the social interest in order and morality.[6]

In *Chaplinsky*, the Court framed these as categories of speech that do not call for any fresh balancing of competing interests. By the Court's reasoning, the relevant balancing occurred long ago and remains valid. As a matter of history and tradition, we recognize these categories of speech as posing substantial risks to the public order and ethos while offering little or no value or benefit.

This may have been the proper framing of the issue when the Court decided *Chaplinsky*, but First Amendment doctrine evolved and things changed. As we have already seen, the Court has construed the First Amendment to afford substantial protection to the lewd (provided it does not meet the definition of obscenity), the profane (because one person's vulgarity is another's lyric), and the insulting (as long as they do not constitute fighting words). Today, it would be inaccurate to describe any of those categories of speech as "exceptions" to the First Amendment.

In this chapter, we take a closer look at some of the categories that might still fairly be viewed as exceptions, like libel and obscenity. Even here, however, we will see that over time the Court has narrowed substantially the scope of those exceptions. Indeed, a great deal of speech that the average person might view as libelous or obscene remains protected because it does not fit within the very specific definitions and standards that the Court has adopted.

DEFAMATION

The law of defamation has a long history and has evolved in complex and technically intricate ways. A book of this nature can explore only some of its most important dimensions. Nevertheless, defamation deserves our close attention because of its significance to the development of free speech doctrine and because of the lessons it conveys concerning the Court's approach to the exceptions more generally.

We begin with some basic ideas and terminology. In sum, a plaintiff in a defamation case claims that the defendant made a false and negative statement about the plaintiff that injured the plaintiff's reputation. As a technical matter, a "libel" claim is one in which the defendant made the offending statement in writing and a "slander" claim is one in which the statement was spoken. That distinction has faded in importance and, today, "defamation" and "libel" are commonly used interchangeably, as we will do in this chapter.

Over the years, the Supreme Court has reviewed many cases involving defamation claims. Because the values that underlie the First Amendment require room for free and robust debate, the Supreme Court in time became increasingly concerned about the potential of libel claims to inhibit speech on matters of public

[6] *Id.* at 571–572.

importance. Prior to 1964, the Supreme Court viewed defamation as a matter of state tort law and criminal law and did not think that it implicated First Amendment concerns at all. But, starting with *New York Times v. Sullivan* in 1964, the Court began to "constitutionalize" libel law, limiting defamation claims so that they do not undermine core First Amendment values.

Prior to 1964, the Supreme Court left it to state law to determine the level of fault on the part of a defendant that a libel plaintiff had to prove in order to prevail. The common law allowed for a strict liability regime, which held defendants responsible for their defamatory statements without regard to whether they had any reason to know those statements were false. Most states did not go so far, adopting a negligence standard that basically required only that the plaintiff show that the defendant committed an error that reasonable effort would have avoided. This standard still made it relatively easy for a plaintiff to prove defamation.

In *New York Times Co. v. Sullivan*, the Court effected two major changes in defamation law. First, the Court recognized that substantial adverse jury verdicts in libel cases could chill the discussion of important public issues in a manner inconsistent with bedrock First Amendment principles. The law of defamation therefore could not be left entirely to the states; libel law had to comply with the speech protections afforded by the First Amendment.

Second, the Court declared that in certain types of cases a negligence standard did not adequately protect speech. In operation, so low a standard of fault would result in some adverse verdicts even where the defendant had made an understandable mistake or where the question of falsity was a close one. Perhaps even more importantly, the mere *threat* of such verdicts would chill individuals and media entities from speaking out on matters of public interest and concern.

In this case and its progeny, the Supreme Court therefore announced a "federal rule" that the First Amendment "absolutely prohibits punishment of truthful criticism."[7] Furthermore, the Court declared, even if the criticism is proved untrue, public officials can only recover damages for defamatory speech when "the statement was made with 'actual malice' – that is, with knowledge that it was false or with reckless disregard of whether it was false or not."[8]

The actual malice standard imposes a significantly higher burden of proof on a public official libel plaintiff than on other libel plaintiffs. Under this standard, a jury cannot find liability based on negligence or on the defendant's "reasonable belief" that statements were false.[9] Rather, to find for the plaintiff the jury must conclude, based on clear and convincing evidence, that the defendant made statements "with knowledge of their falsity or in reckless disregard of whether they are true or false."[10]

7 Garrison v. Louisiana, 379 U.S. 64, 79 (1964) and Rosenblatt v. Baer, 383 U.S. 75 (1966).
8 *New York Times Co.*, 376 U.S. at 280.
9 Garrison v. Louisiana, 379 U.S. 64, 78 (1964).
10 *Id.*

As the Court's definition makes clear, "actual malice" is a term of art. It does not mean "malice" in the sense in which we ordinarily think of it – that is, as hatred, spite, or animosity. Indeed, the Court has stated expressly that it is not enough for the plaintiff to prove "ill will, evil motive, or intention to injure."[11] Those states of mind, which the courts sometimes confusingly call "common law malice," are not the same as *New York Times* actual malice and proof of one does not constitute proof of the other.

In this context, "recklessness" also has its own special meaning. Proof of recklessness requires more than simply showing a "failure of [the defendant] to make a prior investigation"[12] or some other form of extreme negligence. Rather, proving recklessness requires a showing that the "false statements [were] made with the high degree of awareness of their probable falsity,"[13] or that the author "in fact entertained serious doubts as to the truth of his publication."[14]

The Supreme Court thus made clear that, in order to prove actual malice, a public official libel plaintiff must show clearly and convincingly that the defendant made the offending statement with a very specific state of mind: the defendant either must have *known* that the statement was false when they made it (that is, they must have intentionally *lied*) or they must have *entertained serious doubts* about its truth. The Court recognized that this would make it difficult for public official plaintiffs to prevail in defamation cases. But it concluded that this is precisely what the First Amendment requires in order to protect free expression.

Over the years, the Supreme Court has continued to endorse the actual malice standard and to expand its application. For example, in later cases, the Supreme Court held that this standard applies not just to public officials but to certain types of "public figures."[15] These include "general purpose" public figures (people whose pervasive fame and influence render speech about them a matter of substantial public interest) and "limited purpose" public figures (people who inject themselves into specific public controversies).[16] Oprah Winfrey might be an example of the former; a parent who becomes an advocate for gun control after losing a child in a school shooting might be an example of the latter.

In addition, the Supreme Court has been firm that a plaintiff cannot avoid the demanding actual malice standard through the simple expedient of labeling their claim as something other than one for libel. The Court has therefore applied the actual malice standard in cases involving statutory invasion of privacy claims[17] and

[11] *See e.g.* Rosenblatt v. Baer, 383 U.S. 75, 84 (1966).
[12] Beckley Newspaper Corp. v. Hanks, 389 U.S. 81, 84–85 (1967). *See also* St. Amant v. Thompson, 390 U.S. 727 (1968).
[13] *Garrison*, 379 U.S at 74.
[14] *St. Amant*, 390 U.S. at 731.
[15] Gertz v. Robert Welch, Inc. 418 U.S. 323 (1974).
[16] *Id.*
[17] Time Inc. v. Hill, 385 U.S. 374 (1967).

claims for intentional infliction of emotional distress.[18] The Court has preserved the strength and integrity of the protections afforded by the actual malice standard by preventing end runs around it.

The actual malice standard has been controversial and the subject of a great deal of public debate. Ever since its adoption, some frustrated public officials and public figures have condemned the standard as allowing the media to say whatever they want with impunity and as granting them a license to lie. The *New York Times* decision may have its puzzles and imperfections,[19] but this criticism is obviously wrong. After all, even under this more demanding standard, media entities remain potentially liable for their defamatory statements. Also, the actual malice standard applies only in cases involving certain kinds of plaintiffs. And the actual malice standard allows for punishment of a proven lie – indeed, that's what "actual malice" is: a knowing falsehood.

The criticism also misses the point. The actual malice standard makes it more difficult for public officials and public figures to prevail in defamation cases because that is precisely how it should be if we want to ensure that debate over issues of public importance has sufficient breathing room. A regime in which public officials and prominent public figures could easily prevail in libel cases would not foster the wide-open expression or provide the latitude for error that are essential to a robust principle of free speech.

In addition to fault, a defamation claim includes an element of falsity. At the common law, the court presumed a statement was false once the plaintiff proved it was defamatory. This left defendants in libel cases with the burden of establishing the truth of their statements. Nevertheless, many states opted to follow a rule that placed the burden of proving falsity on the plaintiff.

Just as the Supreme Court in 1964 constitutionalized the fault element of a libel claim, in 1986 it constitutionalized the falsity element. In *Philadelphia Newspapers, Inc.* v. *Hepps*,[20] the Court held that, in a libel case based on a statement about a matter of public interest, the plaintiff has the burden of proving falsity. As noted, many states already had allocated the burden of proof this way; but *Hepps* made clear that the First Amendment requires as much.

In order to prevail, a libel plaintiff must show that the offending statement is not just false but *materially* so.[21] This means that the plaintiff must prove that the published statement had "a different effect on the mind of the reader" than that which the precise truth would have produced.[22] Small mistakes or inaccuracies

[18] Hustler Magazine v. Falwell, 485 U.S. 46 (1988).
[19] *See, e.g.*, Len Niehoff, Three Puzzling Things about *New York Times* v. *Sullivan*: Beginning the Anniversary Conversation, 29 COMM. LAW 10 (2012–2013).
[20] Philadelphia Newspapers, Inc. v. Hepps, 475 U.S. 767 (1986).
[21] Masson v. New Yorker Magazine, 501 U.S. 496, 517 (1991).
[22] *Id.*

therefore do not suffice.[23] And a statement is not false for purposes of a defamation claim if its "substance," "gist," or "sting" is the same as that of the literal truth.[24]

The requirement that a libel plaintiff prove factual falsity has an important consequence. It means that if the statement is not the *kind* of expression that can be proved objectively true or false then it cannot serve as the basis for a defamation claim. This principle effectively immunizes from libel claims a statement that constitutes rhetorical hyperbole, that uses loose and figurative language, that amounts to a subjective assessment, or that comes in the context of parody or satire.[25] To offer a simple example, a statement that a public official accepted a monetary bribe on a specific date can be proved true or false and so could give rise to a libel claim; in contrast, a statement that the official's public policies are unwise cannot be proved objectively true or false and so is not actionable in defamation.

The Court in *Chaplinsky* broadly stated that the First Amendment offers no protection for libelous statements and that defamation claims therefore do not present "any constitutional problem." As the preceding discussion indicates, however, things are vastly more complicated. In time, the Supreme Court came to recognize that libel claims do indeed implicate First Amendment concerns. As a result, the Court constitutionalized various elements of the tort, including fault and falsity. Along the way, the Court limited the kinds of statements that qualify as actionable in libel and made it more difficult for certain defamation plaintiffs to prevail. In sum, the Court has construed narrowly the so-called libel exception. Many statements that fit within the general definition offered earlier – a negative statement that injures the plaintiff's reputation – will therefore not support a defamation claim. We see this pattern in the Court's treatment of the other "exceptions" as well.

OBSCENITY

Chaplinsky indicated that another exception to the First Amendment exists with respect to speech deemed "obscene." Indeed, the Court historically has viewed obscenity regulation as an acceptable tool for preserving "public morals."[26] But, because "morality" is neither universally defined nor socially static, the Court has faced the daunting task of formulating a definition of obscenity that is sufficiently specific to qualify as a "test" but also sufficiently flexible to accommodate diverse communities and changing sensibilities. And the Court has had to ensure that laws

[23] *Id.*

[24] *Id.*

[25] *See, e.g.*, Milkovich v. Lorain Journal Company, 497 U.S. 1, 22 (1990); Hustler Magazine v. Falwell, 485 U.S. 46 (1988); and Dun & Bradstreet v. Greenmoss Builders, 472 U.S. 749 (1985).

[26] *Chaplinsky*, 315 U.S. at 571–572.

limiting the availability of materials "injurious to public morals"[27] do not run afoul of the constitutionally guaranteed freedom to advocate ideas and express oneself.[28]

Early decisions reflected this tension between restricting materials deemed injurious to the public good while upholding principles of free speech. Over time, the Court struck down many obscenity laws due to issues such as vagueness or overbreadth.[29] The Court's obscenity decisions tend to fall on the far ends of a spectrum that ranges from those based on determinations of community standards of morality, at one end, to those based on fervent adherence to constitutional principles of liberty, on the other end. The early cases generally fall at the former end of the spectrum. The later cases, where the Court often struck down obscenity laws on vagueness and overbreadth grounds, at the other end.

The Court's modern efforts to arrive at a proper standard for addressing obscenity began in 1957 with *Roth* v. *United States*.[30] Justice Brennan, writing for the Court, started from the premise that obscenity (properly defined) did not deserve the protection of the First Amendment. He then laid out a test for determining when speech could be deemed obscene: "whether to the average person, applying contemporary community standards, the dominant theme of the material taken as a whole appeals to prurient interest."[31]

Both Justice Douglas and Justice Harlan dissented in *Roth*, criticizing the notion that obscenity was unworthy of First Amendment protections. Justice Harlan argued that the assumption that obscenity "is a peculiar genus of 'speech and press,' which is as distinct, recognizable, and classifiable as poison ivy is among other plants" was far too generalized.[32] Justice Douglas too took issue with *Roth*'s harsh classification of obscenity: "There is no special historical evidence that literature dealing with sex was intended to be treated in a special manner by those who drafted the First Amendment."[33]

Nevertheless, the *Roth* test remained the benchmark in many subsequent obscenity cases,[34] although it did evolve. Justice Brennan sought to rework the standard he

27 Winters v. New York, 333 U.S. 507, 515 (1948).

28 Kingsley v. Regents of the Univ. of New York, 360 U.S. 684 (1959).

29 *See e.g.*, *Winters*, 333 U.S. at 518 (striking down an obscenity law for vagueness); Joseph Burstyn v. Wilson, 343 U.S. 495 (1952) (finding a New York obscenity law unconstitutional because it created an unlawful opportunity for a censor to arbitrarily limit speech through an unclear standard); Smith v. California, 361 U.S. 147 (1959) (finding law criminalizing possession of obscene literature unconstitutionally vague where it did not provide an adequate definition of obscene); and Bantam Books, Inc. v. Sullivan, 372 U.S. 58, 59 (1963) (striking down a Rhode Island policy on the grounds that it sought to censor or suppress certain materials without providing procedures that protect against the suppression of protected speech).

30 Roth v. United States, 354 U.S. 476, 484 (1957).

31 *Id.* at 489.

32 *Id.* at 497 (Harlan, J., dissenting).

33 *Id.* at 514 (Douglas, J., dissenting).

34 *See, e.g.*, Jacobellis v. Ohio, 378 U.S. 184 (1964) (validity questioned in Kaplan v. California, 413 U.S. 115 (1973)) (applying *Roth* to determine that the film in question was not obscene); and

had set forth in *Roth* and to create a more finely tuned formulation for determining obscenity in the case *A Book Named "John Cleland's Memoirs of a Woman of Pleasure"* v. *Attorney Gen. of Massachusetts*,[35] often simply called the *Memoirs* case. Justice Brennan there reasoned that for speech to qualify as obscene "three elements must coalesce: it must be established that (a) the dominant theme of the material taken as a whole appeals to a prurient interest in sex; (b) the material is patently offensive because it affronts contemporary community standards relating to the description or representation of sexual matters; and (c) the material is utterly without redeeming social value."[36]

The *Memoirs* standard created a heavy burden of proof, requiring prosecutors to show that the speech was *completely* devoid of any value whatsoever. This made obscenity prosecutions almost impossible to win; after all, even materials filled with outrageously graphic sexual content may have *some* component that has *some* value. It quickly became clear that the test required further refinements.

Those adjustments came in *Miller* v. *California*.[37] Drawing on parts of the *Memoirs* test and rejecting others, the Court in *Miller* outlined the three key elements necessary to determine obscenity:

> The basic guidelines for the trier of fact must be: (a) whether "the average person, applying contemporary community standards" would find that the work, taken as a whole, appeals to the prurient interest; (b) whether the work depicts or describes, in a patently offensive way, sexual conduct specifically defined by the applicable state law; and (c) whether the work, taken as a whole, lacks serious literary, artistic, political, or scientific value.[38]

Miller sought to establish a bright-line test and to provide fairly specific instruction to the states about what their obscenity laws needed to include to pass constitutional muster.

The Court's language clearly suggests that this was not just a matter of First Amendment rights but also of due process:

> Under the holdings announced today, no one will be subject to prosecution for the sale or exposure of obscene materials unless these materials depict or describe patently offensive "hard core" sexual conduct specifically defined by the regulating state law, as written or construed. We are satisfied that these specific prerequisites

Ginzburg v. United States, 383 U.S. 463 (1966) (finding pornographic materials distributed via mail to be obscene under the *Roth* standard and not protected from charges under the Federal Obscenity Statute by the First Amendment).

35 A Book Named "John Cleland's Memoirs of a Woman of Pleasure" v. Attorney Gen. of Mass, 383 U.S. 413 (1966).

36 *Id.* at 418.

37 Miller v. California, 413 U.S. 15 (1973).

38 *Id.* at 24 (1973) (internal citations omitted).

> will provide fair notice to a dealer in such materials that his public and commercial activities may bring prosecution.[39]

This standard continues to guide obscenity litigation today,[40] although (apart from child pornography) such prosecutions in the United States have become relatively rare.

The Court clarified aspects of the *Miller* test in later cases. For example, the Court observed that, while jurors must base their determination of what is "hard core" and "patently offensive" on the standards of the *community*, the determination regarding the *value* of the speech is not similarly localized.[41] Instead, a general standard of how the "reasonable person"[42] would assess the value of the speech applies. This principle helps guard against the difficulties that would follow if, for example, Ann Arbor, Michigan and Grand Rapids, Michigan had different localized views of the value of Henry Miller's *Tropic of Cancer*, James Joyce's *Ulysses*, or Vladimir Nabokov's *Lolita*.

The Court in *Miller* thus made clear that the obscenity "exception" is, like the defamation "exception," technically constructed and narrowly construed. Many things that many people will find sexually offensive will not meet the test. Indeed, the Court expressly distinguished obscenity from pornography, allowing for the criminalization of only those materials that could be deemed "hard core" or "patently offensive."[43] As a result, the memoirs of Catherine Millet, the photographs of Robert Mapplethorpe, films like *Last Tango in Paris*, and endless numbers of rap songs may contain strong sexual content and may deeply offend some readers, viewers, and listeners. But they plainly do not qualify as "obscene" under *Miller* because of their literary and artistic merit.

On the same day *Miller* was decided, the Court also handed down its opinion in *Paris Adult Theatre I* v. *Slaton*.[44] Justice Brennan, who dissented in *Miller*, receded from his former attempts to define obscenity in *Roth* and *Memoirs* and filed yet another dissent. Here, he seemingly gave up on the notion that obscenity could be adequately captured in a judicial definition: "No one definition, no matter how precisely or narrowly drawn, can possibly suffice for all situations, or carve out fully suppressible expression from all media without also creating a substantial risk of encroachment upon the guarantees of the Due Process Clause and the First

39 *Id.* at 27–28.

40 *See, e.g.*, Kaplan v. California, 413 U.S. 115 (1973); Jenkins v. Georgia, 418 U.S. 153 (1974); Hamling v. United States, 418 U.S. 87 (1974); Brockett v. Spokane Arcades, 472 U.S. 491 (1985); and Ashcroft v. American Civil Liberties Union, 535 U.S. 564 (2002).

41 Smith v. United States, 431 U.S. 291, 301 (1976).

42 Pope v. Illinois, 481 U.S. 497 (1987). "The proper inquiry is not whether an ordinary member of any given community would find serious literary, artistic, political, or scientific value in allegedly obscene material, but whether a reasonable person would find such value in the material, taken as a whole." *Id.* at 500–501.

43 *Miller*, 413 U.S. at 28 (1973).

44 Paris Adult Theatre I v. Slaton, 413 U.S. 49 (1973).

Amendment."[45] Justice Brennan reasoned that while formulaic tests, such as the one he laid out in *Roth* and the one promulgated in *Miller*, could provide some stability to the field of obscenity law, they did so at the expense of First Amendment values.[46]

Justice Brennan observed that, to avoid constitutional issues, a definition of obscenity must be narrowly drawn.[47] He concluded, however, that the Court's repeated and strenuous efforts to arrive at such a definition had failed:

> Of course, the vagueness problem would be largely of our own creation if it stemmed primarily from our failure to reach a consensus on any one standard. But after 16 years of experimentation and debate I am reluctantly forced to the conclusion that none of the available formulas, including the one announced today, can reduce the vagueness to a tolerable level while at the same time striking an acceptable balance between the protections of the First and Fourteenth Amendments, on the one hand, and on the other the asserted state interest in regulating the dissemination of certain sexually oriented materials. Any effort to draw a constitutionally acceptable boundary on state power must resort to such indefinite concepts as "prurient interest," "patent offensiveness," "serious literary value," and the like. The meaning of these concepts necessarily varies with the experience, outlook, and even idiosyncrasies of the person defining them.[48]

The fact that, after *Miller*, the Court has shown almost no interest in wading back into the definitional morass to see if it can do better may validate Justice Brennan's conclusion that the concept of obscenity resists an adequately clear and workable definition.

The Court's struggle to define obscenity highlights a crucial dilemma in this area of doctrine. Obscenity regulations derive from moral and, with an assist from *Miller*, communal judgments.[49] At its basic level, however, the First Amendment denies the government the "power to restrict expression because of its message its ideas, its subject matter, or its content."[50] In this sense, the *Miller* test is at odds with the very foundations of the First Amendment. After all, the Court has repeatedly held that feelings of offense and "disgust [are] not a valid basis for restricting expression,"[51] and obscenity doctrine is fundamentally about speech that provokes just those sorts of feelings.

It is important to note that *Roth*, *Memoirs*, and *Miller* shared a common background: each involved a prosecution of someone who published or distributed the

45 *Id.* at 85 (1973) (Brennan dissenting).
46 *Id.* at 73.
47 *Id.* at 89.
48 *Id.* at 83–84.
49 Mark Huppin and Neil Malamuth, *The Obscenity Conundrum, Contingent Harms, and Constitutional Consistency*, 23 *Stan. L. & Pol'y Rev.* 31, 32 (2012).
50 Brown v. Entm't Merchs. Ass'n, 131 S. Ct. 2729, 2733 (2011) (quoting Ashcroft v. American Civil Liberties Union, 535 U.S. 564, 573 (2002)).
51 *Brown*, 564 U.S. at 798 (2011).

offending material. Those cases therefore left open the question of whether the same analysis applies with respect to an individual's mere *possession* of obscene material, especially in sanctity of their own home. Prosecuting someone for possession of sexually explicit material, without more, raises privacy concerns that publication and distribution arguably do not.

The Supreme Court recognized at least some right to privacy in *Griswold* v. *Connecticut*,[52] a case involving a law that prohibited the dispensing of birth control to married couples.[53] The right arose from the idea that a number of constitutional provisions recognized certain zones of privacy. These included the rights to be free from quartering soldiers, unreasonable searches, and bars to association.[54]

In *Stanley* v. *Georgia*,[55] the Court determined that the First Amendment created another category of protected privacy, particularly in regards to the possession of obscene materials.[56] This right prevented the government from creating and enforcing obscenity laws that would "reach into the privacy of one's own home."[57] "Whatever the power of the state to control public dissemination of ideas inimical to the public morality," the Court declared, "it cannot constitutionally premise legislation on the desirability of controlling a person's private thoughts."[58]

Thirty years later, the Court still further extended constitutional protection of private sexual intimacy in *Lawrence* v. *Texas*.[59] The Court declared: "The case does involve two adults who, with full and mutual consent from each other, engaged in sexual practices common to a homosexual lifestyle. The petitioners are entitled to respect for their private lives. The State cannot demean their existence or control their destiny by making their private sexual conduct a crime."[60] The dissent, authored by Justice Scalia, warned that the majority's opinion "effectively decrees the end of all morals legislation [including obscenity laws]."[61]

As noted above, for now *Miller* remains the law of the land and the applicable standard in obscenity prosecutions. Justice Scalia's dissent, however, raises provocative and intriguing questions: Does *Lawrence* mean that the government must refrain from legislating *all* sexual morality as between consenting adults? And, if

[52] Griswold v. Connecticut, 381 U.S. 479, 484 (1965) (recognizing the First Amendment right to privacy).
[53] *Id. See generally* E. THOMAS SULLIVAN AND TONI M. MASSARO, THE ARC OF DUE PROCESS IN AMERICAN CONSTITUTIONAL LAW (2013).
[54] *Id.* at 484.
[55] Stanley v. Georgia, 394 U.S. 557 (1969).
[56] *Id.* at 565.
[57] *Id.*
[58] *Id.* at 566.
[59] Lawrence v. Texas, 539 U.S. 558 (2003).
[60] *Id* at 578.
[61] *Id.* at 599 (Scalia, J., dissenting).

so, then does the *Miller* test – which seeks to restrict the access of adults to sexually explicit materials – go by the wayside? One scholar observes:

> In fact, for many years already (since 1969's *Stanley* v. *Georgia*) the Court has permitted the private possession of obscenity. Thus, granted that *Lawrence* helps to bar government from dictating what our sexual morals should look like and by whose eyes, we'd nonetheless be reluctant to overstate what this should mean, or to mistake it for something it's not. Taken together, *Lawrence* and *Stanley* indicate that government may not control how we think about or conduct our sexual selves in the privacy of the home.[62]

Although, at least for now, the *Miller* test still governs obscenity law, reasonable people can question how long it will do so and how to understand its significance in light of *Lawrence* and the ongoing shifts in the membership of the Supreme Court.

Of course, no such privacy or consent arguments hold where a law targets a form of sexually explicit speech that necessarily entails the victimization of nonconsenting persons, as child pornography does.[63] In those instances, the state does not seek simply to enforce a moral standard; it seeks also to prevent and punish conduct that causes severe physical and emotional harm. Because there are special considerations at play in regulating child pornography – specifically, the abuse and exploitation that are intrinsically involved in its production – states have the ability to punish the mere possession of this content.[64] This is a stark but necessary departure from the principles that the Court announced in *Stanley* v. *Georgia*.[65]

Today, obscenity law faces even greater challenges than the definitional problems highlighted by Justice Brennan or the questions raised by Justice Scalia. With the advent of the internet, policing the distribution of obscene materials has become increasingly difficult, if not practically impossible. Indeed, the stuff of the early obscenity prosecutions – where the government seized stockrooms or mailings filled with sexually explicit books, magazines, and 8 mm films – has little relevance to the present online environment.

Nevertheless, in the early years of the internet the federal government launched several ambitious legislative attempts to control online access to obscene material, particularly on the part of minors. One of the first came in the Communications Decency Act,[66] which was challenged in *Reno* v. *American Civil Liberties Union*[67] and which sought "to protect minors from 'indecent' and 'patently offensive' communications on the Internet."[68] The Court struck down much of the Act on grounds of constitutional overbreadth. Among other things, the Court held that some of the

62 Huppin, *supra*, at 52.
63 *See* New York v. Ferber, 458 U.S. 747 (1982).
64 Osborne v. Ohio, 495 U.S. 103 (1990).
65 *Id.*
66 42 U.S.C.S. § 223.
67 Reno v. American Civil Liberties Union, 521 U.S. 844, 849 (1997).
68 *Reno*, 521 U.S. at 844. See chapter 16.

Act's terms, like "indecent" and "patently offensive," covered "large amounts of nonpornographic material with serious educational or other value."[69]

In evaluating this regulation, Justice Stevens, writing for the majority, set the standard for future consideration of restrictions of digital online speech:

> The dramatic expansion of this new marketplace of ideas contradicts the factual basis of this contention. The record demonstrates that the growth of the Internet has been and continues to be phenomenal. As a matter of constitutional tradition, in the absence of evidence to the contrary, we presume that governmental regulation of the content of speech is more likely to interfere with the free exchange of ideas than to encourage it. The interest in encouraging freedom of expression in a democratic society outweighs any theoretical but unproven benefit of censorship.[70]

In sum, the Court viewed the internet as analogous to the classic town square "marketplace of ideas," where viewpoints and information are freely shared and content-based regulation is very rarely permissible. We return to this theme in Chapter 16.

Similar concerns arose in *United States* v. *American Library Association*.[71] There, complainants challenged the validity of the Children's Internet Protection Act,[72] which made federal funding for public libraries' internet access contingent on the installation of "software to block images that constitute obscenity or child pornography, and to prevent minors from obtaining access to material that is harmful to them."[73] The Court upheld the policy as consistent both with the longstanding tradition of libraries to curate their content to facilitate "learning and cultural enrichment," as well as the government's power to make "content-based judgments in deciding what private speech to make available to the public."[74] Ultimately, the Court held that there was no difference between the internet and the printed materials offered at the library, which had never included pornography. Blocking internet pornography on library computers was therefore constitutional.[75]

The holding in *Reno* notwithstanding, it remains clear that the government has an interest in protecting "the welfare of children" and in ensuring that they are "safeguarded from abuses" that might prevent their "growth into free and independent well-developed men and citizens."[76] It is therefore constitutionally permissible for a state to prohibit selling to children materials that would not be deemed obscene

69 *Id.* at 877.
70 *Id.* at 885.
71 United States v. American Library Association, 539 U.S. 194, 199 (2003).
72 20 U.S.C.S. § 9101 (1996).
73 *American Library Association*, 539 U.S. at 199.
74 *Id.* at 203–04.
75 *Id.*
76 Ginsberg v. New York, 390 U.S. 629, 641 (1968).

when sold to adults. These distinctions simply allow consideration of the "social realities" that certain materials are fit for adults but not children.[77]

In the pre-internet age, sexually explicit material was often displayed and distributed through "adult" movie theaters and bookstores. This prompted the adoption of local zoning laws that limited the locations of these facilities. The Court addressed such a regulation in *Renton* v. *Playtime Theatres*,[78] holding that a zoning ordinance that prohibited "adult motion picture theaters from locating within 1,000 feet of any residential zone, single- or multiple-family dwelling, church, park, or school" did not violate the First Amendment.[79] In sum, the Court found that the ordinance constituted a reasonable and content-neutral time, place, and manner restriction on the location of such businesses and was therefore valid.

If the Court's analysis were correct, then this would amount to a straightforward application of the public forum doctrine. The Court's thinking in *Renton* has been questioned, though, and for good reasons. Indeed, the Court's conclusion that the ordinance was content-neutral seems puzzling because, by its terms, the regulation pertained only to motion picture theaters that showed *adult* films.

In order to get around this problem, the Court reasoned that the ordinance was not directed toward the content of the speech shown in such theaters but rather toward the "secondary effects" that such businesses may have in the surrounding community, lowering the overall quality of life. This rationale seems like a dodge, because the alleged secondary effects necessarily result from the content of the speech exhibited. No one would make a similar claim if the zoning ordinance applied only to movie theaters showing musicals.

Doctrinal infirmities aside, one can easily question the continued relevancy of a case like *Renton*. The quantity and range of sexually explicit materials now available on the internet eclipse that which is available in any adult bookstore or movie theater. And the risks posed by obscenity on the internet are overwhelmingly greater given its much easier accessibility. Still, many communities continue to have such zoning laws on their books and to enforce them as they deem necessary.

For the reasons discussed, the Court's categorical statement in *Chaplinsky* that "the lewd and the obscene" fall outside of the protections of the First Amendment turns out to be a gross overstatement. Under *Miller*, a great deal of material that the average person might find "lewd" falls within the scope of the right to free expression and "obscenity" is narrowly defined. As with the so-called defamation exception, the obscenity "exception" carves out much less than we might expect. This approach is consistent with the Court's view that, in order to give speech the breathing space it requires, we must protect some expression that on its face seems of little value to the furtherance of a good society.

77 *Id.* at 638.
78 Renton v. Playtime Theatres, 475 U.S. 41 (1986).
79 *Renton*, 475 U.S. at 43.

Critics from both sides have questioned the wisdom and efficacy of current obscenity doctrine. On one hand, some argue that this doctrine is overprotective of speech, rendering lawful numerous forms of pornography that perpetuate and promote the objectification, oppression, and sexual victimization of women.[80] On the other hand, others argue that in an internet-dominated world the idea of restraining speech based on localized "community standards" is outdated, dangerous, and unpredictable in application. In any event, given the Court's struggles in this area of doctrine, it seems unlikely that it will be inclined to revisit the currently controlling standard anytime soon.

SPEECH CRIMES

Although *Chaplinsky* did not include this category in its famous list, an exception to First Amendment protection also has existed historically for crimes that are effectuated through speech. Many familiar crimes fall into this category, such as blackmail, extortion, bribes, conspiracy, and insider trading. The fact that the perpetrator uses words in the commission of the crime obviously does not insulate them from prosecution; common sense tells us that an armed robber who says "give me all your money" cannot invoke a First Amendment defense. "It rarely has been suggested," the Court observed in *United States v. Williams*,[81] "that the constitutional freedom for speech and press extends its immunity to speech or writing used as an 'integral part' of conduct in violation of a valid criminal statute."

Intriguingly, this principle applies even when there is no proof a crime would or could have been committed, as *Williams* itself demonstrates. That case involved a prosecution for "pandering" child pornography in violation of federal law. The statute defined "pandering" so broadly that it applied even where the materials in question were *not* child pornography, although the defendant intended prospective purchasers to believe that they were. The defendant in *Williams* argued that, because the statute punished speech that was not actually connected with the distribution of actual child pornography, it was unconstitutionally overbroad.

The Supreme Court rejected this argument. Writing for the Court, Justice Scalia observed that laws punishing the "braggart, exaggerator, or outright liar" for advertising the sale of illegal materials are plainly constitutional; indeed, those fraudulent statements are actually "doubly excluded from the First Amendment."[82] First, even if a person was mistaken about the illegality of the underlying transaction, their effort to sell something illicit is akin to other inchoate crimes that are frequently punished,

[80] *See, e.g.*, CATHERINE MACKINNON, ONLY WORDS (1993).
[81] United States v. Williams, 553 U.S. 285 (2008).
[82] *Id.* at 299.

such as attempt or conspiracy.[83] And, second, the Court previously had held that the government can punish "fraudulent offers" of sale of illegal goods.[84]

Within the category of speech crimes, threats may pose the most serious challenges. As with obscenity, the primary problem here is definitional. Many of us might feel threatened in some sense by language that nevertheless deserves constitutional protection – for example, phrases like "you'll be sorry" or "I think you'll regret doing that" or "I have a long memory." The question is how to distinguish that sort of vaguely threatening language from what the courts have called a "true threat": a threat so serious that the government should have the authority to punish it.

The Supreme Court has yet to set forth a fully developed "true threat" doctrine. It has described true threats as "those statements where the speaker means to communicate a serious expression of an intent to commit an act of unlawful violence to a particular individual or group of individuals."[85] And it has held that some speech plainly does not qualify, like the hyperbolic statement of a teenage antiwar protestor who declared: "If they ever make me carry a rifle, the first one I want to get in my sights is [President Johnson.]"[86] But most of the efforts at defining a true threat have come from lower courts, which have not arrived at a single consistent definition.

In addition to not protecting speech that effectuates a crime or that attempts to do so, the First Amendment does not protect speech that incites *others* to act unlawfully. As discussed in Chapter 7, over time the Court limited the types of speech that qualify as punishable incitement, distinguishing "[t]he mere abstract teaching . . . of the moral propriety or even moral necessity for a resort to force and violence," which the First Amendment does protect, from speech that is "directed to inciting or producing imminent lawless action and is likely to incite or produce such action, which the First Amendment does not."[87] Anti-incitement laws thus remain on the books, but the definition of incitement is narrow and prosecutions for it are rare.

As with defamation and obscenity, the Court has generally viewed speech crimes narrowly. Furthermore, the Court has shown little enthusiasm for expanding the universe of constitutionally prohibitable speech-based crimes, even in sympathetic cases. For example, it has on various grounds struck down laws that punish speech that features sexually fetishistic animal abuse[88] and laws that punish lying about one's military service[89] – even though a reasonable person might struggle to explain how either of these forms of expression contributes to the marketplace of ideas.

[83] *Id.* at 300.

[84] *Id.* (citing Illinois ex rel. Madigan v. Telemarketing Associates, Inc., 538 U.S. 600, 611–612 (2003)).

[85] Virginia v. Black, 538 U.S. 343 (2003).

[86] Watts v. United States, 394 U.S. 705 (1969).

[87] Brandenburg v. Ohio, 395 U.S. 444, 449 (1969).

[88] United States v. Stevens, 559 U.S 460 (2010).

[89] United States v. Alvarez, 567 U.S. 709 (2012).

FIGHTING WORDS

The final exception to First Amendment protections identified in *Chaplinsky* was fighting words: "those which by their very utterance inflict injury or tend to incite an immediate breach of the peace."[90] Indeed, *Chaplinsky* was a case *about* such provocative speech. There, a city marshal instructed Walter Chaplinsky to cease distributing religious pamphlets. Chaplinsky responded by verbally attacking the marshal, resulting in Chaplinsky's arrest. The Supreme Court upheld Chaplinsky's conviction on the basis that his verbal assault constituted unprotected fighting words.

Although *Chaplinsky* suggests that the fighting words exception might broadly apply to personal insults and offenses, over the years the Supreme Court repeatedly has narrowed it. In *Terminiello* v. *Chicago*[91] and *Feiner* v. *New York*,[92] the Court held that fighting words could be punished only if they satisfied the then-controlling "clear and present danger" test. In *Street* v. *New York*,[93] the Court described fighting words as a "narrow class" of speech that did not include the merely "disrespectful." And, in *Cohen* v. *California*,[94] the Court limited fighting words to those that satisfied the *Brandenberg* "likely to incite or produce imminent lawless action" standard. Along the way, the Court repeatedly has held that mere offensiveness, by itself, is not a basis on which to proscribe or punish speech.

In the fighting words doctrine, we therefore see the same pattern we have seen with respect to the other so-called exceptions. The Court in *Chaplinsky* suggested that the First Amendment offers no protection whatsoever to these forms of speech. But the subsequent case law makes clear that these exceptions are narrow and do not necessarily align with our expectations about what the First Amendment does or should embrace. And that case law makes equally clear that the Court has had little or no interest expanding the number of exceptions.

The very limited scope of the exceptions to First Amendment protections has significant meaning for contemporary conversations about free expression. For example, as we explore in Chapter 12, proponents of hate speech regulation often point to doctrines like incitement or fighting words in support of their argument that such speech can be constitutionally restrained. It turns out, however, that these doctrines usually offer much less opportunity for restricting speech than their simple labels might suggest.

Furthermore, the narrowness of the exceptions enables relativists to argue that First Amendment protection extends too far. They can point to numerous examples of speech that seems defamatory, obscene, threatening, degrading, or repulsive; that

90 *Chaplinsky*. at 572.
91 Terminiello v. Chicago, 337 U.S. 1 (1949).
92 Feiner v. New York, 340 U.S. 315 (1951).
93 Street v. New York, 394 U.S. 576 (1969).
94 Cohen v. California, 403 U.S. 15 (1971).

adds little or no value to public discourse; that common sense suggests the government should be able to restrain; but that the Supreme Court has held the First Amendment protects. In Chapter 5, we alluded to some of the cautionary tales that absolutists have to tell. These make for some of the most powerful cautionary tales the relativists have to offer.

PART IV

Current Controversies

12

Hate Speech

Throughout the history of First Amendment jurisprudence, the Supreme Court has struggled with the question of how to treat speech that offends and insults an individual or group of people. Proponents of restrictions on such speech generally have relied upon three arguments. First, the speech often has little value and contributes nothing to the marketplace of ideas. Second, such speech amounts to a verbal assault that injures its target, even if not physically. And, finally, such speech may prompt the *targeted group or individual* to respond with violence of their own.

In recent years, this issue has attracted increased attention as legislators, policy makers, and college and university administrators have searched for tools to address concerns about "hate speech." Under existing First Amendment doctrine, no precise legal definition of hate speech exists. The Supreme Court has not carved out an exception for hate speech or recognized it as a disfavored category. To the contrary, the Court consistently and resolutely has declared that speech does not fall outside of First Amendment protections simply because it offends someone, even severely.

Nevertheless, hate speech is a real phenomenon with serious consequences for individuals and society. Furthermore, although the Supreme Court has not defined hate speech, a shared understanding of what the phrase means exists, at least in general terms. It is commonly understood that "hate speech" refers to words that expresses animosity or that encourages violence against a person or group based on characteristics like race, gender, ethnicity, LGBTQ status, national origin, disability, or religion.

Despite these points of agreement, the subject of hate speech has fostered a tremendous amount of controversy. People have voiced good faith disagreements over what qualifies as hate speech and how to measure its effects. Debate has raged over whether our laws can limit this speech without encountering insurmountable problems of vagueness, overbreadth, and uneven enforcement.[1] And opinions differ as to whether we *should* prohibit hate speech, assuming that the law gives us room to do so.[2]

The Court's hate speech jurisprudence began in 1949 with its decision in *Terminiello* v. *City of Chicago*.[3] In that case, a priest who gave a fiery anti-Semitic speech was convicted under a breach of peace law that criminalized expression that "stirs the public to anger, invites dispute, brings about a condition of unrest, or creates a disturbance."[4] Writing on behalf of the Court, Justice Douglas explained why the law was unconstitutionally overbroad:[5]

> [A] function of free speech under our system of government is to invite dispute. It may indeed best serve its high purpose when it induces a condition of unrest, creates dissatisfaction with conditions as they are, or even stirs people to anger. Speech is often provocative and challenging. It may strike at prejudices and preconceptions and have profound unsettling effects as it presses for acceptance of an idea. That is why freedom of speech, though not absolute, is nevertheless protected against censorship or punishment, unless shown likely to produce a clear and present danger of a serious substantive evil that rises far above public inconvenience, annoyance, or unrest. There is no room under our Constitution for a more restrictive view. For the alternative would lead to standardization of ideas either by legislatures, courts, or dominant political or community groups.[6]

The Court in *Terminiello* did not foreclose the theoretical possibility that the state could proscribe some of the expression we think of as hate speech. But it clearly signaled that the government cannot punish speech on the sole basis that it offends someone. And it made plain that overly broad regulations will not pass constitutional muster.

Several years later, the Court seemed to take a more sympathetic view in *Beauharnais* v. *Illinois*.[7] In that case, the Supreme Court upheld the constitutionality of a statute similar to the sort of hate speech laws for which some people advocate today. In sum, the statute made it unlawful for anyone to engage in speech that exposed any "class of citizens" to "contempt, derision, or obloquy" because of their race, color, creed, or religion. The Court viewed the statute as an extension of defamation law – protecting against the libel of a group – and so concluded it passed constitutional muster.

1 *See* Leonard Niehoff, *Policing Hate Speech and Extremism: A Taxonomy of Arguments in Opposition*, 52 U. Mich. J. L. Ref. 859 (2019).
2 *Id.*
3 Terminiello v. City of Chicago, 337 U.S. 1 (1949).
4 *Id.* at 4.
5 *Id.*
6 *Id.* at 4–5.
7 Beauharnais v. Illinois, 343 U.S. 250 (1952).

That result probably made sense under then-existing legal doctrine, which, as we discussed in Chapter 11, viewed defamation as lying entirely outside of the protection of the First Amendment. But it seems extraordinarily unlikely that the Supreme Court would reach the same result today. After all, the Court has constitutionalized the law of libel; and the Court almost certainly would find the statute at issue in *Beauharnais* unconstitutionally vague and overbroad. *Beauharnais* may have suggested a viable path toward a constitutional hate speech law, but the prospect proved to be short-lived.

In the 1960s and 1970s, it became increasingly apparent that mere offensiveness did not place speech outside the protections of the First Amendment. In 1977, a case arose that tested the limits of that principle: *National Socialist Party* v. *Skokie*.[8] In that case, the National Socialist Party of America, a neo-Nazi organization, planned to march in Skokie, Illinois, the home to a large population of Holocaust survivors. The trial court issued an injunction against the march and the Illinois appellate courts refused to stay the effect of that injunction.

It is perhaps difficult to imagine speech more hateful in its intention or effect. Nevertheless, the Supreme Court reversed the lower court's denial of the stay. In a brief order, the Supreme Court held that by refusing to stay the injunction the Illinois courts had not provided sufficient procedural safeguards to protect rights guaranteed by the First Amendment. Although issued on procedural grounds, the order sent a clear message: the state cannot summarily silence speech, even where it promotes a vile and meritless ideology that has a horrific history and that deeply and intentionally offends people.

As concerns over hate speech escalated, communities began to experiment with laws that attempted to define and directly proscribe such expression. In its 1992 decision in *R.A.V.* v. *St. Paul*,[9] the Court addressed the St. Paul, Minnesota ordinance that we discussed in Chapter 10. As you will recall, the ordinance provided:

> Whoever places on public or private property a symbol, object, appellation, characterization or graffiti, including, but not limited to, a burning cross or Nazi swastika, which one knows or has reasonable grounds to know arouses anger, alarm or resentment in others on the basis of race, color, creed, religion or gender commits disorderly conduct and shall be guilty of a misdemeanor.[10]

Given the Court's decision in *Beauharnais*, political leaders in St. Paul may have believed that existing First Amendment doctrine gave them the latitude to adopt such a law.

As noted in Chapter 10, although the law at issue in *R.A.V.* may have been well intended, it suffered from serious problems of vagueness and overbreadth. The Court did not, however, decide the case on this basis. The Minnesota courts had

[8] National Socialist Party v. Skokie, 432 U.S. 43 (1977).
[9] R.A.V. v. St. Paul, 505 U.S. 377 (1992).
[10] *Id.* at 380.

saved it from these difficulties by rather torturously interpreting the language of the ordinance as applying only to speech exempted from First Amendment protection as "fighting words." So, instead, the Supreme Court focused on the fact that the ordinance favored some speech over other speech based on its content and found the law unconstitutional on this basis.[11]

The Court's reasoning may seem puzzling. After all, didn't we learn in Chapter 11 that the First Amendment doesn't protect fighting words? And isn't a prohibition against fighting words necessarily based on the content of the speech? Why, then, did the St. Paul ordinance fail to pass constitutional muster?

An example helps explain the Court's thinking. Imagine that, in a face-to-face encounter, one person makes an anti-Semitic remark to another person so antagonizing that it is likely to provoke imminent lawless action. The St. Paul ordinance allows for the punishment of *those* fighting words. But, now, imagine that, in a different face-to-face encounter, one person makes a derogatory remark about *anti-Semites* so insulting that it is similarly likely to provoke imminent lawless action. The St. Paul ordinance does *not* allow for the punishment of *those* fighting words.

The problem with the St. Paul ordinance was therefore that it punished only those fighting words that the political leaders in St. Paul disfavored based on their *content*. And, as we have discussed, this sort of content-based discrimination rarely survives constitutional scrutiny. It failed to do so here.

Eleven years after *R.A.V.*, the Supreme Court decided *Virginia* v. *Black*.[12] The Court there upheld a law that, at first glance, may seem indistinguishable from the St. Paul ordinance. *Black* involved a law that criminalized all cross-burnings done with "intent of intimidating any person or group of persons." The Court deemed the law constitutional, given the history of cross-burning in America and its strong likelihood to incite violence or be perceived as a real threat.[13]

Despite their apparent inconsistency, we can reconcile the outcomes in *R.A.V.* and *Black*. The law at issue in *Black*, unlike the one in *R.A.V.*, punished *all* threats made through cross-burning, regardless of their ideological content. In this sense, the law in *Black* did not discriminate between the *content* of the threats or the *viewpoints* they reflected. That law proscribed a threatening cross-burning on the lawn of a racist, just as it proscribed a threatening cross-burning on the lawn of a racial minority.

The Court in *Black* made clear that Congress did not have to prohibit *every* threat in order to pass a valid law. Lawmakers can choose to punish some threats and not others. But, in doing so, they cannot discriminate so as to disfavor some threats *based on their content or viewpoint*: "[T]he First Amendment does not prevent Congress from passing a law that prohibits true threats against the life of the President of the

[11] *Id.* at 382.
[12] Virginia v. Black, 538 U.S. 343 (2003).
[13] *Id.* at 348.

United States, but the First Amendment *does* preclude it from passing a law that prohibits true threats against the President because of his or her policies toward inner cities."[14] This principle leaves the proponents of hate speech laws with a blunt instrument: the government can pass laws banning threats generally or singling out certain threatening behaviors, like cross-burning; but it cannot pass laws that ban only those threats that reflect specific hateful viewpoints.

Existing legal doctrine also renders it difficult, if not impossible, to police hate speech through the use of tort law claims, like intentional infliction of emotional distress. As discussed in Chapter 1, in *Snyder* v. *Phelps*[15] the Court rejected such a claim based on speech that by any standard qualified as extreme and outrageous. And it was speech that the Court acknowledged had emotionally injured a parent grieving the loss of a beloved child.

Nevertheless, the Court defended the right of the protestors there to voice their ideas. Chief Justice Roberts explained:

> Speech is powerful. It can stir people to action, move them to tears of both joy and sorrow and – as it did here – inflict great pain. On the facts before us, we cannot react to that pain by punishing the speaker. As a Nation we have chosen a different course – to protect even hurtful speech on public issues to ensure that we do not stifle public debate.[16]

Although it may not align with our intuitions about which speech the First Amendment should protect, the Court's ruling in *Snyder* rested on the core values and basic principles we discussed previously: the First Amendment creates a strong presumption that all ideas are allowed entry into the marketplace and a chance to compete; an idea should not be punishable simply because it is offensive; and a standard like "outrageousness," which applies in tort claims of intentional infliction of emotional distress, is too vague and overbroad to satisfy First Amendment requirements for precision and narrowness.

The challenges posed by existing doctrine have prompted some proponents of hate speech laws to urge the Supreme Court to create a new exception. As noted in Chapter 11, however, the Court's decisions reflect a clear pattern of narrowly construing even those exceptions that it has historically recognized. And the Court has balked at invitations to create new ones, even in compelling cases.

It may be worthwhile to say more about the cases where the Court has rejected proposed new exceptions, because they demonstrate the Court's keen reluctance to exclude speech from First Amendment protection. Consider, for example, *United States* v. *Alvarez*.[17] There, the Court refused to create a new exception for speech involving false claims of military service awards. Surely, most people would strongly

14 *Id.*
15 Snyder v. Phelps, 562 U.S. 443 (2011).
16 *Id.* at 460–461.
17 United States v. Alvarez, 567 U.S. 709 (2012).

condemn such acts of "stolen valor," reasoning that they perpetrate a kind of fraud and degrade the significance of the military decorations of those who actually earned them. Nevertheless, the Court held a federal law criminalizing such false claims to be unconstitutional. Justice Kennedy, writing for the Court, observed, "[t]he Nation well knows that one of the costs of the First Amendment is that it protects the speech we detest as well as the speech we embrace."[18]

Or consider *United States* v. *Stevens*.[19] *Stevens* involved a federal statute that criminalized so-called crush videos, in which an animal is tortured as a form of sexual fetish. Such videos do not qualify as "obscene" under the *Miller* test discussed in the last chapter because, among other things, they do not depict any actual sexual activity. But, surely, everyone except enthusiasts for such speech would condemn it as cruel, worthless, and disgusting.

Nevertheless, the Court held the statute unconstitutional. The Court began by reiterating its reluctance to create new exceptions to the First Amendment.[20] The Court went on to reject, as dangerous and inconsistent with existing doctrine, the idea that it should evaluate the statute by weighing its value against its harm. The "First Amendment's guarantee of free speech," the Court declared, "does not extend only to categories of speech that survive an ad hoc balancing of relative social costs and benefits."[21] The Court held that First Amendment protection for speech is not contingent on whether it "is deemed valueless or unnecessary, or so long as an ad hoc calculus of costs and benefits tilts in a statute's favor."[22]

Or consider *Brown* v. *Entertainment Merchants Association*.[23] In that case, the Court struck down a California statute restricting the sale of violent videogames to minors.[24] As in *Stevens*, the Court applied the strict scrutiny test and found the law unconstitutionally overbroad.[25] Again, the Court rejected the idea that it should apply a balancing test and deem this speech unworthy of protection. The Court acknowledged that the games included grotesque and horrific images but declared that "disgust is not a valid basis for restricting expression."[26]

You will note how distant this reasoning is from that which we encountered in *Chaplinsky*.[27] In that early case, the Supreme Court suggested that exceptions might arise whenever speech failed this sort of balancing: "It has been well observed that such utterances are no essential part of any exposition of ideas, and are of such slight

[18] *Id.* at 729–730.
[19] United States v. Stevens, 559 U.S. 460 (2010).
[20] *Stevens*, 559 U.S. at 473.
[21] *Id.* at 470.
[22] *Id.* at 471.
[23] Brown v. Entm't Merchs. Ass'n, 564 U.S. 786 (2011).
[24] *Brown*, 564 U.S. at 805.
[25] *Id.*
[26] *Id.* at 798.
[27] Chaplinsky v. New Hampshire, 315 U.S. 568, 571–572 (1942).

social value as a step to truth that any benefit that may be derived from them is clearly outweighed by the social interest in order and morality."[28]

In time, however, the Court recognized that an ad hoc balancing test does not adequately protect speech. To the contrary, it leaves room for the punishment of *any* form of unpopular expression – precisely what the First Amendment exists to prevent. Balancing is the model favored by relativists, who see free speech as an important value but not necessarily more important than others. As the Court moved toward an increasingly absolutist model, in which free expression has primacy, it necessarily moved away from the concept of balancing.

A number of scholars have argued that the Court largely has gotten things right here and should not carve out a new exception for hate speech. After all, any hate speech regulation will necessarily entail content-based and viewpoint-based judgments,[29] which First Amendment doctrine generally views as constitutional anathema. And those judgments will, in turn, unavoidably involve moral determinations, ideological choices, and subjective assessments.

What separates the United States in part from other democracies is the primacy of allowing for the expression of diverse – and often divisive – opinions.[30] Creating a categorical exception for hate speech, the argument goes, would undermine this uniquely American tradition. And any such project would face daunting definitional hurdles:

> [A] court would have to first decide to create a pseudo category of *speech*, hateful symbols, that is less deserving of protection. This determination would be based on a weighing of costs and benefits that is subjective and arbitrary, may reflect impermissible government motive, and removes a lot of *speech* from the safeguards of strong First Amendment protection.[31]

In addition, a hate speech exception would "prescribe what shall be orthodox" and would place boundaries around the exercise of the human conscience, which the Court repeatedly has held to be sacrosanct.[32]

To be clear, those who take a more absolutist approach to this issue do *not* maintain that the government is powerless to take *any* steps to proscribe speech that targets individuals because of their race, gender, ethnicity, religion, or other characteristic. Even our fairly absolutist Court has recognized that the state can punish such speech insofar as it meets the standard for fighting words or incitement. And, as

[28] *See also* United States v. Alvarez, 132 S. Ct. 2537, 2548 (2012) (the Court refuses to employ ad hoc balancing tests, and instead uses the "most exacting scrutiny").
[29] Erica Goldberg, *Free Speech Consequentialism*, 116 Col. L. Rev. 687, 740–741 (2016).
[30] *Id.*
[31] *Id.* at 742.
[32] *See* Leonard Niehoff, *Policing Hate Speech and Extremism: A Taxonomy of Arguments in Opposition*, 52 U. Mich. J. L. Ref. 859 (2019).

Black demonstrates, laws of general application (like those prohibiting threats) can be used to penalize such speech.

Furthermore, an obvious overlap exists between the forms of expression we call "hate speech" and those we call "discrimination." A barrage of racist epithets, for example, could fall into either category, depending on context. The First Amendment does not preclude the government from adopting anti-discrimination measures that help ensure equal treatment in areas like employment, access to public facilities and housing, and education. The fact that the discriminatory treatment occurs through words, rather than through conduct, does not prevent the government from adopting a remedy. A pervasive environment of sexist language can deprive someone of the opportunity to work or learn unhindered just as much as a pervasive environment of sexist conduct.

Proponents of a hate speech exception to the First Amendment point out that such anti-discrimination laws are limited in their utility. They apply only in certain contexts and with respect to particular relationships. They often come into play only where the offending conduct is "so severe, pervasive and objectively offensive" as to adversely interfere with the person's positive experiences and opportunities.[33] And, for the most part, to qualify as discrimination the speech or conduct may not be directed toward a general audience; instead, it must target a specific individual or group (for example, Black employees).[34]

The various doctrines described so far in this chapter give the proponents of a hate speech exception some – but certainly not all – of what they want. Critics of existing doctrine charge that this gap leaves a significant amount of valueless and injurious speech unaddressed. They cite the march of neo-fascists in Skokie as a prime example of the failures of doctrine, pointedly asking: "Must we defend Nazis?"[35]

The proponents of a hate speech exception also point to European countries, which have adopted a variety of aggressive anti-hate measures. Those countries do so because they take a more relativist view of free speech, seeing it as one value among many and as needing to be weighed against considerations like equality and human dignity. Absolutists respond by pointing out that the results under those European laws, some of which are distressingly absurd, prove their point.

In her 2018 book *Hate Speech: Why We Should Resist It with Free Speech, Not Censorship*, First Amendment scholar and former American Civil Liberties Union President Nadine Strossen provides a number of examples. For instance, in 2013, musician, poet, and Nobel Prize winner Bob Dylan was charged with "incitement to racial hatred" under French law because of a brief statement he made during an interview with *Rolling Stone* magazine in which he compared Croatians with the

[33] See Erwin Chemerinsky and Howard Gillman, Free Speech on Campus, 118–123 (2017).

[34] *Id.* at 120–121.

[35] Indeed, this is the title of a 2018 book by Critical Legal Studies scholars Richard Delgado and Jean Stefancic, as discussed in Chapter 2.

Ku Klux Klan and with Nazis.[36] In 2014, political leader Paul Weston was arrested and charged with committing a "racially aggravated crime" under British law when, during one of his speeches, he quoted a statement by Winston Churchill that was critical of Islam.[37] Professor Strossen notes the numerous obstacles that exist to writing an anti-hate-speech law that is sufficiently clear, specific, and narrow to pass constitutional muster, using the results under European laws to support her point.

Calls for greater regulation of hate speech have been particularly pronounced on college campuses, where those demands have been met with an equally forceful insistence on the preservation of universities as bastions of free expression. Numerous controversies have ensued: one public university expelled fraternity members for singing racist slurs while riding on a bus; another expelled students for using such epithets while walking through an open area on campus; a private university cut funding for a student newspaper that published an op-ed criticizing the tactics of the Black Lives Matter movement; a college's Bias Response Group declared it a "racialist targeted attack" when the pro-Trump slogan "Make America Great Again" was posted in a classroom, offending some students of color; a law professor was threatened with dismissal for using the "N" word in a class where racial examples were relevant to the material being taught; a university found faculty members to be in violation of its anti-harassment policies for wearing "Blackface" as part of a Halloween costume; students disrupted controversial speakers on campus and pressed for the cancellation of speaker invitations; and so on. We return to the unique challenges posed by the higher education environment in Chapter 14, where we talk about campus speech, and Chapter 15, where we address academic freedom.

These campus controversies are a microcosm of our broader struggle as a society. On one hand, our polity seeks to promote environments where all people feel welcomed, included, respected, and secure. This goal supports an argument for prohibiting hate speech. On the other hand, proscribing an ill-defined category of speech because it is offensive and runs against popular sensibilities is fraught with peril. It directly conflicts with the core values that we considered at the beginning of this book and the basic principles that emerge from First Amendment doctrine as it has developed.

In his opinion in *Barnette*, Justice Jackson reminded us that the whole point of the Bill of Rights was to deprive political majorities of such choices, even when well intentioned:

> Struggles to coerce uniformity of sentiment in support of some end thought essential to their time and country have been waged by many good as well as by evil men . . . Nationalism is a relatively recent phenomenon but at other times and places the ends have been racial or territorial security, support of a dynasty or

[36] Nadine Strossen, Hate: Why We Should Resist It with Free Speech, Not Censorship 95 (2018).

[37] *Id.* at 96.

> regime, and particular plans for saving souls. As first and moderate methods to attain unity have failed, those bent on its accomplishment must resort to an ever-increasing severity. As governmental pressure toward unity becomes greater, so strife becomes more bitter as to whose unity it shall be … Compulsory unification of opinion achieves only the unanimity of the graveyard.
>
> It seems trite but necessary to say that the First Amendment to our Constitution was designed to avoid these ends by avoiding these beginnings …
>
> We can have intellectual individualism and the rich cultural diversities that we owe to exceptional minds only at the price of occasional eccentricity and abnormal attitudes. When they are so harmless to others or to the State as those we deal with here, the price is not too great. But freedom to differ is not limited to things that do not matter much. That would be a mere shadow of freedom. The test of its substance is the right to differ as to things that touch the heart of the existing order.[38]

As Justice Jackson recognized, these principles come at a cost: we will have to endure speech that we find upsetting and unsettling, even when it threatens the very heart of the existing order. Importantly, we must never forget that this burden will fall more heavily on some of us than on others.

Some scholars and commentators have suggest that the way out of this dilemma is to modify First Amendment doctrine in order to protect only "true beliefs" – that is, those beliefs that can be justified on the basis of truthful and defensible knowledge and information.[39] Any such proposal, however, necessarily entails the idea of an arbiter who determines which things qualify as "truthful and defensible" and who directs citizens in their choices and decision making within the marketplace of ideas. And this leads us right back to the evils that Justice Jackson described: some official prescribing what shall be orthodox in thought and opinion, censoring out the rest, and pushing us toward "the unanimity of the graveyard." Isaiah Berlin observed "that there [is] a deep human yearning to find 'One Great Truth.'" But, he warned, "that's a dead end: Our fate is to struggle with a 'plurality' of values, with competing truths, with trying to reconcile what may be irreconcilable."[40]

Nevertheless, it is true that hate speech exists. It is true that such speech is far too pervasive in our society. It is true that such speech does real harm. It is true that such speech undermines equality: another constitutional value and one that is essential to the fulfillment of liberty's promise.

The impulse to address the harm caused by hate speech is therefore understandable and honorable, even if the obstacles to doing so are formidable if not insurmountable. Accordingly, in our conversations about free expression, we must never dismiss that impulse as mere "political correctness" or "cancel culture" or the like.

38 West Virginia Bd. of Education v. Barnette, 319 U.S. 624 (1943).

39 Joseph Blocker, *Free Speech and Justified True Belief*, 133 Harv. L. Rev. 439 (2019).

40 As quoted by Nicholas Kristof, *Mizzou, Yale, and Free Speech*, New York Times A29 (Nov. 12, 2015).

To do so is to deny these obvious truths. And, just as importantly, it is to deny the power of speech itself – the very power that makes it worth protecting.

It would be a sad paradox if our society concluded that our cherished principle of free expression prohibited us from freely expressing our concerns about the harm that hate speech does and exploring what tools we have to address it – even though those tools may be limited, given our core values and basic principles. After all, forced unanimity is not the only way by which humankind has made graveyards. Prejudice and oppression have had no small role in multiplying them as well.

13

Campaign Finance Regulation

Some of the greatest challenges in interpreting the free speech clause of the First Amendment have come in the field of campaign finance regulation. It is arguably the doctrinal area where we see the Court's most extreme swings, overruling established precedent and ignoring empirical realities because of ideological shifts among its members. Furthermore, as we will see, the Court's missteps began early: by initially framing the campaign finance debate as one focused on problems of "corruption," the Court foreclosed a more nuanced understanding of the influence of money in politics.

Things did not improve with the passage of time. In recent years, the Supreme Court has abandoned decades of judicial efforts to adopt a flexible understanding of "corruption" that would accommodate political realities. In one of its historically most controversial opinions, *Citizens United* v. *FEC*,[1] the Court uprooted a line of precedent by holding that expenditure limitations on corporations unconstitutionally burdened their First Amendment rights. *Citizens United* sparked so much popular outrage that a number of presidential candidates have included in their platforms a vow to work to overturn the decision.

Much of the popular debate over campaign finance and *Citizens United* has been misinformed and therefore unhelpful to moving discussions on the issue forward. For example, as this chapter discusses, the ideas that we use money to express ourselves and that entities like corporations have First Amendment rights are sensible, unremarkable, and predate *Citizens United*. Nevertheless, people who oppose the outcome in *Citizens United* often target these ideas with slogans like "Corporations are not people!" and "If money is speech, speech is not free!" There

[1] Citizens United v. FEC, 558 U.S. 310 (2010). In retirement, Justice Stevens remarked that Justice Kennedy's opinion for the Court in *Citizens United* "was a disaster for our election law." Justice Stevens wrote a dissent in the case. *See* John Paul Stevens, *The Making of a Justice: Reflections on my First* 94 YEARS 501 (2019).

are good reasons to doubt the wisdom and validity of *Citizens United*, but they have nothing to do with these sorts of overly simplistic arguments.

We begin at the beginning. The legislative effort to control the influence of money in political campaigns goes back at least to the 1907 Tilman Act, in which Congress first sought to regulate direct corporate gifts. These early rules arose during the presidency of Theodore Roosevelt but resurfaced again in 1940 to prohibit direct financing by unions. It was not until the 1970s, when Congress and states began campaign reform efforts in the wake of the Nixon-era Watergate scandal, that the judiciary intervened in a significant manner. Those reforms focused on campaign fundraising abuses, among other areas.[2]

The most critical early campaign finance decision came in the 1976 case *Buckley v. Valeo*.[3] Before dissecting the "intricate statutory scheme" of the Federal Election Campaign Act of 1971,[4] the Court began by expounding more generally on the critical nature of election-related speech. The Court observed that "[i]n a republic where the people are sovereign, the ability of the citizenry to make informed choices among candidates for office is essential, for the identities of those who are elected will inevitably shape the course that we follow as a nation."[5]

Against this backdrop, the Court went on to determine that the use of money in this context constitutes a form of "speech."[6] It rejected the lower court's reasoning that spending money on a campaign should be deemed less protected "expressive conduct," finding instead that such expenditures were entitled to full First Amendment protection.[7] Though a broad equation of money and speech has invited significant criticism,[8] the connection between being able to speak and being able to pay for it seems obvious. As the Court noted, "virtually every means of communicating ideas in today's mass society requires the expenditure of money."[9]

2 *See* JOAN BISKUPIC, THE CHIEF: THE LIFE AND TURBULENT TIMES OF CHIEF JUSTICE JOHN ROBERTS 204 (2019).

3 Buckley v. Valeo, 424 U.S. 1 (1976).

4 *Id.* 12–13 (citing 18 USC § 608 (a–e)).

5 *Id.* at 14–15.

6 *Id.* at 18.

7 The *Buckley* Court also distinguished campaign finance restrictions from the reasonable time, place, or manner restrictions that the Court regularly upholds in other circumstances, finding that the campaign finance law restricted the *quantity* of speech. *Buckley*, 424 U.S. at 18. A focus on protecting the quantity, rather than ideological diversity, of election speech has continued through the Court's campaign finance jurisprudence.

8 *See id.* at 262 (White, J., concurring in part) (contesting "the argument that money is speech" and that "limiting the flow of money to the speaker" was unconstitutional); *see also* J. Skelly Wright, *Politics and the Constitution: Is Money Speech?*, 85 YALE L. J. 1001 (1976).

9 *Buckley*, 424 U.S. at 19. The Court noted the cost of speaking, from the "humblest handbill" to the most expensive media spots, and compared a First Amendment right to speak circumscribed by spending limits with a hypothetical right to drive a vehicle without the right to purchase gasoline to refill the tank. *Id.* at 19, n. 18. As Justice Scalia pointed out decades later, effective communication to a large constituency requires a division of labor, which, in turn,

And, of course, a corresponding proposition holds true as well: government restraints on the ability to pay for speech are effectively government restraints on speech itself.

The *Buckley* Court then proceeded to make its second lasting contribution to campaign finance law. The Court distinguished political *expenditures* from political *contributions*. The Court ruled that, while money spent on political messaging independent of a specific political campaign was highly protected speech, money that was contributed to a particular campaign was subject to greater regulation.[10] This analytic approach has been criticized by academics, politicians, and members of the Court from across the ideological spectrum as empirically meaningless.[11] It is easy to see why: a particular political message can in many instances serve as a straightforward proxy for a particular candidate.

The Court based this dubious distinction on the argument that restrictions on monetary contributions to campaigns serve a "constitutionally sufficient" government interest in "limit[ing] the actuality and appearance of corruption."[12] In particular, the Court expressed concern regarding contributions made to secure political "quid pro quos" from successful candidates, undermining democratic integrity.[13] The Court found "deeply disturbing" the revelations of attempts to curry governmental favor in exchange for contributions during in the 1972 election.[14] And the Court noted that the damage to public faith in democracy stemming from the *appearance* of corruption was "[o]f almost equal concern" to that caused by *actual* corruption.[15]

The Court believed that this anticorruption interest justified the contribution-versus-expenditure distinction. In the Court's view, money transferred into a politician's campaign account created greater risks of an unsavory quid pro quo arrangement than did more general political expenditures. At a minimum, it created greater risks of the appearance of such a backroom deal.

By identifying "corruption," or its appearance, as the driving rationale for campaign finance restrictions, the Court limited the legislative response going forward. The decision effectively tasked reformers with the project of finding anticorruption rationales that would justify further measures. Other possible justifications, which may have been not only valid but more persuasive, necessarily went by the wayside.

Of course, one such justification is that the government has a legitimate interest in addressing the distorting effects of disproportionate political spending. Uncapped

"requires a means of mediating exchange, and in a commercial society, that means is supplied by money." McConnel v. FEC, 540 U.S. 93, 252 (2003) (Scalia, J., dissenting).

[10] This is not to say that all restrictions on contributions are permissible. In 2006, the Supreme Court held unconstitutional a Vermont state election contribution limit of $400, which was the lowest in the country and not indexed for inflation. Randall v. Sorrell, 548 U.S. 230 (2006).

[11] *See, e.g., Buckley*, 424 U.S. at 241, 244 (Burger, C.J., concurring in part).

[12] *Buckley*, 424 U.S. at 26.

[13] *Id.* at 26–27.

[14] *Id.* at 27.

[15] *Id.*

spending allows the better-resourced side of a debate to have outsized access to channels of communication – and a correspondingly outsized influence over voters. Commercial markets are regulated to prevent excessive concentrations of power, and it can be argued that the political marketplace of ideas should be monitored similarly.

In *Buckley*, the Supreme Court rejected this argument. The Court declared that restricting the speech of some in order to increase the relative voice of others was "wholly foreign" to our conception of the First Amendment as promoting the "widest possible dissemination of information."[16] In keeping with its adherence to a largely unregulated marketplace of ideas model of speech, the Court prioritized maximizing the total amount of speech over its equitable distribution or the diversity of viewpoints represented.[17] Dismissing concerns that political campaigning had become a spending arms race leading to prohibitively skyrocketing costs, the Court responded that the government may not "determine that spending to promote one's political views is wasteful, excessive, or unwise."[18]

At the turn of the twentieth century, during the so-called *Lochner* era, the Supreme Court had used a wide-ranging free market ideology to strike down various progressive economic regulations.[19] In doing so, the Court took on an activist role, usurping power assigned to the legislative branch. By time the Court decided *Buckley* in 1976, it had long abandoned the *Lochner* framework as judicially immodest and overreaching.[20] But, as *Buckley* demonstrates, that framework proved to be more enduring as a model for free speech jurisprudence than it did in other areas of constitutional law. And, in the area of campaign finance as elsewhere in First Amendment doctrine, the model of a free market prevailed and dominated.

Buckley thus enshrined three critical principles of campaign finance jurisprudence. First, campaign spending is protected speech. Second, campaign contributions raise concerns that general political expenditures do not. And, third, those concerns relate to actual and apparent corruption. The fact that massive expenditures can distort the political process, marginalize voices and perspectives, and frustrate the search for the truth and for the best policies was not viewed as a consideration. Despite the manifest disconnection between this doctrine and political reality, it attracted the five-justice majority necessary for the opinion.

16 *Id.* at 49 (quotes omitted).

17 The abandonment of an equalizing interest has been controversial, ruling out the potentially most coherent theory supporting upper limits on campaign finance spending. *See, e.g.*, Marlene Arnold Nicholson, *Buckley v. Valeo: The Constitutionality of the Federal Election Campaign Act Amendments of* 1974, 1977 WIS. L.REV. 323, 336 (1977).

18 *Buckley*, 424 U.S. at 57.

19 Named for the Court's decision in Lochner v. New York, 198 U.S. 45, 61 (1905).

20 West Coast Hotel Co. v. Parish, 300 U.S. 379 (1937) (overruling Lochner v. New York, 198 U.S. 45 (1905)).

For our purposes, the next major development came just two years after *Buckley*, in *First National Bank of Boston* v. *Bellotti*.[21] In that case, the Supreme Court held that corporations have First Amendment rights, including to make contributions to ballot initiative campaigns. The Court therefore struck down a Massachusetts law that prohibited corporate donations to ballot initiatives under certain circumstances.

Buckley and *Bellotti*, read together, thus yield two central principles: first, that election-related spending is speech; and, second, that corporations have First Amendment rights. As we will see, the Court's controversial decision in *Citizens United* relied on both of these ideas; when it did so, they had been a settled part of First Amendment doctrine for roughly forty years. Someone can therefore disagree with these principles or the way in which the *Citizens United* Court applied them; but criticisms based on the notion that *Citizens United* invented them are wrong by a magnitude of four decades.

Fourteen years after *Buckley*, in the 1990 case of *Austin* v. *Michigan Chamber of Commerce*,[22] Justice Marshall pushed back against the notion that government restrictions on campaign spending cannot be based on equality concerns. In *Austin*, the Court addressed a Michigan law that prevented corporations from making contributions or independent expenditures from their general corporate treasuries.[23] The law required that corporations instead collect and dispense money for these purposes through a segregated fund, or a Political Action Committee (PAC).[24] The Michigan Chamber of Commerce, a nonprofit corporation comprising mostly for-profit businesses, challenged the restriction during a 1985 special election campaign. The chamber wished to use money from its general treasury, rather than a separate political fund, to place a newspaper ad for a specific candidate, an undertaking that would have been punishable as a felony under the Michigan law.[25]

Writing for the Court, Justice Marshall adopted an intriguing strategy. He echoed *Buckley*'s anticorruption language.[26] But then, careful to avoid the term "equalizing," he identified what he termed a "different type of corruption in the political arena: the corrosive and distorting effects of immense aggregations of wealth that are accumulated with the help of the corporate form and that have little or no correlation to the public's support for the corporation's ideas."[27]

Austin thus focused on the corporate identity of the "speaker." In particular, the Court found that corporations enjoyed unique "state-created advantages," including

21 First National Bank of Boston v. Bellotti, 435 U.S. 765 (1978).
22 Austin v. Michigan Chamber of Commerce, 494 U.S. 652 (1990).
23 *Id.* at 655.
24 *Id.*
25 *Id.* at 656.
26 *Id.* at 659.
27 *Id.* at 658–659.

perpetual life and limited liability, that allowed them to use "'resources amassed in the economic marketplace' to obtain 'an unfair advantage in the political marketplace.'"[28] This type of corporate influence was "unfair," according to the Court, because "the resources in the treasury of a business corporation are not an indication of popular support for the corporation's political ideas. Instead, these resources reflect the economically motivated decisions of investors and customers."[29]

The *Austin* decision accordingly expanded the scope of the acceptable government objective of preventing corruption. Under *Austin*, the government could act to rein in the influence of "political war chests funneled through the corporate form"[30] and to ensure that "expenditures reflect actual public support for the political ideas espoused by corporations."[31] Rather than overruling *Buckley*'s expenditure-versus-contribution distinction, the Court simply created a corporate exception. Still, the Court struggled a bit to convincingly articulate why corporations deserved such different treatment.[32] This is unsurprising: after all, it would seem that *anyone* with a massive war chest has an unfair advantage in the political arena, regardless of whether they are a corporation.

This issue was not lost on the four dissenting justices, who took issue with the Court's "animosity and distrust" for corporations.[33] Rather than "assum[ing] that the corporate form has an intrinsic flaw that makes it corrupt," the dissenting justices viewed corporations as a "segment of the political community" with "unique views of vital importance."[34] Corporations, accordingly, should be viewed not as predatory entities but simply as associations of individuals who "may find that the nonprofit corporate form is the only feasible way of organizing so that they can transmit important views to the public as a whole."[35]

Although Justice Kennedy's dissent focused primarily on the nonprofit nature of the chamber, the core of the debate between the factions of the Court rested on

[28] *Id.* at 658–659 (quoting FEC v. Massachusetts Citizens for Life, Inc., 479 U.S. 238, 257 (1986)).

[29] *Id.* at 659 (internal quotes omitted).

[30] *Id.* at 659 (quoting FEC v. National Conservative Political Action Committee, 470 U.S. 480, 500–501 (1985)).

[31] *Id.* at 660.

[32] *Id.* at 660. Justice Stevens, in a concise concurring opinion, advocated for abandoning the distinction from the *Buckley* compromise, in favor of more robust campaign finance regulation. *Id.* at 678 (Stevens, J., concurring). The dissent, for its part, protested that the majority's hostile treatment of corporations was really nothing more than an unprincipled attempt to make an end run around the central holding of *Buckley*: that expenditure limitations were unconstitutional because there was no valid government interest in equalizing political speech. *Id.* at 702 (J. Kennedy, dissenting) (citations omitted).

[33] *Austin*, 494 U.S. at 695–696 (J. Kennedy, dissenting).

[34] *Id.* at 699–700, 704 (J. Kennedy, dissenting). Justice Scalia argued that corporations formed a much needed counterweight to the "dominant power of government." *Id.* at 694 (J. Scalia, dissenting).

[35] *Id.* at 711 (Kennedy, J., dissenting).

more fundamental questions. First, are corporations profit-hunting entities capable of capturing the reins of government from the people, or are they a trusted form of association that individuals can use to make their voices heard by their government?[36] And second, is more speech always better, or could the volume of particularly amplified positions effectively silence other views?

Thirteen years later, in 2003, the Supreme Court took yet another opportunity to review campaign finance regulation. Through the 273 pages of the massive *McConnell* v. *FEC* decision,[37] the members of the Court issued eight separate opinions. The result was a comprehensive navigation of the labyrinth of campaign finance restrictions contained in the Bipartisan Campaign Reform Act of 2002 (BCRA).[38]

Writing for the Court, Justices O'Connor and Stevens cobbled together a five-justice majority to uphold many of the BCRA's core regulatory provisions. The joint opinion began with a long and detailed history of Congressional attempts to rein in "the pernicious influence of 'big money' campaign contributions."[39] It described a "cautious advance, step by step,"[40] of "steady improvement"[41] in federal election law continuing through a set of 1974 reforms in response to the "unseemly" practices of the 1972 elections during President Richard Nixon's term.[42]

Despite these sustained Congressional efforts to reduce the effect of money in politics, candidates continued to find ways to access so-called soft money, financing not expressly directed toward any particular candidate that fell outside the reach of the Federal Election Campaign Act's (FECA) regulations on money intended to influence a federal election.[43] The Federal Election Commission (FEC) narrowly construed its mandate under the FECA and adopted a regulatory framework that allowed political parties to fund "mixed-purpose activities," such as generic advertising and get-out-the-vote drives, in part with "soft money."[44] The result was that the parties (and, indirectly, individual candidates) benefited from donations that were well in excess of the limits on FECA-regulated "hard money."[45]

36 Kennedy's dissent referred to "the corporate form *used by* the speaker," rather than corporations *as* speakers, suggesting that he viewed them less as self-propagating pseudo-organisms than as simple groupings of individuals choosing to exercise their First Amendment rights in a coordinated fashion. *Id.* at 713 (J. Kennedy, dissenting) (emphasis added).

37 McConnell v. FEC, 540 U.S. 93(2003), overruled by Citizens United v. Fed. Election Comm'n, 558 U.S. 310 (2010).

38 The new law amended the Federal Election Campaign Act of 1971 (FECA) and various other scattered provisions of federal election law. *Id.* at 114.

39 *Id.* at 115 (quotations omitted).

40 *Id.* at 117 (quotations omitted).

41 *Id.* at 117–118.

42 *Id.* at 118.

43 *Id.* at 122.

44 *Id.* at 123.

45 *Id.* at 124–125, 131.

The Court noted that, in 1995, the FEC had borrowed *Buckley* v. *Valeo*'s[46] narrow interpretation of FECA's expenditure limits and had determined that parties could use soft money for advertisements that did not "expressly advocate" the election or defeat of a particular candidate.[47] This led to a proliferation of what the Court termed so-called issue ads, which only needed to eschew "magic words" such as "elect Jane Doe" in order to avoid FECA regulation.[48] Although these ads were ostensibly about issues rather than elections, the Court noted that almost all aired within sixty days of the election that they were clearly intended to influence.[49] By avoiding FECA's disclosure requirements, corporations and unions spent hundreds of millions of dollars from their general funds on ads while concealing their identities.[50] Most troubling of all, these financing efforts appeared to achieve their desired effect: the buying and selling of political influence. The Court examined lengthy findings and numerous examples of campaign finance money being solicited in exchange for special access to candidates and senior government officials.[51]

The Court observed that Congress had responded to these developments by enacting the BCRA in 2002. The Act, among other things, attempted to "take national parties out of the soft-money business"[52] and remedy the functionally meaningless "magic words" requirement for express advocacy.[53] These reforms, intended to plug the loopholes that *Buckley* left open, were at the center of the Supreme Court showdown.

Justices O'Connor and Stevens borrowed from *Austin*'s playbook, continuing to use the accepted vocabulary of "corruption," while expanding the definition to encompass forms of influence outside of the term's commonly understood meaning.[54] The *McConnell* Court's view of corruption included "undue influence" over elected officials stemming from "substantial donations to gain access to high-level government officials" and resulting in public cynicism.[55] This was very different from the dissent's view of corruption as limited to instances of quid pro quo exchange, which the majority derided as "crabbed" and out of touch with "common sense and the realities of political fundraising."[56]

46 424 U.S., at 80 (construing FECA's expenditure limitations, as well as disclosure and reporting requirements, "to reach only funds used for communications that expressly advocate the election or defeat of a clearly identified candidate" (footnote omitted)).

47 *McConnell*, 540 U.S. at 124 (citing FEC Advisory Op. 1995-25).

48 *Id*. at 126, 127.

49 *Id*. at 127–128.

50 *Id*.

51 *Id*. at 128–130.

52 *Id*. at 133.

53 *Id*. at 132.

54 *Id*. at 138–139.

55 *Id*. at 144, 150 (quotes omitted).

56 *Id*. at 152.

Having situated the threat of disproportionate influence within the realm of "corruption," the Court concluded that using political parties to dodge existing campaign finance laws had proven sufficiently problematic to warrant a Congressional response. The majority therefore upheld the BCRA's loophole-closing amendment, declaring that "the hard lesson of circumvention by the entire history of campaign finance regulation" confirmed the provision's validity and importance.[57]

The Court next addressed the "electioneering communications" provision of the BCRA, which sought to replace the FEC's "functionally meaningless" test with a more robust definition that would encompass ads clearly intended to sway an upcoming election.[58] The Court found that the regulation was another sensible loophole-closing measure, designed to prevent the circumvention of FECA regulations through the avoidance of "magic words." The Court reasoned that the narrow "express advocacy" rule that the FEC had adopted based on *Buckley* was the result of statutory construction, not constitutional law, and thus was amenable to redesign by the legislature.[59]

In sum, the majority opinion told a cat-and-mouse tale of a century-long effort by Congress to catch and stop attempts by innovative financiers to purchase outsized political influence. It was a story that counseled deference to those Congressional responses and regulatory experiments, which continually faced new challenges and strategies. "Money, like water, will always find an outlet," the Court observed. The Court signaled a willingness to think expansively about what constitutes a corrupting influence in order to grant regulators broad discretion in their ever-evolving battle against the dangers posed by influxes of large amounts of money into the political process.

McConnell was decided by a bare majority and included many concurring and dissenting opinions. It is a fractured piece of jurisprudence that makes for hard reading. But its central lesson was clear: Congress was attempting to deal with a serious problem – the development of ever-shifting and complex mechanisms to inject money into politics and the threats that these expenditures pose to democracy. Five justices thought Congress had the leeway to do so. In essence, the Court recognized that while money may be speech, it is also still money – and it can distort the political process in pernicious and dangerous ways.

Just four years after *McConnell*, the Supreme Court took another opportunity to address the constitutionality of the BCRA's loophole-closing provision regarding communications. In *Federal Election Commission* v. *Wisconsin Right to Life, Inc.*,[60] a nonprofit ideological corporation challenged the prohibition of advertisements it

57 *Id.* at 165.
58 *Id.* at 189, 193.
59 *Id.* at 190.
60 Federal Election Commission v. Wisconsin Right to Life, Inc., 551 U.S. 449 (2007).

wanted to run shortly before the 2004 federal election. The ads decried filibusters by Senate Democrats and urged viewers to call two named senators up for reelection to express their discontent.[61]

Chief Justice John Roberts, who recently had replaced William Rehnquist at the center of the bench, wrote the operative opinion for the fragmented Court. He did not challenge *McConnell's* central holding that the BCRA could constitutionally regulate "sham" issue ads or those ads that were the "functional equivalent" of speech "expressly advocating the election or defeat of a candidate."[62] He did, however, construct an exceedingly narrow test for identifying a constitutionally proscribable "sham." The Chief Justice indicated that only those ads that were "susceptible of no reasonable interpretation other than as an appeal to vote for or against a specific candidate" could be regulated as "express advocacy."[63]

Applying this newly articulated test to Wisconsin Right to Life's proposed ads, the Court rejected the argument that "any appeal to citizens to contact their elected representative" necessarily rendered the communication "the functional equivalent" of express advocacy.[64] The Court was equally unconvinced by record evidence demonstrating the extent to which such potential sham issue ads influenced election outcomes.[65] This decision laid the groundwork for a future restructuring of campaign finance laws.

Thirty-four years after *Buckley*, and only three years after the *Wisconsin Right to Life* opinion, the Court in *Citizens United* issued a sweeping ruling that uprooted campaign finance jurisprudence and returned it to where it had stood before *Austin*. In January of 2008, an incorporated political activist group, Citizens United, released a ninety-minute documentary film entitled *Hillary: The Movie*.[66] The film was highly critical of then Senator Hillary Clinton, who was a candidate in the upcoming 2008 presidential primary. Citizens United wished to use money from its general fund to make *Hillary* available through video-on-demand, and also produced several short advertisements promoting it.[67]

Citizens United sought a declaratory judgment holding that these materials did not fall within the prohibitions of the BCRA. Neither party requested a ruling on the facial constitutional validity of the statute. Nevertheless, in a move unusual for a Court that generally seeks to avoid the appearance of a judicial activism, the Court requested further briefing and reargument to specifically address that much broader

61 *Id.* at 458–459.
62 *Id.* at 456.
63 McConnell v. Fed. Election Comm'n, 540 U.S. 93 (2003) (subsequent history omitted); *WRTL*, 551 U.S. at 469–470 (2007).
64 *Id.* at 470.
65 *Id.* at 471.
66 Citizens United v. Fed. Election Comm'n, 558 U.S. 310, 319–320 (2010).
67 *Id.* at 320.

issue.[68] In sum, the Court intentionally bypassed alternative approaches that would have avoided a constitutional ruling.

The Court held that, because the BCRA imposed an "outright ban, backed by criminal sanctions" on elements of corporate speech, it was necessary to reexamine the doctrinal framework set forth in *Austin*.[69] Challenging the principle that formed the core of Austin – that disproportionate wealth in politics can distort democracy – Justice Kennedy wrote that "[a]ll speakers, including individuals and the media, use money amassed from the economic marketplace to fund their speech. The First Amendment protects the resulting speech."[70] He rejected *Austin*'s concern that corporations might use disproportionate financial resources to achieve an outsized dissemination of their messages, concluding that it unacceptably "interfered with the open marketplace of ideas."[71] And he stressed that "political speech cannot be limited based on a speaker's wealth . . . or identity."[72]

The *Citizens United* Court took an "absolutist" view of the First Amendment, consistent with the decisions of this most recent era: "it is our law and our tradition that more speech, not less, is the governing rule."[73] And the Court essentially shrugged off all competing concerns. Indeed, Justice Kennedy even suggested that the growing sums of corporate money spent during political campaigns indicated democracy was thriving, not withering. "The fact that a corporation, or any other speaker, is willing to spend money to try to persuade voters presupposes that the people have the ultimate influence over elected officials."[74]

In short, the Court explicitly overruled *Austin*, striking down corporate expenditure limitations as unconstitutional.[75] Further, it overruled those aspects of *McConnell* that extended *Austin*'s rationale.[76] The Court concluded that, under such campaign finance laws, "[s]peech would be suppressed in the realm where its necessity is most evident: in the public dialogue preceding a real election. Governments are often hostile to speech, but under our law and our tradition it seems stranger than fiction for our Government to make this political speech a crime."[77] "Choices and assessments" regarding the validity of differing political opinions "are not for the Government to make."[78]

[68] Instead, Citizens United had argued that, as in the *WRTL* case, BCRA could not be constitutionally applied to Citizens United's ads in particular. *Id.* at 321. In the alternative, Citizens United maintained that their proposed materials were not even prohibited by BCRA, and could be exempted as a simple matter of regulatory interpretation. Citizens United claimed that *Hilary* did not fit the definition of "electioneering communication" under FEC regulation, because it was available on demand and not "publicly distributed." *Id.* at 323.

[69] *Id.* at 337.

[70] *Id.* at 351.

[71] *Id.* at 353–354 (citations and internal quotes omitted).

[72] *Id.* at 347, 358.

[73] *Id.* at 361.

[74] *Id.* at 360.

[75] *Id.* at 365.

[76] *Id.* at 365.

[77] *Id.* at 372.

[78] *Id.* at 372.

From a legal standpoint, the consequences of *Citizens United* are not difficult to understand. The Court's decision largely returned to the world of campaign finance that existed before *Austin*. And, at least for now, *Buckley*'s embattled division between contributions and independent expenditures remains.

From a broader jurisprudential standpoint, however, *Citizens United* leaves us with numerous problems and puzzles, some of which go well beyond the First Amendment. For example, the case raises serious questions about the Court's commitment to judicial restraint. As a general proposition, in order to prevent the appearance of judicial overreach, the Supreme Court labors to address only the narrowest issue necessary to resolve the case that the litigants bring before it and tries to avoid unnecessarily broad rulings, issues of policy, and constitutional holdings. This incremental and precedent-respecting approach lends stability and predictability to the law and is essential to the perception of the Court as impartial and legitimate. In *Citizens United*, however, the Court decided to reach questions the parties did not present, to dismiss Congress's concerns and efforts, to upend existing doctrine, and to issue a ruling so broad that it may be impossible to change absent a constitutional amendment.

Citizens United has met with both approval and strong condemnation. These conflicting views of the opinion often reflect differing beliefs about why the Constitution protects free speech. As we discussed at the beginning of this book, some arguments in support of free speech focus on the opportunity that such expression affords for personal autonomy, fulfillment, development, and exercises of conscience.[79] Because corporations are not human beings, those sorts of arguments do not align well with claims that corporations should have First Amendment rights.[80] The mantra that "corporations are not people" reflects the general understanding that corporations were created to serve humans (shareholders and other stakeholders), not the reverse.[81]

Other arguments that we discussed at the beginning of the book, however, *do* support the notion that corporations should enjoy First Amendment protection. For example, as we have noted, one of the leading arguments in support of protecting free expression is that the resulting marketplace of ideas leads to the discovery of the truth and plays a critical role in sound democratic decision making.[82] Under this

[79] *See* Kent Greenfield, Corporations Are People Too (and They Should Act Like It) 115 (2018).

[80] *Id.* at 119.

[81] Justice Stevens' dismay at the majority's sympathy for corporate rights echoes this sentiment. *Citizens United*, 558 U.S. at 466 (Stevens, J., dissenting) (pointing out that corporations "have no consciences, no beliefs, no feelings, no thoughts, no desires" to be protected). As Justice Scalia pointed out in his concurrence, however, allowing corporations to speak may further the speech rights of their human members. *Id.* at 391–392 (Scalia, J., concurring) ("the individual person's right to speak includes the right to speak *in association with other individual persons*").

[82] *See* Alexander Meiklejohn, Free Speech and Its Relation to Self-government 24 (1948).

argument, any effort to regulate the marketplace of ideas – particularly based on the identity of the speaker or the speaker's message – is fraught with peril and should be summarily rejected. The Supreme Court decision in *Citizens United* reflects this perspective.

Still, critics maintain that the rationale underlying *Citizens United* is simplistic and naïve. And they contend that it is not even consistent with the best arguments in favor of granting corporations First Amendment protection, including the one just noted. After all, they observe, disproportionate power in the marketplace of ideas, as in any other kind of market, has attendant evils. Huge infusions of corporate cash tend to drown out other voices, frustrating the very search for truth and fully informed decision making that free speech is supposed to foster.[83] In this sense, *Citizens United* raises questions about which reasonable people can disagree but that is foundational to our thinking about the First Amendment: Why do we protect freedom of speech? And, if we do so in order to empower people to find their way toward the truth, then is that goal best served by a regulated or unregulated marketplace of ideas?

Although the *Citizens United* decision foreclosed certain types of regulations, efforts to mitigate the influence of concentrated wealth in politics have continued. Campaign finance reformers turned to alternative strategies at the state and local levels. Still, many of these attempts have not fared well in the courts, including the Supreme Court.

For example, in *Arizona Free Enterprise Club's Freedom Club PAC* v. *Bennett*,[84] the Court examined an Arizona state law that granted candidates choosing to conduct a publicly funded campaign an opportunity to receive financing in an amount equivalent to that spent in support of their opponent. The Court delivered yet another ruling divided along ideological lines. Chief Justice Roberts, writing for the five-justice majority, declared the law unconstitutional on the grounds that it burdened speech by deterring privately funded candidates from spending more on their campaigns, knowing that doing so would trigger the flow of funds to their opponents. Even though the law purported to increase, rather than reduce, the total amount of speech, the Court judged that it would have the opposite effect. The Court also suggested that the law would penalize the privately funded candidate's speech by reducing its impact: "an advertisement supporting the election of a candidate that goes without a response is often more effective than an advertisement that is directly controverted."[85]

83 *See Citizens United*, 558 U.S. at 470 (Stevens, J., dissenting) (pointing to the potential "drowning out of noncorporate voices").

84 Arizona Free Enterprise Club's Freedom Club PAC v. Bennett, 564 U.S. 721 (2011).

85 *Id.* at 747. The dissent responded: "that, after all, is the whole idea of the First Amendment." *Id.* at 769 (Kagan, J., dissenting).

Some creative alternative schemes that have arisen have not yet been tested before the Supreme Court. For example, New York City has had success with a public financing that matches small donations to a particular candidate on a six-to-one basis, thereby increasing the relative influence of small donors compared to large donors.[86] Others have suggested granting $50 "democracy vouchers" to citizens who can then allocate them to any candidate who rejects large contributions.[87] This scheme was enacted in Seattle and was recently proposed in Arizona.[88] The Washington State Supreme Court upheld the so-called democracy dollars scheme, distinguishing it from the matching mechanism at issue in *Arizona*.[89]

But reforms that have been subjected to Supreme Court review have continued to fare poorly. Thus, in its 2014 decision in *McCutcheon* v. *Federal Election Commission*,[90] the Court issued yet another five-to-four decision striking down a campaign finance law. The provision at issue sought to limit the total amount that spenders could contribute across all candidates in a given time period, imposing so-called "aggregate limits." Writing for the Court, Chief Justice Roberts held that "[t]he Government may no more restrict how many candidates or causes a donor may support than it may tell a newspaper how many candidates it may endorse."[91] While leaving *Buckley*'s allowance for reasonable contribution limits to *individual* candidates undisturbed, the Court in *McCutcheon* doubled down on a narrow quid pro quo anticorruption interest as the only acceptable interest in regulating campaign spending.[92]

The Court's campaign finance decision in *Citizens United* and its progeny have been the subject of ongoing, heated, and seemingly unresolvable debate. It is now easy to see why. As we discussed in the Introduction, people tend to take absolutist or relativist views of free speech. The simplicity and clarity of the commands of *Citizens United* appeal to absolutists, even if the practical consequences of the decision may not. But relativists think that the opinion does not adequately account for competing values and concerns, including those that go to the very integrity and sustainability of our democracy.

86 *See*Michael J. Malbin, Peter W. Brusoe and Brendan Glavin, *Small Donors, Big Democracy: New York City's Matching Funds as a Model for the Nation and States*, 11 ELECTION L.J. 3 (2012).

87 Lawrence Lessig, *More Money Can Beat Big Money*, NEW YORK TIMES A31 (Nov. 16, 2011). http://www.nytimes.com/2011/11/17/opinion/in-campaign-financing-more-money-can-beat-big-money.html?_r=0.

88 Jeremy Duda, *"Democracy Dollars" Could Pump Millions of Dollars of Public Funding into Elections*, ARIZONA MIRROR (Nov. 1, 2019). http://www.azmirror.com/2019/11/01/democracy-dollars-could-pump-millions-of-dollars-of-public-funding-into-elections/.

89 Elster v. City of Seattle, 193 Wash. 2d 638, 643–644, 444 P.3d 590, 593 (2019). Opponents of the law subsequently filed a petition for writ of certiorari with the US Supreme Court. *Id.*, *petition for cert. filed*, 19 USL.W. 608 (US Nov. 12, 2019).

90 McCutcheon v. Federal Election Commission, 572 U.S. 185 (2014).

91 *Id.* at 204.

92 *Id.* at 207.

Furthermore, as just noted, some arguments in favor of free speech lend greater support to providing full protection to corporations than others. Whether you believe that corporate speech should receive such protection largely depends on why you think we have a First Amendment in the first place. If you believe that we protect free speech so that ideas and information can be exchanged without restriction, then there is no obvious reason to treat corporations differently when they speak. But if you believe that we protect free speech so that individuals can fulfill their human potential, then affording corporations the same liberties seems nonsensical and like excellent fare for eye-rolling bumper stickers.

For these reasons, *Citizens United* serves like something of a First Amendment Rorschach test: our reactions to it tell us a great deal about how we see things more generally. This explains why it has been the subject of such sharp disagreement. And, for better or worse, it also explains why it may be a stubborn precedent that an absolutist Court with a deep commitment to a largely unregulated marketplace of ideas will be inclined to preserve and follow.

14

Speech in Public Schools

In this chapter, we turn to the complex and contentious issue of speech in the public schools, focusing on problems related to student speech. The Supreme Court has issued a number of important rulings in this area. Unfortunately, they leave us in a doctrinally puzzling place, for several reasons.

First, unlike most areas of First Amendment doctrine, over time the Supreme Court cases addressing speech in K-12 schools have trended toward *less* protection rather than *more*. Second, the precise basis for the Court's ruling in some cases is occasionally less than completely clear. Third, a few of the leading K-12 cases involved such idiosyncratic facts that it is difficult to determine their meaning and their significance as precedent. And, finally, changes in the social and technological landscape raise questions not fully answered by the Court's decisions. Little wonder student speech, particularly in the K-12 context, remains so controversial.

This chapter discusses the major Supreme Court decisions in this area and the major principles that they appear to yield. It then discusses some recent and important lower-court decisions regarding student speech. Those lower courts have had to struggle with such nettlesome contemporary issues as discriminatory speech, identity-based harassment, threats of violence, and bullying. Furthermore, they have had to do so in an environment complicated by the fact that a great deal of potentially concerning and disruptive student speech now occurs off-campus or online and not during regular school hours.

For much of the twentieth century, public school students enjoyed only limited free speech protection. In a sense, this is understandable. After all, schools need to maintain order, to protect more vulnerable students from their more aggressive peers, to inculcate students in certain behavioral norms, and to achieve academic and educational goals. In light of these considerations, it seemed appropriate for administrators to enjoy almost absolute authority to control their students, including their speech while at school.

Over time, however, it became increasingly clear that these are not the only relevant considerations with respect to student expression. In their effort to please parents and other constituents, and to prevent problems before they materialize, school administrators may overestimate the risks posed by student expression. They may foreclose students from engaging in debate over the important issues of the day, depriving them of the opportunity to learn how to become politically engaged and responsible participants in our democracy. In a country that prides itself on the primacy of free speech, repressive school policies may provide only a harsh lesson in the primacy of censorship.

The critical and foundational change in our thinking about student speech came in the Supreme Court's 1969 decision in *Tinker* v. *Des Moines Independent School District*.[1] That case arose when a handful of teenage students were suspended for wearing black armbands to school in protest of the Vietnam War. In an opinion written by Justice Fortas, the Court flatly rejected the notion that "either students or teachers shed their constitutional rights to freedom of speech or expression at the schoolhouse gate."[2]

It is difficult to overstate the importance of this ruling. It acknowledges that minors have First Amendment rights *away* from school. And it makes clear that those rights do not vaporize the instant a minor takes on the identity of a student. Justice Fortas's use of the image of the "schoolhouse gate" suggests a porous border between the extracurricular and curricular environments, making it important that rights continue to be recognized as a student passes from the one to the other.

Of course, the *Tinker* Court recognized that the right of students to speak in school is not absolute. The Court acknowledged that administrators have a legitimate interest in controlling the conduct of the students in their charge. But it also concluded that the Des Moines school administrators had "sought to punish petitioners for a silent, passive expression of opinion, unaccompanied by any disorder or disturbance."[3]

The Court effectively declared that student speech was presumptively protected by the First Amendment, provided that it did not "substantially interfere with the work of the school or impinge upon the rights of other students."[4] The Court thus suggested that there were two – and only two – circumstances under which a school could restrain student speech. The speech at issue here did not fall into either category.

A "substantial interference" standard might afford little protection if courts simply deferred to the judgments of school districts. But *Tinker* also made clear that unsubstantiated fears of disruptions were not to be taken at face value. After all,

1 Tinker v. Des Moines Indep. Cmty. Sch. Dist., 393 U.S. 503 (1969).
2 *Id.* at 506.
3 *Id.* at 508.
4 *Id.* at 509.

the Court observed, "[a]ny word spoken, in class, in the lunchroom, or on the campus, that deviates from the views of another person may start an argument or cause a disturbance."[5]

The Court recognized that this standard means that some disruptions will escape prevention and will occur in the natural and inevitable order of things. But the Court held that our constitutional commitment to the "hazardous freedom" of vigorous and open debate demands that "we must take this risk."[6] Accordingly, mere "discomfort" or "unpleasantness" stemming from the expression of an "unpopular viewpoint" did not justify the institutional censorship of student speech.[7] Unless it "materially" and "substantially" interferes with the "appropriate discipline in the operation of the school," student speech is protected.[8]

In so ruling, the Court noted the danger that school restrictions on student speech could easily lead to viewpoint discrimination – which, as we discussed in Chapter 9, is a grave evil under our First Amendment doctrine. Indeed, the Court saw evidence of such discrimination in this case. It observed that other students in the school had worn political campaign buttons – some had even donned the Nazi Iron Cross – but had suffered no official repercussions.[9]

One of the most striking things about *Tinker* is that the Court viewed the school context as one in which it is particularly important to preserve First Amendment freedoms. The Court emphasized that public schools are not "enclaves of totalitarianism," where students can only express those "sentiments that are officially approved."[10] To the contrary, the Court declared, school classrooms are the physical embodiment of the marketplace of ideas, where thoughts and perspectives are freely exchanged.[11] "The Nation's future depends upon leaders trained through wide exposure to that robust exchange of ideas," the Court concluded.[12]

Such a sweeping view of First Amendment protection for student speech drew fierce responses from those who saw the decision as an assault on the traditionally absolute authority of school officials to control what happens on school grounds. In his fiery dissenting opinion, Justice Black (who in other contexts took on the role of a First Amendment absolutist) objected to what he saw as an undermining of school discipline, leading to a "new revolutionary era of permissiveness."[13] The ruling, according to Justice Black, subjected schools to the "whims and caprices of th[e]

5 *Id.* at 508–509.
6 *Id.* at 508–509 (citation omitted).
7 *Id.* at 509.
8 *Id.* at 509 (quote omitted).
9 *Id.* at 510–511.
10 *Id.* at 511.
11 *Id.* at 512.
12 *Id.* at 512.
13 *Id.* at 518 (Black, J., dissenting). He predicted the ruling would spawn a concomitant parade of horribles such as allowing voting or school board membership for those under age eighteen or twenty-one. *Id.* at 518 (Black, J., dissenting).

loudest-mouthed" pupils as they "defy and flout orders of school officials to keep their minds on their own schoolwork."[14] Though less strident in tone, Justice Harlan's dissent echoed Justice Black in suggesting that school officials merited significant deference and "the widest authority in maintaining discipline."[15]

Despite its breadth and its controversial implications, the expansive protection of student speech recognized in *Tinker* remained solidly in place until the mid-1980s. Then, in the 1986 case of *Bethel School District* v. *Fraser*,[16] the Supreme Court appeared to take a step back from *Tinker*. The Court's confusing reasoning in the case, however, left things less than perfectly clear.

Fraser involved a high school student who, during a mandatory assembly, gave a campaign speech that the Court described as using an "elaborate, graphic, and explicit sexual metaphor."[17] Approximately 600 high school students, many of whom were fourteen-year-olds, attended the assembly. Apparently, the student's bawdy speech had its intended effect, as some members of the audience responded by hooting and yelling or making sexual gestures.[18] Others were less amused: one teacher reported forgoing part of her scheduled lesson to discuss the matter,[19] and the school responded by suspending the student and removing his candidacy for graduation speaker.[20]

Writing for the majority, Chief Justice Burger labored to distinguish the *Tinker* case. He emphasized that *Tinker* had involved only the "nondisruptive, passive expression of a political viewpoint" and he implied that the loud and at least somewhat disruptive use of a sexual joke deserved less protection under the First Amendment.[21] Seizing on *Tinker*'s statement that such protection did not extend to speech that either "intrudes upon the work of the schools or the rights of other students," the Court found the speech at the assembly to be materially different from the wearing of black armbands.[22] Moving away from the Court's view in *Tinker* that schools should not be places of indoctrination, the *Fraser* Court stressed that the

[14] *Id.*

[15] 393 U.S. 503, 526 (Harlan, J., dissenting). As a compromise between disciplinary needs and free speech principles, he advocated for a rule that would require complaining students to bear the burden of showing that school officials acted with illegitimate motives. *Id.* (Harlan, J., dissenting).

[16] Bethel School District v. Fraser, 478 U.S. 675 (1986).

[17] *Id.* at 677–678.

[18] *Id.* at 678.

[19] *Id.* at 678. The Court, writing in 1986, described the fourteen-year-old students in the audience as "on the threshold of awareness of human sexuality" and noted a previously recognized "interest in protecting minors from exposure to vulgar and offensive spoken language." *Id.* at 683–684.

[20] *Id.* at 678.

[21] *Id.* at 680.

[22] *Id.* (quotation omitted).

"work of the schools" included the "inculcation" of the values of "a civilized social order" by forbidding modes of expression that are vulgar and offensive.[23]

The Court offered several additional explanations for reaching a result different than that in *Tinker*. First, the Court was concerned that the younger members of the audience were being forced to hear a "sexually explicit monologue directed towards an unsuspecting audience."[24] Second, the Court noted that the school's actions were not related to any intent to silence an unpopular political viewpoint, as in *Tinker*.[25] Third, the Court believed that school officials needed the ability to guard against "vulgar and lewd speech ... [that] would undermine the school's basic educational mission."[26] Finally, the Court reasoned that the school had a valid interest in "dissociat[ing] itself" from such vulgarities that are "inconsistent with fundamental values of public school education."[27]

In his concurring opinion, Justice Brennan – one of the Court's great champions of First Amendment freedoms – sought to limit the scope of the holding in *Fraser*. He approved of the suspension only because of the specifics of the school assembly, which administrators sought to have "proceed in an orderly manner" without disruption and wanted to use as a means to teach "civil public discourse."[28] Under different circumstances, Justice Brennan concluded, the student's speech may have been protected.[29] Justice Marshall, in dissent, expressed doubt that any real "disruption of the educational process" had occurred, arguing that the student's speech should be protected by *Tinker* without any modification of the constitutional test established there.[30]

The *Fraser* decision engendered considerable confusion. It seemingly expanded *Tinker*'s limited exception for disruptive expression so as to also allow restrictions on speech that impacted the school's "basic educational mission."[31] But what, exactly, constituted a school's basic education mission? And how much deference should be shown to the judgment of school administrators in that regard?

Some of the language in the opinion regarding "inculcation" of the values of "a civilized social order" suggested that school administrators enjoy broad discretion in setting limits on student speech.[32] But other parts of the opinion (and Justice Brennan's concurrence) suggested that *Fraser* was narrowly limited to its specific facts: an "offensively lewd and indecent" speech that took place at a mandatory

[23] *Id.* at 683.
[24] *Id.*
[25] *Id.* at 685–686.
[26] *Id.*
[27] *Id.* (quote omitted).
[28] *Id.* at 688–689 (Brennan, J., concurring).
[29] *Id.* at 688–689 (Brennan, J., concurring).
[30] *Id.* at 690 (Marshall, J., concurring).
[31] *Fraser*, 478 U.S. 675, 685–686.
[32] *Id.* at 683.

assembly attended by a large number of fourteen-year-old students.[33] But which of these components drove the analysis here? The lewdness of the speech? *Tinker* did not identify that as an exception. The nonpolitical nature of the expression? Maybe, although Fraser's speech took place in the context of a school election. The "captive audience" context? Perhaps, although students had no choice but to observe the black armbands in *Tinker*, either.

The Court's decision may have rested on the combination of these factors, which would make some sense. After all, in other contexts the Court has been reluctant to extend protection to sexually explicit speech where there is a substantial risk that children will be exposed to it.[34] And the Court also has indicated an interest in protecting so-called captive audiences, those unable to avoid speech they find offensive.[35] Still, trying to extricate a straightforward legal principle from *Fraser* proves extraordinarily difficult, and courts and scholars have disagreed about the meaning and precedential significance of the case.

Two years later, the Court seemed to retreat still further from *Tinker* in its 1988 decision in *Hazelwood School District* v. *Kuhlmeier*.[36] In that case, a high school principal redacted two pages from student articles in a newspaper that was written and published as part of a journalism class. One of the articles discussed three students' experiences with teen pregnancy, and another discussed the impact of divorce on some of the school's students.[37] Although no real names were used in the articles, the school's principal cited concern that the pregnant students' identities would be readily ascertainable and that the divorce piece – which was critical of one of the student's parents – should have provided the parent with an opportunity to print a response.[38] The student authors sued on the grounds that the principal's censorship of their articles violated their First Amendment rights. *Tinker* may have suggested that the students had a case. After all, they could have written and published such articles outside of school. If they do not shed their rights at the schoolhouse gate, then why shouldn't they be able to write and publish them here? Nevertheless, the Court thought about this case quite differently.

Writing for the *Hazelwood* majority, Justice White cited *Fraser* for the proposition that the free speech rights of students while in school are not necessarily the same as those of adults. He reiterated the school's interest in regulating speech at odds with its "basic educational mission."[39] And he distinguished *Tinker*, which he

[33] 478 U.S. 675, 685.

[34] *See* F.C.C. v. Pacifica Found., 438 U.S. 726, 749 (1978) (upholding FCC broadcasting restrictions on George Carlin's "Filthy Words" monologue in part because "broadcasting is uniquely accessible to children, even those too young to read").

[35] Kovacs v. Cooper, 336 U.S. 77 (1949); *see also* Con Edison v. Public Service, 447 U.S. 530 (1980); Mn. Alliance v. Mansky, 138 S. Ct 1876 (2018).

[36] Hazelwood Sch. Dist. v. Kuhlmeier, 484 U.S. 260 (1988).

[37] *Id.* at 263.

[38] *Id.*

[39] *Id.* at 266.

characterized as involving personal expression that happened to occur on school premises, on the one hand, from speech that occurred in "school-sponsored publications" and that is part of the "school curriculum," on the other.[40]

According to Justice White, such curricular productions, "supervised by faculty members and designed to impart" learning upon the students, could reasonably be perceived to carry the "imprimatur" of the school.[41] As such, the school had a legitimate interest in declining to publish student speech from which it wished to dissociate itself.[42] The majority reasoned that, because the paper here was produced as part of a journalism class, the school was justified in setting high academic standards and in eschewing work that was "ungrammatical, poorly written, inadequately researched, biased or prejudiced, vulgar or profane, or unsuitable for immature audiences."[43]

In particular, the Court believed school officials were justified in protecting immature audiences from the dissemination of materials on "sensitive topics."[44] The Court further noted that schools could refuse to sponsor expression that "might reasonably be perceived to advocate drug or alcohol use."[45] In sum, under *Hazelwood*, educators can constitutionally exercise "editorial control over the style and content of student speech in school-sponsored expressive activities so long as their actions are reasonably related to legitimate pedagogical concerns."[46] The Court concluded that the principal's conduct here met this test.

Hazelwood plainly brings the K-12 environment very far away from the relatively freewheeling marketplace of ideas described in *Tinker*. Despite *Tinker*'s bold and famous declaration that students do not lose their First Amendment rights at the schoolhouse gate, *Hazelwood* indicated they might well do so at the classroom door – or anywhere else where school sponsorship or the academic curriculum is implicated. Furthermore, reiterating a theme we saw in *Fraser*, the *Hazelwood* Court was sympathetic with the idea that certain topics or modes of expression were

[40] *Id.* at 271.

[41] *Id.*

[42] *Id.* at 270–271.

[43] *Id.* at 271–272.

[44] *Id.* at 272 (such topics might "range from the existence of Santa Claus in an elementary school setting to the particulars of teenage sexual activity in a high school setting"). According to the dissent, the school had no legitimate interest in wielding such "Orwellian" "thought control" over its students. *Id.* at 286–287 (Brennan, J., dissenting). Official determinations of the "vaporous" metric of "potential topic sensitivity" could all too easily be manipulated to achieve unconstitutional viewpoint discriminatory ends, perhaps even library book bans. *Id.* As a possible example, Justice Brennan pointed to the case at hand: the school principal apparently had not objected to other articles on the topic of teenage sex in the same issue of the school paper. *Id.* at 287–288 (Brennan, J., dissenting). Rather, he had singled out for censorship the article that could have been interpreted as potentially *advocating for* such behavior. *Id.*

[45] *Id.* at 272. Stepping beyond the facts of the case, Justice White's remark provided fuel for future decisions restricting student speech during the war on drugs.

[46] *Id.* at 273. Censorship of such materials creates a constitutional violation only when it "has no valid educational purpose."

inappropriate for immature audiences and that school administrators should have some authority to restrict their students' exposure to them.

Even with *Hazelwood*, however, the Supreme Court was not done limiting the free speech rights of students. The next blow came in the 2007 case, *Morse v. Frederick*.[47] Few Supreme Court cases involve such unique facts that they acquire nicknames, but this one did: it is often referred to as the "Bong Hits for Jesus" case.

Morse arose from the 2002 Olympic Torch Relay, which passed through Juneau, Alaska, on its way to the Salt Lake City Olympic Games. The procession traveled along the street in front of the local high school. The principal decided to allow staff and students to attend as an "approved social event or class trip."[48]

As the torchbearers passed by, a group of students unfurled a fourteen-foot banner emblazoned with the phrase "BONG HiTS 4 JESUS."[49] The principal spotted the banner and, believing it to encourage illegal drug use in violation of school policy, directed the students to take the banner down.[50] One student refused to comply. The principal responded by confiscating the banner and suspending the student.[51] The student filed an action for damages against his principal for violating his First Amendment rights.

No single rationale for disposing of the case earned the vote of a majority of the justices. In his plurality opinion, Chief Justice Roberts acknowledged that *Fraser*'s meaning "is not entirely clear." He nevertheless distilled two principles from the case: first, that the constitutional rights of students in school were not necessarily the same as those of adults or outside of the school context, and, second, that *Tinker*'s "substantial disruption" test was not the only analysis available in school speech cases.[52] The latter was important because the speech at issue here did not substantially disrupt school order or interfere with the learning process.

Furthermore, Chief Justice Roberts believed that the student's banner posed no danger of being mistaken for an expression carrying the "imprimatur" or approval of the school.[53] And, indeed, no sensible person would have mistaken it as a school-endorsed message, whatever its meaning – if it had one. (The student maintained that the phrase was a nonsensical one that he used simply to try to attract the attention of the television cameras.) The case therefore did not fall cleanly within the analytic approaches taken in either *Fraser* or *Hazelwood*.

Chief Justice Roberts nevertheless concluded that the principal's actions were justified under a different rationale – as a salvo in the war on drugs. He noted the serious consequences of drug abuse among young people. And he declared that the

47 Morse v. Frederick, 551 U.S. 393 (2007).
48 *Id.* at 397.
49 *Id.*
50 *Id.*
51 *Id.*
52 *Id.* at 404–405.
53 *Id.* at 405.

school accordingly had an interest in deterring drug use by school children and in educating students of the dangers associated with it.[54]

The Chief Justice stopped short of endorsing the principal's argument that she was justified in censoring the speech because it was "offensive."[55] He found that a "stretc[h]," expressing concern that such reasoning could lead to proscribing political and religious speech, which is often perceived as offensive by some listeners.[56] The student could be disciplined for displaying the banner, the Chief Justice reasoned, not because it was offensive but because it could have been reasonably understood to promote illegal drug use.[57]

The idea that "Bong Hits for Jesus" promotes illegal drug use may strike many people as a "stretch" as well. We can count among those people Justice Stevens, who filed a strident and colorful dissent. He found it inconceivable that any reasonable student would have viewed the slogan as advocating much of anything, let along the unlawful consumption of drugs, memorably observing that students do not "check their brains" at the schoolhouse gate.

In any event, Justice Alito's concurring opinion, joined by Justice Kennedy, supplied the key fifth vote in upholding the principal's decision. Justice Alito concurred to the extent that the Court's holding applied to speech reasonably interpreted as advocating for illegal drug use. But he rejected any implication that a school could prohibit speech on such broad and vague grounds that the expression interfered with its "educational mission."[58] Justice Alito cautioned that such a standard could "easily be manipulated in dangerous ways," for example targeting disfavored speech that was for or against a war or other government policy.[59]

Morse leaves the law of student speech in considerable disarray. The opinion of Justice Roberts seems to create a "drug exception" to student free speech, under which school administrators can discipline students for making almost any statement that they believe promotes drug use. But, surely, drugs aren't the only significant concern of school administrators. Do exceptions exist for those other concerns as well? For alcohol consumption? Tobacco use? Teenage pregnancy? Contraception? Plus, Justice Roberts spoke here only for a plurality. How would a majority of the Court rule on these questions? We simply do not know.

Recent developments in the K-12 context have placed tremendous pressure on school administrators. They have seen spikes in student suicides and witnessed the harmful effects of bullying.[60] They have observed an increase in malicious attacks

[54] *Id.* at 407.
[55] *Id.* at 401.
[56] *Id.*
[57] *Id.* at 409.
[58] *Id.* at 423 (Alito, J., concurring).
[59] *Id.* (Alito, J., concurring).
[60] *See* Francisco M. Negrón, Jr., *Maddening Choices: The Tension between Bullying and the First Amendment in Public Schools*, 11 First Amend. L. Rev. 364, 365 (2013) (describing the

on students of color, LGBTQ students, and others. They have witnessed a drumbeat of reports of horrific school shootings. And they know that the internet and social media now allow students to disrupt educational processes when they are not even on school grounds.

Each of these pressures has led to an understandable, if not always advisable or constitutional, impulse to restrict speech. In attempting to assess what they can and cannot do, schools find little guidance in the four Supreme Court decisions just discussed. Three of those cases were decided before the internet had become a factor and two were decided before it was even invented. Most were decided before bullying was recognized for the scourge that it is, before school shootings became epidemic, and before high school students openly identified as gay. A review of some leading lower-court cases reveals the struggles that have ensued.

In a 2006 case, *Harper* v. *Poway Unified School District*, a student group sponsored an event to raise awareness of gay rights issues.[61] While the event was going on, a student with different views wore shirts that bore the phrases "I will not accept what God has condemned" and "homosexuality is shameful 'Romans 1:27.'" The school detained the student in the principal's office for doing so. In upholding the school's decision, the Ninth Circuit relied on the rarely invoked second prong of *Tinker*, finding that the T-shirt "collid[ed] with the rights of other students in the most fundamental way."[62] The dissent objected that this reasoning would seriously endanger First Amendment rights by granting students an affirmative right not to be offended.[63]

An interesting contrast to *Harper* comes in the 2008 *Nuxoll* decision from the Seventh Circuit.[64] That case addressed a school ban on a T-shirt that bore the slogan: "Be Happy, Not Gay." The school found that the shirt violated its rule against "derogatory comments ... that refer to race, ethnicity, religion, gender, sexual orientation, or disability."[65] Writing for the court, Judge Richard Posner found the school's rule to be *facially* constitutional. After all, the policy targeted derogatory comments aimed at "major components of [one's] personal identity unalterable or deeply rooted personal characteristics."[66] And, given that adolescent students may be particularly sensitive to such comments, it was foreseeable that they could lead to a "deterioration in the school's ability to educate."[67]

But Judge Posner found that this policy could not, consistent with the First Amendment, be applied to the shirt at issue there. Echoing the *Harper* dissent,

difficulty school administrators face when protecting students from bullying while avoiding First Amendment infringements).

61 Harper v. Poway Unified School Dist., 445 F.3d 1166 (9th Cir. 2006).

62 *Id.* at 1178 (quotation omitted).

63 *Id.* at 1198 (Kozinski, J., dissenting).

64 Nuxoll ex rel. Nuxoll v. Indian Prairie School Dist. No. 204, 523 F.3d 668 (7th Cir. 2008).

65 *Id.* at 670.

66 *Id.* at 671.

67 *Id.* at 672.

Judge Posner noted that "people do not have a legal right to prevent criticism of their beliefs or for that matter their way of life."[68] And he found that the shirt at issue here was only "tepidly" anti-gay and that there was no evidence it had resulted in the kind of disruption described in *Tinker*.[69]

A school administrator who reviewed those two cases might justifiably conclude they offer less than completely clear guidance. A school can apparently have a policy that prohibits derogatory comments about characteristics like LGBTQ status. But, in enforcing it, the school will have to determine whether the comment is grievously offensive or just tepidly so. How would a school make such a judgment? And how much deference should courts show those decisions?

Racially charged speech has also challenged school administrators. In a 2010 case, the Sixth Circuit upheld a school district's ban on Confederate flags in school.[70] One judge wrote separately that reducing racial tension in schools was an interest analogous to that of deterring drug use in schools, which had justified the drug speech exception apparently endorsed in *Morse*.[71]

Given the perhaps uniquely inflammatory nature of the Confederate flag, and its arguable infringement of the right of minority students to learn in a nondiscriminatory educational environment, the court's ruling may make sense – even under *Tinker*. But the invocation of *Morse* is worrisome. In *Morse*, Justice Breyer's concurring opinion had warned that the new exception for pro-drug speech could easily proliferate, because drugs were just one of many hazards faced by students. The Sixth Circuit decision appears to make his concurring opinion prophetic.[72] As Justice Breyer feared, *Morse* seems to have opened the door to a dangerous particularization of First Amendment rights, where school administrators will silence speech whenever they think an analogy can be drawn between their goals and the goal of deterring drug use.

All four of the Supreme Court decisions discussed involved speech that took place on campus or at a school-sponsored event. This left open the question of whether school administrators have any authority to control student speech when it occurs elsewhere. In a pre-internet 1979 case, the Second Circuit seemed to limit school authority to the school premises, ruling against a school that had suspended students

68 *Id.*

69 *Id.* at 676.

70 Defoe v. Spiva, 625 F.3d 324 (6th Cir. 2010).

71 *Id.* at 339 (Rogers, J. concurring) ("If we substitute 'racial conflict' or 'racial hostility' for 'drug abuse,' the analysis in *Morse* is practically on all fours with this case.") The distinction between political context and advocacy for drugs that were a crime was apparently lost on the court.

72 Morse v. Frederick, 551 U.S. 393, 426–427 (2007) (Breyer, J., concurring). In 2011, a federal district court in California granted summary judgment in favor of a school district which had prevented students from wearing American flag T-shirts on Cinco de Mayo. Dariano v. Morgan Hill Unified School Dist. 89, 822 F Supp. 2d 1037 (N.D. Cal. 2011). The court cited evidence supporting a finding of a potential for substantial disruption and even violence resulting from the shirts. *Id.* at 245.

for publishing and distributing an allegedly "morally offensive" tabloid at a local store.[73]

Over the years, though, courts became more comfortable with the idea that off-campus conduct can have in-school consequences and so should not be immune from regulation. Thus, in 2017, the Ninth Circuit ruled in favor of a school that had suspended a seventh-grader for sexually harassing two sixth-grade students with disabilities in a public park several hundred feet from school shortly after the school day ended.[74] Relying on *Tinker*, the court reasoned that sexual harassment interferes with the rights of others.[75] Though the incident had not occurred on school grounds, the court found that the offending speech was "closely tied" to the school and that the effects of the harassment could be expected to "spill over into the school environment," justifying institutional intervention.[76]

The problems presented by off-campus speech have been made greatly more acute and complex by the internet and the prevalence of social media. Courts have differed in their approaches to such speech. In 2011, the Third Circuit addressed a pair of cases in which students had created fake and very unflattering MySpace profiles of their school principals.[77] The court found that the off-campus internet speech was beyond the purview of school officials, noting a lack of substantial disruption to the school in one case and an insufficient "nexus" between the online speech and the school in the other.[78]

That same year, the Fourth Circuit seemed to reach an opposite result while addressing a student MySpace page dedicated to harassing a classmate. The page featured photographs of the classmate with drawn-on red dots intended to indicate herpes on her face and pelvic region.[79] It labeled the targeted student a "slut" and a "whore," and included various derogatory comments and photos.[80] Noting the serious consequences of student harassment and bullying, the Fourth Circuit found both a disruption and a "nexus" between the speech and school's "pedagogical

[73] Thomas v. Bd. of Ed., Granville Cent. Sch. Dist., 607 F 2d 1043, 1052 (2d Cir. 1979) ("When school officials are authorized only to punish speech on school property, the student is free to speak his mind when the school day ends").

[74] C.R. v. Eugene Sch. Dist. 4J, 835 F.3d 1142 (9th Cir. 2016), *cert denied*, 137 S.Ct. 2117 (2017).

[75] *Id.* at 1153 ("Because [the seventh-grader's] speech interfered with the younger students' rights to be secure and let alone, we conclude that his suspension was permissible under *Tinker*").

[76] *Id.* at 1150–1151.

[77] J.S. ex rel. Snyder v. Blue Mountain Sch. Dist., 650 F.3d 915, 920 (3d Cir. 2011); Layshock v. Hermitage Sch. Dist., 650 F.3d 205, 214–215 (3d Cir. 2011).

[78] *Snyder*, 650 F 3d at 920 (holding that the fake profile insinuating that the principal was a sex addict and a pedophile could not have been reasonably forecast to cause substantial disruption in school); *Layshock*, 650 F.3d 205, 214–215 (holding that the creation of the extremely unflattering fake profile did not have a sufficient "nexus" to the school to justify school intervention).

[79] Kowalski v. Berkeley Cty. Sch., 652 F 3d 565, 568 (4th Cir. 2011).

[80] *Id.* at 572–573, 577.

interests" sufficient to justify administrators' "good faith efforts" to protect its students.[81]

In the same vein, the Fifth Circuit recently upheld the punishment of a student who posted a vulgar and profane rap song containing lyrics deemed to threaten violence against two teachers at the student's high school.[82] The court stressed the "near-constant student access to social networking sites," noted that the offending lyrics were "directed at school officials," and concluded that the speech was (via Facebook) "directed toward the school community," where it could reasonably be anticipated to impact the classroom.[83] The Fifth Circuit also gave a nod to *Fraser* in considering the school's role in teaching students "the boundaries of socially appropriate behavior."[84]

In light of the horrific escalation in student-on-student violence over the years, off-campus student speech containing threats, particularly those involving potential school shootings, raise special safety concerns. Courts generally have responded sympathetically, ruling in favor of schools that have punished such messages, even when the threat was not directly conveyed to its target. Thus, in 2011 the Eighth Circuit upheld the suspension of a student for sending instant messages from home to a friend, threatening to shoot students at the school.[85] The court found it "reasonably foreseeable" that by sending such a message – even to a friend – a "substantial disruption" to the school could occur.[86] Similarly, in 2013, the Ninth Circuit upheld a suspension and temporary expulsion of a student for a sending instant messages to friends from home that bragged about his weapons and "threaten [ed] to shoot specific classmates."[87] The court relied on both of the justifications for restricting student speech outlined in *Tinker*, finding a risk of disruption at school and an interference with the rights of other classmates.[88]

It is easy to sympathize with a school's impulse to prohibit and swiftly punish any student speech that could possibly lead to violence. But, in their zeal to preserve safety, some schools plainly have gone too far.[89] For example, students have been punished for silently protesting new security measures with *Tinker*-like armbands, commenting on the possibility of a mass shooting at their own schools, publishing satirical student newspaper articles, and writing violently themed works in creative

[81] *Id.*
[82] Bell v. Itawamba Cty. Sch. Bd., 799 F 3d 379, 383 (5th Cir. 2015).
[83] *Id.* at 393, 400.
[84] *Id.* at 389–390 (quotations omitted). See also *Pulaski Cty. Special Sch. Dist.*, 306 F 3d 616, 619 (8th Cir. 2002) (en banc).
[85] D.J.M. v. Hannibal Public School District # 60, 647 F.3d 754 (8th Cir. 2011).
[86] *Id.* at 760.
[87] Wynar v. Douglas Cnty. School Dist., 728 F.3d 1062, 1064–1066 (9th Cir. 2013).
[88] *Id.* at 1065.
[89] Clay Calvert, *Free Speech and Public Schools in a Post-Columbine World: Check Your Speech Rights at the Schoolhouse Metal Detector*, 77 DENV. U. L. REV. 739 (2000); David L. Hudson, *Fear of Violence in Our Schools: Is "Undifferentiated Fear" in the Age of Columbine Leading to a Suppression of Student Speech?* 42 WASHBURN L.J. 79, 80 (2002).

writing classes.[90] Perhaps the clearest example of an overreaction was the arrest and imprisonment of a seventh-grade student for writing a violent Halloween story for a class assignment – an effort that was lauded by his teacher and received an "A" grade.[91] And, even when a particularly dark artistic expression does justify concern, we may wonder about the wisdom of responding with punitive measures that further isolate angry students and silence troubled teens who would have otherwise alerted officials of the need to make a precautionary intervention.[92]

School administrators and First Amendment scholars thought that the Court might shed some additional light on these issues in 2021 when it decided the case of *Mahanoy Area School District* v. *B. L.*[93] In that case, B. L. – a high school student who failed to make the varsity cheerleading squad – responded to her misfortune by posting on the social media platform Snapchat an image of herself with her middle finger raised and the caption: "Fuck school fuck softball fuck cheer fuck everything." The coaches of the junior cheerleading squad suspended B. L. from the team as a result.

In an opinion written by Justice Breyer, the Court decided the case on very narrow and fact-specific grounds. The Court held that B. L.'s speech was presumptively protected as criticism of circumstances she thought unfair. The Court found it important that her speech took place outside of school hours and away from school property. And the Court noted that there was little or no evidence that her speech resulted in material disruption at the school itself. Those who hoped the Supreme Court would use this case as an opportunity to offer broad clarifications of the doctrine in this area were almost certainly disappointed by its ruling. Indeed, it seems fair to say that the only principle for which the case clearly stands is that this particular student had the right to use these particular vulgarities under these particular circumstances.

Student speech in K-12 schools has proven to be one of the most vexing areas of First Amendment doctrine because compelling concerns pull us in opposing directions. On the one hand, the wisdom and optimism of *Tinker* continue to resonate with us. Students should not leave their First Amendment rights at the schoolhouse gate. If they do, then how will they become effective participants in the marketplace

[90] Clay Calvert, *Free Speech and Public Schools in a Post-Columbine World: Check Your Speech Rights at the Schoolhouse Metal Detector*, 77 Denv. U. L. Rev. 739, 739–743 (2000).

[91] *Id.* at 741.

[92] *See, e.g.*, Lavine v. Blaine Sch. Dist., 257 F.3d 981, 990 n.7 (9th Cir. 2001) ("Simply expelling a student without providing some kind of counseling or supervision might not be the best response to a school's concern for potential violence"); Lavine ex rel. Lavine v. Blaine Sch. Dist., 279 F.3d 719, 729 (9th Cir. 2002) (mem.) (Kleinfeld, J., dissenting from denial of en banc review) (warning that "[a]llowing the school to punish a student for writing a poem about a school killer may foster school killings, drying up information from students about their own and other students' emotional troubles").

[93] 141 S. Ct. 2038 (2021).

of ideas? How will they learn to think critically? How will they acquire the intellectual and communicative skills they need to contribute as members of a democracy?

On the other hand, school administrators have valid arguments for imposing some restraints. Schools must be able to accomplish the task of educating, a goal sometimes in conflict with the First Amendment ideal epitomized by a freewheeling public square. The young age of the students entrusted into the care of school administrators supports affording them narrower speech rights and broader protections from harmful speech than adults receive. Furthermore, the impressionable minds of younger students may not always carry the same capacity for discernment as their more fully developed counterparts, such as college students, leaving them vulnerable to troublesome influences and unwise counsel. And, of course, students must learn about the responsibilities that go with free expression; that speech carries consequences is certainly a lesson better learned young.[94]

In contrast to the Supreme Court's ongoing retreat from the free speech rights of K-12 students recognized in *Tinker*, the free speech rights of university students have fared much better. In 1972, the Supreme Court upheld the First Amendment rights of a leftist student group that had been denied recognition based on its alleged advocacy of "destruction" and other acts of civil disobedience.[95] The Court approvingly cited *Tinker* in support of student rights against encroaching government "enclaves immune from the sweep of the First Amendment."[96] But the Court seemed to go even further than *Tinker*, holding that college campuses bear a "heavy burden" to demonstrate that censorship was required to avoid serious disruption.[97] The Court also appeared to do away with the controversial second *Tinker* exception in the college context when, in its concluding paragraph, it listed "infringement of the rights of others" as one of the necessary costs of free speech.[98]

The next year, the Supreme Court once again protected university student speech rights, this time in a short but illuminating *per curiam* decision. In *Papish* v. *Board of Curators of the University of Missouri*,[99] a graduate student in the school of journalism was expelled for distributing a school newspaper article entitled "Motherfucker Acquitted," which included a cartoon of police raping the Statue of Liberty.[100] The school found the article to be in violation of its policy against "indecent conduct or

[94] *See, e.g.*, Kowalski v. Berkeley Cty. Sch., 652 F 3d 565, 568 (4th Cir. 2011) (finding for school which punished student for defamatory social media page targeting classmate as a "slut" and a "whore" and claiming she had herpes); Doe v. Pulaski Cty. Special Sch. Dist., 306 F 3d 616, 619 (8th Cir. 2002) (en banc) (upholding expulsion of eighth-grader who wrote a threatening letter to his ex-girlfriend).

[95] Healy v. James, 408 U.S. 169, 187–188 (1972).

[96] *Id.* at 180.

[97] *Id.* at 184.

[98] *Id.* at 194.

[99] Papish v. Board of Curators of the University of Missouri, 410 U.S. 667 (1973).

[100] *Id.*

speech."[101] The Court upheld the student's challenge to the expulsion, finding that the "mere dissemination of ideas – no matter how offensive to good taste – on a state university campus may not be shut off in the name alone of conventions of decency."[102]

Although elementary and high school students lost all three of the Supreme Court decisions that immediately followed *Tinker*, university student speech rights went undefeated during this same period.[103] The reasons for the difference in the outcomes are perhaps obvious. College students are older and should enjoy the freedoms that go with adulthood.[104] And, in our society, universities have a special role in fostering open debate, rather than indoctrination.[105] As discussed in Chapter 4 and in our consideration of the Everyday First Amendment, the Supreme Court has recognized institutions of higher education as our quintessential marketplaces of ideas. Though lower courts occasionally have riled critics by imposing unprotective secondary school speech case law onto the university level, Supreme Court decisions have come down firmly on the side of protecting university student speech.[106]

In the 1960s and 1970s, campus free speech issues largely revolved around the right to protest. In the 1980s, the focus shifted. In response to growing concerns about the demeaning and stigmatizing effects of speech that targeted members of historically marginalized groups, hundreds of colleges adopted so-called hate speech codes.[107] The creation and implementation of such codes was complicated by the fact that, as discussed in Chapter 12, the Supreme Court has never carved out hate speech as a category of expression that falls outside the protections of the First Amendment.

The issue raised significant debates centered around the competing goals of free speech, dignity, and equality. Proponents of such codes argued for the need to foster

[101] *Id.* at 668.

[102] *Id.* at 670.

[103] Meggen Lindsay, *Tinker Goes to College: Why High School Free-Speech Standards Should Not Apply to Post-secondary Students – Tatro v. University of Minnesota*, 38 WM. MITCHELL L. REV. 1470, 1482–1483 (2012) ("[T]he Supreme Court has never upheld a student-speech restriction at the university level").

[104] *Id.* at 1482–1483 (noting that schools are expected to stand in the role of parents when in custody of minor students, as opposed to adult college students).

[105] The *Healy* Court approvingly referenced academic freedom and the college as "peculiarly the 'marketplace of ideas'" in support of student speech rights. Healy v. James, 408 U.S. 169, 180–181 (1972).

[106] *See, e.g.*, Meggen Lindsay, *Tinker Goes to College: Why High School Free-Speech Standards Should Not Apply to Post-secondary Students – Tatro v. University of Minnesota*, 38 WM. MITCHELL L. REV. 1470, 1482–1483 (2012) (criticizing a lower court's weak application of *Tinker* but noting that the Supreme Court "has not linked high school- and college-speech rights"); Frank D. LoMonte, *The Key Word Is Student: Hazelwood Censorship Crashes the Ivy-Covered Gates*, 11 FIRST AMEND. L. REV. 305, 309 (2013) (criticizing a lower court using *Hazelwood's* curricular exception in the college setting).

[107] *See* TIMOTHY C. SHIELL, CAMPUS HATE SPEECH ON TRIAL 1–5 (2009).

a welcoming environment and protect the safety, mental health, and emotional security of students who were members of traditionally oppressed or stigmatized groups.[108] Constitutional scholars disagreed over whether it was possible to regulate such expression without also punishing obviously protected speech.[109] Opponents warned that such well-intentioned efforts were fatally vague and over-broad, and that they would inevitably become the tools of the powerful to censor minorities.[110]

Conceptual and line-drawing problems abounded. If a state cannot adopt a law that bans flag-burning because it outrages some people, then how can a public university adopt a speech code that bans demeaning speech based on its offensiveness? And questions were raised about whether the proponents of speech codes had thought through the consequences of allowing them. After all, if a public university can impose a "prescribed orthodoxy" on its campus, then what prevents the majority from weaponizing that power to silence minority viewpoints?

The proponents of these codes have good intentions and their arguments have moral force. The goal of fostering a diverse, welcoming, and inclusive campus environment is a critical one, particularly if institutions of higher education seek to prepare their students to live and thrive in a multicultural world. But speech codes have proven themselves a legally unworkable tool for achieving that goal. Indeed, as of the writing of this book, the courts have struck down every public university speech code that has been challenged on First Amendment grounds.[111] They remain a legally viable option for *private* institutions, but, as discussed Chapter 4, many of those schools have rejected the adoption of such codes on the grounds that they are inconsistent with the sort of robust academic freedom they want to foster on campus.

For many years, the debate over these codes (and other campus speech issues) seemed to be at an impasse. Two factions emerged. And their adherents dug in their heels.

Absolutists argued that colleges should not adopt policies that in any way chilled the full and frank discussion of all issues on campus. The absolutists had a point: institutions of higher education have a special role in our society as marketplaces of

[108] *See, e.g.*, JEREMY WALDRON, THE HARM IN HATE SPEECH 8–9 (2012); Richard Delgado, *Words that Wound: A Tort Action for Racial Insults, Epithets, and Name Calling*, in Mari Matsuda et al. (eds.), WORDS THAT WOUND 94 (1993); Mari J. Matsuda, *Public Response to Racist Speech: Considering the Victim's Story*, in Mari Matsuda et al. (eds.), WORDS THAT WOUND 24 (1993); Charles R. Lawrence III, *If He Hollers Let Him Go: Regulating Racist Speech on Campus*, in Mari Matsuda et al. (eds.), WORDS THAT WOUND 62 (1993).

[109] *Compare id.* (all arguing in favor of hate speech codes) with *Chemerinsky*, FREE SPEECH ON CAMPUS 104 (2017) (concluding that hate speech codes are "inherently vague" and "inherently politically charged," chilling speech on critical issues and leading to arbitrary and surprising results).

[110] *Id.* at 104–110 (providing historical and modern examples of hate speech codes used against minorities and for political purposes).

[111] ERWIN CHEMERINSKY AND HOWARD GILMAN, FREE SPEECH ON CAMPUS 97 (2017). *See, e.g.*, Doe v. Univ. of Michigan, 721 F. Supp. 852, 853 (E.D. Mich. 1989).

ideas, and members of healthy university communities will necessarily encounter language and ideas that offend them. Plus, some of the positions taken by the proponents of speech codes were extreme and lent themselves to caricature. Unfortunately, these dynamics led many absolutists to be dismissive of minority concerns.

On the other side, relativists argued that universities had failed to make their campuses welcoming places for minorities. The relativists had a point, too: colleges were not doing enough to address the marginalization, alienation, and discrimination that many minority students (and faculty, for that matter) were experiencing. Plus, absolutists often fulfilled a caricature of their own, glibly elevating an abstract principle over the struggles of those who are most often targeted by its abuses. Unfortunately, these dynamics led many relativists to be dismissive of the value of free speech.

Still, in recent years some absolutists and some relativists have come to take more nuanced approaches. Absolutists have become increasingly conscious of the challenges that minorities face, including because of factors like structural discrimination. Absolutists may continue to believe that speech codes are not the way to address those problems. But at least they have become better at acknowledging that the problems exist, are serious and pervasive, and deserves our best efforts to solve.

For their part, relativists recently have witnessed fresh examples of the power of free speech in amplifying minority viewpoints and mobilizing movements toward equality and justice. The murder of George Floyd (and, tragically, too many others to name here) prompted one of the largest international public demonstrations in the history of the world. Relativists may continue to believe that our First Amendment doctrine does not get things exactly right. But some have become better at recognizing the indispensable role it plays in achieving a more equal and just union.

Controversies and disagreements about free speech on campus will continue. But these movements in the positions of at least some absolutists and relativists provide space for productive dialogue. And such conversations are essential if we are to continue to make progress in addressing problems that have bedeviled us since the foundation of the republic.

15

Academic Freedom

In Chapter 14, we considered the issue of student speech. In this chapter, we shift our attention to faculty and to educational institutions themselves. The right of faculty to engage in the uncensored exchange of ideas, and of institutions to create space for them to do so, is traditionally referred to as "academic freedom."

Although the concept of academic freedom has a long and important history, and although it is frequently invoked in discussions about rights on college campuses, it remains difficult to define. It invites many questions that do not lend themselves to easy answers. Who within the academic community enjoys the right? The school, administrators, faculty, or students? Or all of them? When freedoms collide, whose preferences prevail? For example, if a university wishes to limit the speech of a professor, whose prerogatives have greater force? Is academic freedom just a norm, a widely embraced way of doing business within these institutions? Or is it a contractual concept, made enforceable through the practice of tenure? Or is it a constitutional principle? And, if the last, then where does the Constitution provide for it?

We begin with the long history of institutions embracing academic freedom as a norm. This practice goes back at least to medieval European universities and the idea of a community of teachers and scholars who study and teach in pursuit of the discovery of knowledge.[1] Later, German universities clarified that while this right of expression existed "within the university," it did not extend outside.[2] In the European tradition, universities became enclaves of freer thought than was generally tolerated outside their walls.

Before the American Civil War, academic freedom as a concept was foreign to American universities and colleges. This is perhaps unsurprising, given that these

[1] Thomas I. Emerson, The System of Freedom of Expression 193 (1970).

[2] *Id. See also* Matthew W. Finkin and Robert C. Post, For the Common Good 1, 22 (2009). Despite the originally limited scope of academic freedom, its arrival to the United States did not detract from pre-existing general free speech rights granted by the First Amendment to all citizens wishing to express their thoughts in the community. *Id.*

schools generally viewed their mission as that of transmitting traditional views and established knowledge to their students, many of whom were training for religious work.[3] Faculty members were employed and retained at the preferences of administrators and trustees and had little security in their positions.[4]

In contrast, German institutions embraced the culture of *lehrfreiheit*, literally meaning the freedom to teach what one wants but generally understood to refer to a broader concept of academic freedom. Within this culture, faculty enjoyed the freedom to engage in research and teaching in an "atmosphere of consent that surrounded the whole process of research and instruction," which was well understood by professors, students, and administrators as a "distinctive prerogative of the academic profession," free from administrative interference.[5] By the end of the nineteenth century, as the Industrial Revolution demonstrated the tangible benefits of creating new knowledge through research, the principles of *lehrfreiheit* began to take root in the United States.[6]

In 1913, Professor Arthur Lovejoy at Johns Hopkins University circulated a letter that led to 600 professors agreeing to form the American Association of University Professors (AAUP).[7] By 1915, the AAUP had published a General Declaration that, among other things, explicitly referred to academic freedom as a defining principle of higher education.[8] In a 1940 *Statement of Principles*, the AAUP set forth the rationale for academic freedom:

> Institutions of higher education are conducted for the common good and not to further the interest of either the individual teacher or the institution as a whole. The common good depends upon the free search for truth and its free exposition.

[3] J. Peter Byrne wrote the most influential analysis of a constitutional element of academic freedom, in which he notes the limited purposes of early American colleges. J. Peter Byrne, *Academic Freedom: A "Special Concern of the First Amendment,"* 99 YALE L.J. 251, 269 (1989). Richard Hofstadter and Walter P. Metzger wrote what remains the most comprehensive history of academic freedom's arrival to the United States as a professional norm in their 1955 book. RICHARD HOFSTADTER AND WALTER P. METZGER, THE DEVELOPMENT OF ACADEMIC FREEDOM IN THE UNITED STATES 278–279 (1955).

[4] J. Peter Byrne, *Academic Freedom: A "Special Concern of the First Amendment,"* 99 YALE L.J. 251, 268–269 (1989).

[5] RICHARD HOFSTADTER AND WALTER P. METZGER, DEVELOPMENT OF ACADEMIC FREEDOM IN THE UNITED STATES 386–387 (1955).

[6] Lawrence White, *Fifty Years of Academic Freedom Jurisprudence*, 36 J.C. & U.L. 791, 796–797 (2010) ("Exposure to German academic governance opened the eyes of nineteenth-century American scholars to the hitherto radical notion that academic freedom protected faculty members from the very powers that were responsible for their appointment and continued employment: trustees and administrators"). Johns Hopkins University, founded in 1876, was the first American University offering graduate education in the German model of research and academic freedom. *Id.*

[7] *Id.* at 800.

[8] *General Report of the Committee on Academic Tenure* (1915), in FREEDOM AND TENURE IN THE ACADEMY 393, 393 (William W. Van Alstyne ed., 1993).

> Academic freedom is essential to these purposes and applies to both teaching and research. Freedom in research is fundamental to the advancement of truth. Academic freedom in its teaching aspect is fundamental for the protection of the rights of the teacher in teaching and of the student to freedom in learning. It carries with it duties correlative with rights.[9]

The foundational AAUP statement thus broadly defined academic freedom, although it underscored that with this freedom came responsibility.

In one important respect, the AAUP statement went beyond the German model. In addition to supporting academic freedom in both teaching and research, it defended faculty freedom of expression of personal opinion outside of the university context.[10] The 1940 *Statement* has enjoyed the universal endorsement of major higher education organizations across the United States.[11]

Despite its meteoric rise as an institutional norm, academic freedom struggled to gain footing as a legal principle. The first time the term appeared in a court decision was apparently the 1940 case, *Kay* v. *Board of Higher Education of the City of New York*.[12] That case involved the British philosopher Bertrand Russell, who was not only a respected academic but an emerging public intellectual. His religious skepticism and his advocacy of what were deemed to be "immoral and salacious doctrines" resulted in legal proceedings under state law to revoke his appointment to the City College of New York.[13]

The trial court judge ordered Russell's offer of employment revoked, dismissively referring to academic freedom as so-called.[14] The judge went on to declare that he would "not tolerate academic freedom being used as a cloak to promote the popularization in the minds of adolescents acts forbidden by the Penal Law." Assuming the mantle of the official who (in the words of *Barnette*) decides what shall be orthodox, the court announced that "[t]his appointment affects the public health, safety, and morals of the community and it is the duty of the court to act. Academic freedom does not mean academic license."[15]

Notwithstanding this inauspicious court debut, academic freedom eventually made its way into the lexicon of the United States Supreme Court. In large part, this was due to McCarthy-era attempts to purge public institutions of leftist sympathizers and others. Those purges called the question of when faculty members could be penalized for their speech or ideology.

9 American Association of University Professors, 1940 *Statement of Principles on Academic Freedom and Tenure with 1970 Interpretive Comments*, in AAUP POLICY DOCUMENTS & REPORTS 3–11 (10th ed. 2006).

10 *Id.*

11 J. Peter Byrne, *Academic Freedom: A "Special Concern of the First Amendment,"* 99 YALE L.J. 251, 279 (1989).

12 Kay v. Board of Higher Education of the City of New York, 18 N.Y.S. 2d 821 (1940).

13 *Id.* at 826.

14 *Id.* at 829.

15 *Id.*

Academic freedom made its first appearance in a Supreme Court opinion in Justice Douglas' dissent to the 1952 case, *Adler* v. *Board of Education of the City of New York*.[16] Interestingly, that case arose in the public school context. In *Adler*, the Court upheld a New York statute that denied employment to teachers who were employed by public institutions and who had been shown to be a "subversive person," concluding that such individuals have no right to work for the state in the school system "on their own terms." The phrase "on their own terms" left open the possibility that *some* right to work as a state teacher existed, even if not an expansive one; but that reassurance was frail and ambiguous at best.

Justice Douglas's dissent expressed concern that the law would "raise havoc with academic freedom," causing a "pall [to be] cast over the classrooms."[17] Justice Douglas was no stranger to the academy: he had taught at the Yale Law School before joining the Court. He observed that "[w]here suspicion fills the air and holds scholars in line for fear of their jobs, there can be no exercise of the free intellect."[18]

Later that same year, in *Wieman* v. *Updegraff*,[19] the Court appeared to reverse course. It struck down an Oklahoma law instituting a political loyalty requirement for public employees, a popular tool at the time for trying to weed out leftist faculty. Noting the "time of cold war and hot emotions," the majority avoided the oath's First Amendment implications; instead it concluded that the law suffered from fatal due process infirmities.[20]

In a concurrence joined by Justice Douglas, Justice Frankfurter, a former Harvard Law School professor, lauded the values associated with academic freedom, though not naming it as such. Focusing on the law's implications for classroom teachers, he opined:

> The process of education has naturally enough been the basis of hope for the perdurance of our democracy on the part of all our great leaders, from Thomas Jefferson onwards.
>
> To regard teachers – in our entire educational system, from the primary grades to the university – as the priests of our democracy is therefore not to indulge in hyperbole. It is the special task of teachers to foster those habits of open-mindedness and critical inquiry which alone make for responsible citizens, who, in turn, make possible an enlightened and effective public opinion.
>
> Teachers must fulfill their function by precept and practice, by the very atmosphere which they generate; they must be exemplars of open-mindedness and free inquiry. They cannot carry out their noble task if the conditions for the practice of a

16 Adler v. Board of Education of the City of New York, 342 U.S. 485 (1952).
17 *Id.* at 394 (Douglas, J., dissenting).
18 *Id.*
19 Wieman v. Updegraff, 344 U.S. 183, 189 (1952).
20 *Id.* at 191. Despite acknowledging the obvious First Amendment concern that "[t]o thus inhibit individual freedom of movement is to stifle the flow of democratic expression and controversy at one of its chief sources," Justice Clark rested his decision on the possibility that an individual could unknowingly associate with a group proscribed under the law. *Id.*

> responsible and critical mind are denied to them. They must have the freedom of responsible inquiry, by thought and action, into the meaning of social and economic ideas, into the checkered history of social and economic dogma. They must be free to sift evanescent doctrine, qualified by time and circumstance, from that restless, enduring process of extending the bounds of understanding and wisdom, to assure which the freedoms of thought, of speech, of inquiry, of worship are guaranteed by the Constitution of the United States against infraction by national or State government.[21]

We have quoted this passage at length because it embodies an important idea: it links academic freedom to the First Amendment. And, in turn, it connects free expression with the fostering of democracy: "the one reason," Justice Frankfurter wrote, "that we know that every totalitarian government must fail is that no totalitarian government is prepared to face the consequences of creating free universities."[22]

Justice Frankfurter obviously did not set out here a detailed and comprehensive theory of academic freedom. Distinctions between faculty research, publication, classroom instruction, and personal advocacy were left unexamined. Despite these gaps, however, his concurring opinion laid the groundwork for viewing academic freedom as a constitutional right, rather than merely a professional norm. And it gave that constitutional status a source: the First Amendment.

Five years later, academic freedom made another step toward constitutional status in the Supreme Court opinion in *Sweezy* v. *State of New Hampshire*.[23] During a criminal inquiry by the attorney general pursuant to a state "subversive activities act," Professor Sweezy had refused to answer questions about the contents of a lecture he had delivered in a humanities class at the University of New Hampshire.[24] The lower court was unsympathetic to Professor Sweezy's First Amendment objection to such questioning and ordered him jailed for contempt.[25]

Writing for a four-justice plurality, Chief Justice Warren reasoned that the contempt order was invalid on due process grounds, avoiding the First Amendment issue. Chief Justice Warren, nevertheless, gave a passing nod to the values of academic freedom:

> The essentiality of freedom in the community of American universities is almost self-evident. No one should underestimate the vital role in a democracy that is played by those who guide and train our youth. To impose any strait jacket upon

[21] *Id.* 196–197 (Frankfurter, J., concurring).

[22] *Id.* 197–198 (Frankfurter, J., concurring) (quoting Statement of Robert M. Hutchins (a former president of the University of Chicago and former dean of the Yale School), Associate Director of the Ford Foundation, November 25, 1952, in Hearings before the House Select Committee to Investigate Tax-exempt Foundations and Comparable Organizations, pursuant to H.Res. 561, 82d Cong., 2d Sess).

[23] Sweezy v. State of New Hampshire, 354 U.S. 234 (1957).

[24] *Id.* at 243. One such question was: "Didn't you tell the class at the University of New Hampshire on Monday, March 22, 1954, that Socialism was inevitable in this country?" *Id.*

[25] *Id.* at 244–245.

> the intellectual leaders in our colleges and universities would imperil the future of our Nation. No field of education is so thoroughly comprehended by man that new discoveries cannot yet be made. Particularly is that true in the social sciences, where few, if any, principles are accepted as absolutes. Scholarship cannot flourish in an atmosphere of suspicion and distrust. Teachers and students must always remain free to inquire, to study and to evaluate, to gain new maturity and understanding; otherwise our civilization will stagnate and die.[26]

Chief Justice Warren's opinion followed a pattern that was becoming established in the Supreme Court's references to academic freedom: powerful and expansive rhetoric in support of the idea; dire predictions of where our society would be without it; but little or no detail to render the principle clear or operationally useful.

Sweezy, however, is most often remembered for the concurring opinion written by Justice Frankfurter and joined in by Justice Harlan. Justice Frankfurter once more lauded the societal benefits of fostering pan-disciplinary intellectual exploration at universities, free from political intervention:

> Progress in the natural sciences is not remotely confined to findings made in the laboratory. Insights into the mysteries of nature are born of hypothesis and speculation. The more so is this true in the pursuit of understanding in the groping endeavors of what are called the social sciences, the concern of which is man and society. The problems that are the respective preoccupations of anthropology, economics, law, psychology, sociology and related areas of scholarship are merely departmentalized dealing, by way of manageable division of analysis, with interpenetrating aspects of holistic perplexities. For society's good – if understanding be an essential need of society – inquiries into these problems, speculations about them, stimulation in others of reflection upon them, must be left as unfettered as possible. Political power must abstain from intrusion into this activity of freedom, pursued in the interest of wise government and the people's well-being, except for reasons that are exigent and obviously compelling.

These sentiments, while eloquently expressed, still had not yet found their way into a majority opinion and it remained difficult to understand how this rhapsodic language translated into legal principles of practical utility.

It was not until 1967 that academic freedom finally played a significant role in a Supreme Court majority opinion. In *Keyishian* v. *Board of Regents of the University of the State of New York*,[27] the Court again addressed a state law requiring employees of public colleges and universities to sign a certificate declaring that they were not members of the Communist Party. Although the Court decided the case on the grounds that the law was unconstitutionally vague, its endorsement of academic freedom was its most powerful yet.[28] Writing for the Court, Justice Brennan declared:

[26] *Id*. at 250.
[27] Keyishian v. Board of Regents of the University of the State of New York, 385 U.S. 589 (1967).
[28] *Id*. at 599.

> Our Nation is deeply committed to safeguarding academic freedom, which is of transcendent value to all of us and not merely to the teachers concerned. That freedom is therefore a special concern of the First Amendment, which does not tolerate laws that cast a pall of orthodoxy over the classroom. The vigilant protection of constitutional freedoms is nowhere more vital than in the community of American schools. The classroom is peculiarly the "marketplace of ideas." The Nation's future depends upon leaders trained through wide exposure to that robust exchange of ideas which discovers truth out of a multitude of tongues, rather than through any kind of authoritative selection.[29]

In this passage, the Court does not just link academic freedom to the First Amendment but to the core value of truth-finding and to the marketplace of ideas. This would become some of the Court's most frequently quoted language regarding the principle of academic freedom.

Still, *Keyishian* has not met with universal praise. In particular, some have argued that the references to the "marketplace of ideas" and the "discovery of truth out of a multitude of tongues" seem out of place in the academic context. In the academy, the argument goes, truth is determined not by an idea's popularity but by other criteria, such as the use of falsifiable hypotheses, experimentation, verification, and peer review.[30] According to one scholar:

> [i]f a marketplace of ideas model were to be imposed upon *Nature* or the *American Economic Review* or *The Lancet*, we would very rapidly lose track of whatever expertise we possess about the nature of the world. Contemporary technical expertise is created by practices that demand *both* critical freedom to inquire *and* affirmative disciplinary virtues of methodological care.[31]

This criticism may, however, be unfair. After all, in describing the marketplace of ideas Holmes suggests that he primarily has in mind matters of opinion, not fact. And, with respect to facts, nothing in the marketplace of ideas theory inherently excludes processes like rigorous scientific enquiry in our effort to discern the truth.

Despite *Keyishian*'s strong majority endorsement of academic freedom, questions remained about the depth, breadth, vigor, and application of the principle. As a result, lower-court decisions have been marked by unpredictability and inconsistency.[32] In 1979, for example, the Seventh Circuit deemed "patently frivolous" a

[29] *Id.* at 603 (quotations and alterations omitted).

[30] J. Peter Byrne, *Academic Freedom: A "Special Concern of the First Amendment,"* 99 Yale L.J. 251, 297 (1989).

[31] Robert C. Post, Democracy, Expertise, and Academic Freedom: A First Amendment Jurisprudence for the Modern State xii (2012).

[32] J. Peter Byrne, *Academic Freedom: A "Special Concern of the First Amendment,"* 99 Yale L.J. 251, 291 (1989); *see also* Judith Areen, *Government as Educator: A New Understanding of First Amendment Protection of Academic Freedom and Governance*, 97 Geo. L.J. 945, 999 (2009) ("In 1968, however, the Court began to use public-employee speech jurisprudence to decide faculty-speech cases. That change reduced the amount of constitutional protection provided for academic freedom").

faculty member's claim that the First Amendment forbade the university from declining to renew his contract on the basis that his research area overlapped with that of an already tenured professor at the school.[33] It may seem unclear why such a claim would lack merit, let alone be patently frivolous, if academic freedom offers expansive and robust protection to thought.

In contrast, in 1990, the Second Circuit sided with a professor of Africana studies who alleged that he had been denied tenure for equating some aspects of Zionism with racism in his course on "The Politics of Race."[34] The faculty member – who, the court pointed out, previously had been expelled from his native South Africa for his outspoken criticism of apartheid – became a lightning rod for controversy, engendering complaints from the Anti-Defamation League of B'nai Brith and the American Jewish Committee.[35] The Court cited *Keyishian* and *Sweezy* and held that "for decades it has been clearly established that the First Amendment tolerates neither laws nor other means of coercion, persuasion or intimidation that cast a pall of orthodoxy over the free exchange of ideas in the classroom."[36]

When institutional and faculty preferences have conflicted, the general trend has been toward holding that the former prevail. Thus, in 1998 the Third Circuit brushed aside a faculty member's complaint that his First Amendment rights had been violated when the department and university leadership ordered him to cease using religious "doctrinaire material" in his "Introduction to Educational Media" class.[37] Then Judge Samuel Alito responded to the professor's academic freedom argument by concluding that he did "not have a constitutional right to choose curriculum materials in contravention of the University's dictates."[38]

In a 2000 case that attracted considerable attention, the Fourth Circuit addressed a Virginia statute that restricted faculty use of state-owned or leased computers to access sexually explicit materials without express permission.[39] The court – noting that "the Supreme Court has never set aside a state regulation" on academic freedom grounds – rejected the claim that "academic freedom of professors is not only a professional norm, but also a constitutional right."[40] Rather, the Fourth Circuit reasoned, "the best that can be said" for a claim of faculty academic freedom

[33] McElearney v. Univ. of Illinois at Chicago Circle Campus, 612 F 2d 285, 288 (7th Cir. 1979).

[34] Dube v. State Univ. of New York, 900 F 2d 587, 589 (2d Cir. 1990).

[35] *Id.* at 590.

[36] *Id.* at 598.

[37] Edwards v. California Univ. of Pennsylvania, 156 F.3d 488, 489–490 (3d Cir. 1998).

[38] *Id.* at 492. Grading, like syllabus selection, also has been a subject of controversy. In Lovelace v. SE Massachusetts Univ., 793 F.2d 419, 425 (1st Cir. 1986), the First Circuit rejected a faculty member's claim that academic freedom protected his decision not to "inflate" grades or "lower his expectations" of students at the administration's bequest. The court held that the university was empowered to set grade expectations and that "[t]he first amendment does not require that each nontenured professor be made a sovereign unto himself." *Id.* at 426.

[39] Urofsky v. Gilmore, 216 F.3d 401, 410–412 (4th Cir. 2000).

[40] *Id.* at 411–412.

is that "teachers were the first public employees to be afforded the now-universal protection against dismissal for the exercise of First Amendment rights."[41]

In essence, the Fourth Circuit took the view that academic freedom belongs to the institution, not to the individual faculty member.[42] The Fourth Circuit acknowledged that the First Amendment does afford *some* protection to faculty members at public institutions. But, the court opined, that is simply because they are public employees.

As discussed in Chapter 8, things are not so simple. The *Garcetti* decision addressed the free speech rights of public employees generally.[43] And it signaled that academic freedom may afford faculty members greater rights than other public employees enjoy.

As we noted there, *Garcetti* created a new rule with respect to public employees. It held that "when public employees make statements pursuant to their official duties, the employees are not speaking as citizens for First Amendment purposes. The Constitution therefore does not insulate their communications from employer discipline."[44] In sum, when acting pursuant to "official duties," public employees have *no* First Amendment rights.

In his dissent, Justice Souter stated that he "hope[d] that today's majority does not mean to imperil First Amendment protection of academic freedom in public colleges and universities, whose teachers necessarily speak and write pursuant to official duties."[45] Justice Souter's comment prompted a brief but important response by the majority:

> There is some argument that expression related to academic scholarship or classroom instruction implicates additional constitutional interests that are not fully accounted for by this Court's customary employee-speech jurisprudence. We need not, and for that reason do not, decide whether the analysis we conduct today would apply in the same manner to a case involving speech related to scholarship or teaching.[46]

The majority's language ("there is some argument") hardly stands as a ringing endorsement of faculty rights to academic freedom. The full-throated embrace of the concept that we heard in the opinions of Justices Frankfurter, Warren, and Brennan is conspicuous in its absence. But it is significant that the majority took

[41] *Id.* at 415.
[42] *Id.*
[43] Garcetti v. Ceballos, 547 U.S. 410 (2006).
[44] *Id.* at 421.
[45] *Garcetti*, 547 U.S. at 438 (Souter, J. dissenting) (quotations and alterations omitted).
[46] *Id.* at 425. See also Robert C. Post, Democracy, Expertise, and Academic Freedom: A First Amendment Jurisprudence for the Modern State 93 (2012). Professor Post warns that faculty viewed as mere employees under *Garcetti* would no longer be able to produce necessary new knowledge, leading to "dire" consequences including economic and military failure. *Id.* at 92–93.

Justice Souter's objection seriously and emphasized that it did not intend to foreclose the possibility that the rule announced there should apply differently, or not at all, with respect to faculty employment disputes.

Since *Garcetti*, the Supreme Court has not decided another case addressing the academic freedom of faculty members. This has left lower courts to determine how and when, if at all and ever, *Garcetti* applies to faculty members. The resulting jurisprudence is complex.

Indeed, at first blush it may appear that the post-*Garcetti* higher education decisions in the lower courts are a crazy, inconsistent patchwork. On closer examination, however, a pattern emerges within the decisions.[47] It might be described as a trend in which the courts are inclined to protect "core" academic activity, like classroom teaching, but to be much less protective of public university employees who have nonacademic roles or whose speech does not fit within that "core" category.

It is easiest to begin by considering nonfaculty employees of colleges and universities. Institutions of higher education have many lower- and mid-level employees whose job responsibilities do not differ substantially from those of their nonacademic counterparts. In these circumstances, application of the *Garcetti* standard in the higher education context typically does not pose any distinct challenges. For example, the analysis necessary to determine whether a campus police officer spoke in their official capacity is unlikely to differ substantially from that necessary to determine whether any other kind of police officer spoke in their official capacity.[48]

High-level university leaders and administrators are more complicated. They often have portfolios of management responsibility that are large and diverse. As a result, it may be difficult for them to argue that their speech regarding a university matter fell outside of their duties. Consider, for example, *Vila* v. *Padron*.[49] In that case, the court held that statements made by a vice president of external affairs, a broad policy-making position, related to her expansive authority at the college and so were unprotected. In addition, because these individuals may hold only courtesy faculty appointments (with no research or teaching responsibilities), or no faculty appointment at all, their speech may not implicate issues of core academic freedom.

As we would expect, the most complicated application of *Garcetti* comes with respect to faculty members. This is so for two reasons.

First, as a threshold matter it may be difficult to discern whether certain conduct falls within a faculty member's job responsibilities. Obviously, teaching and research typically do. But what about administrative and quasi-administrative work for which he or she receives no additional compensation? Voluntary committee service?

[47] For an early assessment of the post-*Garcetti* lower court cases, *see* Leonard M. Niehoff, *Peculiar Marketplace: Applying Garcetti v. Ceballos in the Public Higher Education Context*, 35 J. Coll. & Univ. L. 75 (2008).

[48] *See, e.g.*, Bradley v. James, 479 F.3d 536 (8th Cir. 2007).

[49] Vila v. Padron, 484 F.3d 1334 (11th Cir. 2007).

Informal presentations? Counseling, mentoring, and advising students? Writing op-eds for external publications? Appearing on television and radio? Tweeting?

On the one hand, the breadth of activity by many faculty members suggests that a wide array of things may fall within their "responsibilities." On the other hand, many faculty members elect not to engage in some of these activities, like participation in social media. Does that suggest those activities are not part of their academic job description?

Second, if conduct *does* fall within a faculty member's job responsibilities, then – as Justice Souter argued in his dissent – *Garcetti* leaves us with a serious problem. Under *Garcetti*, most public employees have fewer or no rights when they speak as part of their official position. But the job responsibilities of faculty include engaging in speech that academic freedom protects. How, then, does *Garcetti* apply here, if at all?

A few distinct trends have emerged in the lower-court cases where this issue has arisen. Some courts – invoking the objections raised in Justice Souter's dissent and the response from the majority in *Garcetti* – have concluded that the *Garcetti* analysis simply does not apply to faculty members. They therefore proceed directly to the analysis set forth in *Pickering* and *Connick*, discussed in Chapter 8. For these courts, the *Garcetti* analysis isn't complicated – it's nonexistent. This doesn't mean that the college will necessarily be powerless to act; it could do so, for example, if the speech were sufficiently disruptive under the *Pickering–Connick* test. Rather, it means that faculty speech doesn't lose all protection simply because it was made as part of the faculty member's job.

Other courts have concluded that it is at least possible that *Garcetti* applies and have looked closely at the faculty member's conduct, distinguishing those things that typically implicate academic freedom (like teaching and scholarship) from those things that usually do not (like administrative work). This application of *Garcetti* can get complicated quickly.

Some of the early post-*Garcetti* cases involved speech that occurred primarily with respect to administrative matters. Consider, for example, *Hong* v. *Grant*.[50] In that case, Hong, a faculty member, made various negative comments about colleagues in the process of conducting peer reviews and about the faculty assigned to teach certain courses. He sued when the university decided not to give him a merit increase in pay, alleging that it had retaliated against him for engaging in this speech. The court granted summary judgment to the university, finding that Hong had made the statements as part of his job responsibilities. The court noted that in light of the university's strong principle of faculty self-governance, Hong's duties were not limited to instruction and research but also included "a wide range of academic, administrative and personnel functions."

[50] Hong v. Grant, 516 F. Supp. 2d 1158 (C.D. Cal. 2007).

Or consider *Renken v. Gregory*.[51] Renken, a faculty member, served as the principal investigator (PI) of a National Science Foundation (NSF) grant. In the course of administering the grant, he complained about the university's use of the funds. Renken alleged that, as a result of this speech, the university returned the NSF funding and reduced his pay. He sued, claiming a violation of his First Amendment rights. The district court granted summary judgment in the university's favor, finding that Renken had engaged in the speech as part of his official duties as a faculty member and PI, meaning his speech was not constitutionally protected. The Seventh Circuit affirmed. Again, the quasi-administrative quality of the speech in question likely made a difference here.

On the other hand, courts have been much less inclined to apply *Garcetti* where the speech in question arose in the context of classroom teaching or publishing. For example, in *Demers v. Austin*[52] a tenured associate professor at a public university claimed that the school retaliated against him for statements he made in a pamphlet and drafts of an in-progress book. The court concluded that *Garcetti* "does not apply to teaching and writing on academic matters by teachers employed by the state." The court held that the *Pickering–Connick* analysis applied to the speech, which addressed a matter of public concern, and remanded for further proceedings.

A similar holding came in *Adams v. Trustees of the University of North Carolina-Wilmington*.[53] There, a criminology professor claimed that he was denied promotion to full professor in retaliation for the conservative and Christian tone of his writings. Finding that the lower court had erred by applying *Garcetti*, which had expressly reserved the question of whether it applied in academic contexts, the Fourth Circuit remanded the case for consideration under the *Pickering–Connick* test.

As noted earlier in this chapter, the fact that a public employee spoke as a private citizen, and not as a function of their official duties, does not end the analysis. The speech *still* will not receive the protection of the First Amendment if (1) it addresses a matter of private interest rather than one of public concern or (2) the employer reasonably predicts the speech will be substantially disruptive.[54] Many of the cases decided along these lines concern faculty speech about sexual matters.

[51] Renken v. Gregory, 541 F.3d 769 (7th Cir. 2008).

[52] Demers v. Austin, 729 F.3d 1011 (9th Cir. 2013). This opinion was withdrawn and superseded on denial of rehearing in Demers v. Austin, 746 F.3d 402 (9th Cir. 2014). The court there affirmed the district court's holding as to the *Pickering* standard but reversed and remanded on other grounds.

[53] Adams v. Trustees of the University of North Carolina-Wilmington, 640 F.3d 550 (4th Cir. 2011).

[54] *See* Waters v. Churchill, 511 U.S. 661, 673 (1994) (a public employer need only show that it reasonably predicts the speech will interfere with a governmental function); Jeffries v. Harleston, 52 F.3d 9, 13 (2d Cir. 1995) (upholding the employer's "reasonable belief"); and *c.f.* Salaita v. Kennedy, 188 F. Supp. 3d 1068 (N.D. Ill. 2015) (premature to dismiss retaliation claim based on faculty speech communicated via Twitter where complaint alleged facts consistent with no finding of disruption).

Thus, courts have often upheld the reasonableness of a higher education employer's concerns where the employee's speech threatened to create a hostile or discriminatory work or learning environment. Accordingly, courts have found disruption of or interference with the workplace where a faculty member's speech addressed details of their sex life, amounted to inappropriate sexual advances, was wantonly vulgar, or was confrontational, degrading, or conducive to an atmosphere of tension.[55] Courts also seem sympathetic to the argument that sexually oriented speech – particularly when it involves profanity and references to the instructor's own sexual experiences and is not germane to the academic subject matter – does not address a matter of public concern.[56]

Of course, even where an institution decides *not* to punish a faculty member for their speech, the mere process of complaint and investigation can be burdensome. For example, in February of 2015, Northwestern University Professor Laura Kipnis published an article criticizing campus rules prohibiting romantic relationships between students and professors as a "hijack[ing]" of feminism that resulted in students being "committed to their own vulnerability, conditioned to imagine they have no agency."[57] After students complained that the article created a hostile learning environment, Professor Kipnis faced a several months-long investigation. Ultimately she was not disciplined, but it can be argued that the duration of the investigation in itself burdened academic freedom.[58]

Challenges in thinking about academic freedom sometimes arise because a faculty member chooses a provocative method for conveying an idea, resulting in offense and arguably exceeding the bounds of protection. For example, in *Hardy v. Jefferson Community College*,[59] an adjunct professor lecturing on language and communication asked his class to identify terms that majorities had historically used to marginalize minorities. A number of examples were offered, including the "N" word, which the professor repeated. A student in the class complained, the college declined to renew his contract, and the professor sued.

Reasonable people can certainly question this faculty member's judgment. Nevertheless, the Sixth Circuit concluded that the professor's use of the offending language was germane to the subject matter under discussion, not gratuitous, and

55 *See* Michael H. Leroy, *#Academicfreedom: Twitter and First Amendment Rights of Professors*, 90 Notre Dame L. Rev. Online 158 (2015).

56 *See Buchanan*, *supra*, and cases discussed therein.

57 Laura Kipnis, *Sexual Paranoia Strikes Academe*, Chron. Higher Educ. (Feb. 27, 2015), https://www.chronicle.com/article/Sexual-Paranoia-Strikes/190351.

58 She wrote another article, and a book, about the experience, which resulted in yet another complaint by the same student and another Title IX investigation by Northwestern. Jeannie Suk Gersen, *Laura Kipnis's Endless Trial by Title IX*, New Yorker (Sep. 20, 2017), https://www.newyorker.com/news/news-desk/laura-kipniss-endless-trial-by-title-ix (describing a "world where expressing an opinion about sexual harassment can be sincerely perceived as sexual harassment").

59 Hardy v. Jefferson Community College, 260 F.3d 671 (6th Cir. 2001).

related to matters of public interest. It was therefore presumptively protected by the First Amendment.

Other forms of provocative pedagogy have not fared as well. For example, in 2016, the University of Oregon suspended law professor Nancy Shurtz for wearing blackface and a hospital gown at a Halloween party she hosted.[60] The university found that Professor Shurtz had dressed as a character from Dr. Damon Tweedy's book, *Black Man in a White Coat: Reflections on Race and Medicine*, as an earnest expression of her admiration for the author and to express her view that the lack of racial diversity in higher education was reprehensible.[61] She said she hoped to promote a discussion about race.[62] At this, she certainly succeeded: controversy erupted as students and faculty members condemned her costume as insensitive, while others supported her.[63]

Again, reasonable people can question this faculty member's judgment. Nevertheless, her supporters maintained that faculty members must have the latitude to experiment with dramatic ways of conveying important messages.[64] But, despite its robustly worded academic freedom policy,[65] the University of Oregon determined that Professor Shurtz had violated the school's discriminatory harassment policy.[66]

As this discussion shows, in its current form the concept of academic freedom does less to protect the free exchange of ideas in universities than we might have hoped or thought. The limited Supreme Court jurisprudence that exists strongly suggests that, at a minimum, educational institutions enjoy such a right as against government interference. But the dimensions and application of that right remain less than clear.

Individual faculty members have even greater cause for concern. Based in the First Amendment, the *constitutional* right of academic freedom applies within public schools but not private ones. And, even within public schools, the right

[60] University of Oregon Investigative Report (Nov. 30, 2016), http://uomatters.com/wp-content/uploads/2018/04/final_investigative_report_redacted_-_final.pdf.

[61] *Id.* at 9–12.

[62] *Id.* at 12.

[63] *Id.* at 16–19.

[64] Eugene Volokh, *At the University of Oregon, No More Free Speech for Professors on Subjects such as Race, Religion, Sexual Orientation*, WASH. POST (Dec. 26, 2016), www.washingtonpost.com/news/volokh-conspiracy/wp/2016/12/26/at-the-university-of-oregon-no-more-free-speech-for-professors-on-subjects-such-as-race-religion-sexual-orientation/; ERWIN CHEMERINSKY AND HOWARD GILLMAN, FREE SPEECH ON CAMPUS 121–123 (2016).

[65] The University of Oregon holds an academic freedom policy that: "[t]he belief that an opinion is pernicious, false, and in any other way despicable, detestable, offensive or 'just plain wrong' cannot be grounds for its suppression." *Id.*

[66] *Id.* See also Sheldon v. Dhillon, No. C-08-03438 RMW, 2009 WL 4282086 (N.D. Ca. Nov. 25, 2009), where a professor was dismissed after an anonymous student complaint following the instructor's measured response to a question regarding the potential for a genetic component to homosexual behavior.

seems fragile. After all, if the faculty member is not speaking in a "core" academic context then the court may conclude that, under *Garcetti*, the expression receives no protection at all. And even if *Garcetti* does not apply and the expression is presumptively protected, the institution may be able to show that the speech should not be protected because it was unduly disruptive.

It can be argued that the protections provided by tenure (and by high standards for tenure revocation) do much more to foster free thought and expression within the academy. Tenure is essentially a contract between the faculty member and the institution and the enforceability of a contract is often a clearer matter than is the enforceability of a constitutional right. But these legal protections have limits, too. Every year, institutions of higher education rely more heavily on nontenured faculty (like adjuncts) and some schools have made tenure revocation an easier process that can be accomplished more swiftly and summarily.

Unless the Supreme Court clarifies the meaning of academic freedom, and recognizes it as a robust right under the First Amendment, the principle will be only as strong as the support it receives as a norm. That is a perilous circumstance, as it leaves academic freedom subject to the passions of the time and the tyrannies of majorities. That is precisely the sort of vulnerability against which the First Amendment was adopted to protect.

16

Speech on the Internet

A contemporary cliché holds that "the internet changed everything." Certainly, it has had a profound and wide-ranging impact on many aspects of human experience.[1] The pace, quantity, and quality of online communication might prompt a reasonable person to assume that the unique characteristics of such speech have required us to reconsider many dimensions of First Amendment theory and doctrine. After all, if the internet changed everything, then surely it must have altered substantially the way we think about free expression. It turns out, however, that things are much more complicated.

Let's first consider free speech *theory*. In a sense, one could argue that the internet did not change our theoretical models, it just facilitated their actualization in the real world. Think back on Chapters 1 and 2, where we discussed the various theories that have been offered in defense of robust protection for free expression. We can see how the internet arguably offers a strong assist in the accomplishment of the objectives of those theories.

We explored, for example, the foundational marketplace of ideas theory, which we have referred to again and again throughout this book. As we have noted, that theory could fail to operate fairly and effectively if barriers to entry make it difficult or impossible for some ideas to get into the market. Such barriers might exist, for example, because minority voices lack resources that are available to the majority or because a small number of entities control most of the mass media.

The digital divide between those who can and cannot afford the technology necessary to secure effective online access remains a serious concern.

[1] For just three dozen examples of ways in which the internet has made life different, *see* Caitlin Dewey, *36 Ways the Web Has Changed Us*, WASH. POST (Mar. 12, 2014), https://www.washingtonpost.com/news/arts-and-entertainment/wp/2014/03/12/36-ways-the-web-has-changed-us/. For an overview of how the twenty-first-century speech environment threatens "critical pieces of the democratic project," *see* Toni M. Massaro and Helen Norton, *Free Speech and Democracy: A Primer for Twenty-First Century Reformers*, 54 UC Davis L REV 1631 (2021).

Nevertheless, the internet has doubtless lowered the barriers to entry into the marketplace of ideas for countless people and organizations. Today, millions of people can speak to the whole world through a few keystrokes on their laptop or cellphone. In this way, the internet would seem to correct a deficiency in the marketplace of ideas model, helping to bring it closer to a practical reality.

In many other respects, however, the internet has made it more difficult for the marketplace of ideas to operate as Justice Holmes imagined. Reliable information and productive ideas spread more widely and easily than ever before – but so do falsehoods and noxious doctrines. Vastly more communication takes place now than in the past – but the amount and velocity of it can overwhelm us and make it difficult to deliberate over the merits of the material that fills our screens. Individual voices project more expansively and penetrate more deeply than at any time in history – but that includes the voices of those who seek to silence others by harassment, threats, and doxing. And many of the voices that end up directing the conversation on the internet may belong not to human beings but to Russian bots.

So it goes with all of our theories behind protecting speech: the internet has proven to be a mixed blessing at best. On the one hand, it facilitates the flow of information necessary for us to make reasoned judgments as participants in the democratic process; on the other hand, it allows for the viral spread of disinformation and skews our political decision making. On the one hand, it empowers individual expression and self-fulfillment; on the other hand, it facilitates attacks and blowbacks that may have a formidable chilling effect. On the one hand, it provides a "safety valve" that channels anger and frustration away from violence and civic unrest; on the other hand, it feeds and escalates conflict between groups and individuals. The history of the internet is a tale of fulfilled potential, both for better and for worse. This includes with respect to free speech theory.

The effect of the internet on First Amendment *doctrine* has been similarly mixed. In many respects, the fact that speech occurs online does not require us to think differently. For instance, the government cannot constitutionally punish someone for expressing their disapproval of capital punishment, regardless of whether that person speaks through a pamphlet, a newspaper editorial, a magazine article, a blog post, or a tweet. That we frequently get the same legal result regardless of where speech occurs should not surprise us, given that our very new forms of speech often resemble very old forms. The proverbial lone pamphleteer of an earlier age has much in common with the solitary blogger of this one.

Certainly, the internet has required some doctrinal adjustments. But many of them do not dramatically alter the legal landscape or change the core meaning of established principles. Take defamation as an example. The existence of the internet does not challenge the foundational concept that an exception to the First Amendment should exist to allow those whose reputations have been harmed by false statements to seek compensation. The internet does, however, raise a host of intriguing questions about how existing doctrine applies to certain aspects of defamation law – if it applies at all.

Consider, for example, the following: When defamation occurs online, in which state (or, for that matter, in which country) is the plaintiff's reputation injured? Should an individual be liable for retweeting someone else's defamatory tweet? Is sharing a link to an article the legal equivalent of republishing the article? A great deal of online speech does not conform to the standards and practices of traditional journalism; how does that complicate the effort to distinguish statements of fact, which are actionable under libel law, from expressions of opinion, which are not?

Scholars have dedicated whole books to the ways in which the internet may require us to revisit the legal doctrine relevant to specific subjects like hate speech, extremism, privacy, obscenity, indecency regulation, "revenge porn," and so on. We cannot here explore every aspect of the law that online speech affects to greater and lesser degrees. We therefore instead focus on a foundational question of central importance to current discussions about free expression: How do the various platforms that support and drive online communication – entities like Google, Facebook, Twitter, and Instagram – fit into existing free speech theory and First Amendment doctrine, if they do at all? The answer to that question offers important insights not only into the law but into the concept of the Everyday First Amendment that we discussed in Chapter 4.

Again, let's begin with theory. At a simplistic level, the answer to the question of how the internet changed things seems relatively straightforward. Entities like Google and Twitter create generally open-access marketplaces through which participants can exchange information and ideas. They help us learn, find our way toward the truth, become better informed participants in our democracy, blow off steam, express ourselves, and lead better lives. They have become the principal means through which free speech theory currently achieves its ends.

Skeptics point out, however, that this rosy picture ignores a significant problem: the vast and historically unprecedented power that these entities wield in shaping public discourse. Consider some recent statistics. No less than 71 percent of the respondents to a 2019 Pew Research Center poll indicated that they use Facebook. Fifty-two percent said that Facebook serves as a news source for them.[2] A 2018 report found that more than 90 percent of all internet searches took place through a Google-affiliated platform (Google, Google Image, YouTube, and Google Maps).[3] We justifiably become concerned whenever a small group of players has disproportionate influence over a commercial marketplace. The same holds true for the marketplace of ideas.

[2] Laura Hazard Owen, *More Americans than Ever Getting News from Social Media, Even as They Say Social Media Makes News "Worse"*, NIEMENLAB (October 2, 2019), https://www.niemanlab.org/2019/10/more-americans-than-ever-are-getting-news-from-social-media-even-as-they-say-social-media-makes-news-worse/.

[3] https://www.businessinsider.com/how-google-retains-more-than-90-of-market-share-2018–4.

As the power of these entities has grown, questions have arisen about how they exercise it. As we discussed in Chapter 4, serious accusations have been made that these platforms manipulate the flow of information and distort public understanding and discourse. One of the paradoxes of our present internet dependency is that we have come to rely heavily on online sources of information that we think are unreliable. Indeed, the same Pew Research poll cited above – which found that about three-fourths of those surveyed use Facebook and roughly half get news there – also found that well over 90 percent thought that social media promotes one-sided and inaccurate news.[4]

The explanation for why Google and a relatively small number of social media platforms have such tremendous power and influence is complex and multifaceted. It is clear, however, that the law played a major role. Certainly, the First Amendment contributed to this process, but a statute passed by Congress has in many respects proven even more significant. In order to understand why, we need to consider what the law looked like before the advent of the internet, specifically with regard to the question of who qualified as the publisher of a statement.

"Publication" has a specific, but not very complicated, meaning in this legal context: to publish a statement simply means that you made the statement to third parties. And the question of who published a statement matters for a similarly straightforward reason: in general, the law provides that you can be held responsible for what you say to other people – that is, for what you "publish." If Smith makes a false and defamatory statement of fact about Jones to others with whom they both do business, then Jones can sue Smith for libel; if Smith discloses an embarrassing private fact about Jones to members of their shared community, then Jones can sue Smith for invasion of privacy; and so on.

Furthermore, an individual or entity may qualify as the publisher of a statement even if they are just repeating what *someone else* said. Consider *New York Times* v. *Sullivan*, discussed in Chapter 11. As you will recall, the plaintiff there sued the *New York Times* over an advertisement that it printed but did not write, edit, or solicit. The fact that someone other than a *New York Times* employee prepared the text did not matter for the purposes of considering whether the paper could be held liable for falsehoods it contained. The *New York Times* still "published" it.

Even before the advent of the internet, the question of who qualifies as the publisher of a statement had some complex dimensions. Of course, in some instances the answer was obvious. In the hypothetical cases discussed above, Smith clearly made the libelous and invasive statements about Jones to third parties and so published them. Similarly, entities like the *Washington Post*, *The Atlantic*

4 See Laura Hazard Owen, *More Americans than Ever Getting News from Social Media, Even as They Say Social Media Makes News "Worse,"* NiemenLab, footnote 1, *supra* (October 2, 2019), https://www.niemanlab.org/2019/10/more-americans-than-ever-are-getting-news-from-social-media-even-as-they-say-social-media-makes-news-worse/.

magazine, NBC, and Random House would be deemed to have published the statements that they included in their newspapers, periodicals, broadcasts, and books.

But in some cases the answer was considerably less clear. Consider, for example, entities like bookstores, magazine vendors, or libraries. On one hand, they engage in the public dissemination of statements; on the other hand, they do not exercise any direct control over the content of that speech. In light of this difference, the law generally treated these sorts of entities, which it labeled "distributors," differently than it treated publishers. Courts held distributors liable for statements they helped circulate only if the distributors knew or had reason to know that the statements were actionable, for example, as defamatory.

We should note that, at least in theory, a third category may have existed as well. Individuals and entities sometimes create spaces, like bulletin boards or kiosks, that facilitate the making of statements. It is true that such spaces help disseminate information, just like newspapers and libraries do. But, given that those who establish such spaces typically exercise *no* editorial control, make *no* choices with respect to content, and take an entirely *passive* approach to what (if anything) gets posted, it does not make much sense to treat them as either publishers or distributors. Surely, if Smith builds a wall, she cannot be held responsible for the graffiti with which Jones adorns it.

In the early history of online communications, a critical question arose: Into which of these categories do internet service providers fall? The answer had vast implications, because it would decide whether online service providers had full responsibility, some responsibility, or no responsibility for statements that third parties made on their platforms. That decision would, in turn, determine how those entities would behave and what they would allow on their sites. In sum, the answer to the question controlled nothing less than how the entire internet environment would operate.

It is important to underscore what was *not* at stake here. If the internet platform was plainly acting as a publisher – circulating content that it had itself created – then there was no reason to treat it differently than we would treat any other speaker. If Facebook directed an employee to post a knowingly false and defamatory statement about a presidential candidate, then it should have the same liability as the *Wall Street Journal* would if it assigned one of its reporters the identical project. In other words, the critical question was not how to treat an internet service provider when it put *its own* statements in circulation but which standard to apply when it facilitated the circulation of *someone else's* statements. For example, if Smith defames Jones in her Facebook post, should Jones be able to sue Facebook as well as Smith?

The effort to answer that question in the lower courts quickly led to jurisprudential disarray. One early case addressed an internet service provider, CompuServe, that hosted a "Journalism Forum" site where a third party posted a daily "newspaper" called *Rumorville*. The court held that, because CompuServe did not exercise any direct editorial control over *Rumorville*, it served as a distributor but not a publisher of the periodical – analogous, the court declared, to a "for-profit library." As a result, the plaintiffs could only maintain a defamation case against CompuServe if they could show that the service provider knew or had reason to know that *Rumorville* had libeled the plaintiffs.[5]

Although the *CompuServe* court resisted the idea that a service provider qualifies as a publisher, its decision was not spectacularly good news for internet platforms or for the free flow of information. Consider: if a company like CompuServe qualified as a distributor of third-party content, then the specter of potential liability still arose anytime someone complained that a particular post was defamatory, or invaded their privacy, or was otherwise actionable through a civil lawsuit. Unless CompuServe employed a vast staff to investigate each such claim to assess its validity, its simplest recourse was simply to take the content down. As a practical matter, finding that internet service providers were distributors effectively gave veto power to anyone who objected – keeping information and ideas off the internet and out of the marketplace.

As more courts addressed these issues, however, the news got worse for internet platforms. In 1995, a New York state court issued an opinion in a defamation case brought against Prodigy, a computer network that hosted various bulletin boards to which third parties posted content. An anonymous posting on one of those bulletin boards, "Money Talk," accused a securities investment firm (Stratton Oakmont) and its president of fraudulent and criminal acts in connection with a stock offering. Because Prodigy enforced certain content guidelines – for example, asking users to refrain from insulting, harassing, or "grossly repugnant" posts – the court concluded that it qualified as a publisher of third-party statements. Under the applicable law, this meant that Prodigy was fully liable for the content, just as if it had made the statement itself.[6]

The *Stratton Oakmont* decision sent a clear message to internet companies that hosted third-party speech: severe consequences could follow if they exercised *any* editorial control over content. Certainly, such control would eliminate any possible argument that they were functioning as passive bulletin boards that should have no liability whatsoever. Under this case, it seemed clear that any form of content restriction, revision, or even guidance would transform the internet platforms from distributors into publishers. This would dramatically escalate their potential legal exposure.

As a result, *Stratton Oakmont* created a perverse incentive. It encouraged online service providers to take a hands-off approach to their sites in order to reduce the threat of being sued. A company could most easily avoid any claim that it qualified

5 Cubby v. CompuServe, 776 F. Supp. 135 (S.D.N.Y. 1991).
6 Stratton Oakmont, Inc. v. Prodigy Services Co., 23 Media L. Rep. 1794 (1995).

as a publisher by doing absolutely nothing about content posted by third parties, no matter how outrageous, offensive, or harmful.

The case also gave rise to a potential double bind. If a company received a complaint about content posted on its site, then the *CompuServe* case suggested it should take the material down in order to avoid distributor liability. If the company *did* take it down, though, then it would face the argument that it was exercising editorial control over third-party content and so qualified as a publisher under *Stratton Oakmont*.

Because the online service industry was still relatively small in 1995, few members of Congress noticed the implications of these cases. But two did and drafted proposed legislation that would give expansive immunity to online service providers for the third-party content that appeared on their sites. In essence, the draft statute treated an internet service provider like the owner of a bulletin board: it could leave third-party material up or take it down, if it chose to, without fear of somehow transforming itself into a publisher or distributor and incurring the attendant liability. The legislators believed that this would encourage such companies to develop their own standards and to remove offending material voluntarily.

During that same time period, many members of Congress were much more concerned about a different problem: children using the internet to access virulent forms of pornography. Public pressure for lawmakers to do something about this concern mounted in the summer of 1995, after *Time Magazine* published an issue with an arresting cover: an image of a young boy's stunned and ghoulishly screen-lit face staring at a computer over the headline "CYBERPORN." In response, Congress passed a statute that made it a crime knowingly to provide pornography to anyone under the age of eighteen – the Communications Decency Act, or CDA.

Civil liberties groups expressed concern that the CDA was so expansively and imprecisely drafted that it infringed on the First Amendment rights of adults. In contrast, these groups found the proposed immunity statute much less worrisome, because it gave private internet service providers the latitude to adopt and enforce standards voluntarily and to take down pornography without resorting to government censorship. Rather than choose between these approaches, Congress elected to adopt both; the immunity statute thus became Section 230 of the CDA. In 1997, the Supreme Court struck down most of the CDA as unconstitutional, but Section 230 survived.[7]

The immunity granted by Section 230 is extraordinarily broad. Its core provision states that "[n]o provider or user of an interactive computer service shall be treated as the publisher or speaker of any information provided by another information content provider." After its passage, courts swiftly and consistently ruled that this language means exactly what it says. Subject to several explicit exceptions, it immunizes everyone that provides an interactive computer service (like Google,

[7] *See* Reno v. American Civil Liberties Union, 521 U.S. 884 (1997).

LinkedIn, or Twitter) and everyone who employs such a service (like an ordinary Facebook user, the *Washington Post*, and the President of the United States) from liability based on content created by someone else.

The 1997 case of *Zeran* v. *America Online, Inc.* offers an important early example of the judiciary's recognition of the breadth of Section 230's protection.[8] Indeed, the case comes so early in the history of online speech doctrine that the court begins its opinion by explaining what the internet *is* – an "international network of connected computers" with "about 40 million worldwide users." Current estimates place usage at well over four billion.[9]

This first foray into the field involved a remarkable set of facts. America Online (AOL) was an internet service provider that, among other things, made virtual bulletin boards available to third-party subscribers for posting messages. An unidentified third party used an AOL bulletin board to advertise "Naughty Oklahoma t-shirts," which were promoted as featuring offensive and tasteless slogans related to the 1995 bombing of the federal building in Oklahoma City. The advertisement instructed those interested in making a purchase to contact "Ken" and provided the home phone number of one Ken Zeran in Seattle, Washington. There was just one problem: Zeran had nothing to do with such T-shirts or with the advertisements; it was a prank.

The stunt made Zeran's life miserable. Outraged callers flooded his phone line with insults, angry messages, and death threats. Things got worse after additional prank advertisements offered bumper stickers and key chains with similarly offensive slogans and encouraged buyers to "please call back if busy" because of high demand. Matters escalated still further when an Oklahoma City radio station learned of the advertisements and encouraged its listeners to phone Zeran in protest. The calls intensified until Zeran was receiving an abusive message about every two minutes.

Zeran couldn't change his telephone number because he used it to operate the business that he ran out of his home, so he tried to solve his problem through other measures. He turned for assistance with the threats to the police and the FBI. He repeatedly asked AOL to remove the advertisements, publish a retraction on the bulletin board, and close the account of the individual posting the false messages. AOL declined to issue a retraction, but it did repeatedly assure Zeran that it would remove the posts and close the account. Nevertheless, AOL delayed in taking any corrective measures. Zeran had little relief from the onslaught until an Oklahoma City paper published a story that exposed the hoax.

8 Zeran v. America Online, Inc., 129 F.3d 327 (4th Cir. 1997).

9 *See* J. Clement, *Global Numbers of Internet Users 2005–2019*, STATISTA (Jan. 7, 2020), https://www.statista.com/statistics/273018/number-of-internet-users-worldwide/#:~:text=In%202019%2C%20the%20number%20of,billion%20in%20the%20previous%20year.

Zeran filed suit against AOL, claiming that the post was defamatory and that the company had a legal obligation to remove the initial message promptly, to publish a written retraction, and to prevent the posting of the additional phony advertisements. AOL invoked Section 230 as a defense. Even though Zeran obviously made a very sympathetic plaintiff, and even though AOL's handling of the matter left a great deal to be desired, the court agreed that the statute clearly barred the claim. "By its plain language," the court declared, "§ 230 creates a federal immunity to any cause of action that would make service providers liable for information originating with a third-party user of the service."[10]

Subsequent cases – many involving similarly sympathetic plaintiffs – have uniformly interpreted Section 230 in a correspondingly expansive matter. Like the *Zeran* court, other courts have dismissed claims by relying on the plain language of the statute and the manifest intention of Congress to preserve free speech "in the new and burgeoning Internet medium."[11] The statute says that "*no*" provider or user of online services will be treated as the publisher of content created by third parties. Courts essentially have declared that "no" means "no."

It is impossible to overstate the significance of Section 230 to online speech as we know and experience it today. One author has called its central provision "the twenty-six words that created the Internet."[12] Without it, social media sites like Facebook, Twitter, Instagram, Reddit, and Yelp become unimaginable.

To take just one example, think about TripAdvisor, where third parties currently post reviews of hotels, restaurants, attractions, and the like. Try to imagine how, or for that matter whether, the site could operate without the protection afforded by Section 230. Absent that law, whenever TripAdvisor received an objection from a business that was the target of an unfavorable post it would have two choices, neither of them attractive. It could employ an army of researchers to analyze the merits of the review. Or it could simply take the review down – even if it might be true, valid, fair, and important for the public to see. Without Section 230, the flow of information on the internet would be much narrower and more halting than it is today and countless sites on which many people depend daily would function very differently, if they existed at all.

Still, the virtues and benefits of Section 230 do not come without substantial challenges and costs. *Zeran* itself reveals one set of issues. In a pre-internet world, someone like the individual who harassed poor Ken Zeran probably would have had limited opportunities to do him much harm. But the existence of the internet and of service providers like AOL vastly amplified the prankster's voice and the injury he could inflict through his hoax. Paradoxically, Section 230 thus completely

[10] *Id.* at 330.

[11] *Id.* at 330–331. The Electronic Frontier Foundation website maintains a useful compendium of many of the most important cases decided under Section 230. *See* https://www.eff.org/issues/cda230/legal.

[12] Jeff Kosseff, The Twenty-Six Words that Created the Internet (2019).

immunized from liability the very entity that made this severe disruption of Zeran's life possible. Zeran may have taken cold comfort from the idea that he always could pursue a legal claim against the person who posted the advertisements. Doing so may have struck Zeran as difficult (because he didn't know the identity of the person), expensive (because he'd have to hire a lawyer to find out who it was and file a lawsuit), and fruitless (because that unidentified person may not have had the resources to pay an adverse judgment).

These same dynamics play out in a wide variety of unsettling contexts. Section 230 ends up facilitating a great deal of troublesome speech: mass harassment campaigns; propaganda from hate organizations and terrorists; "revenge porn"; and so on and so on. Seeking legal redress against the individual or organization engaging in the speech is often complicated. Seeking it against the online platform that hosts the content is generally impossible. As a result, the law leaves those wronged with no practical remedy.

Section 230 also results in some peculiar asymmetries. Assume, for example, that a third party sends a letter to the editor at the *Wall Street Journal*, which decides to publish the correspondence in its print edition. If that letter is defamatory, then the paper has the same liability as if it had made the statement itself because it qualifies as a "publisher" of the statement under the law. Now assume instead that a third party posts the *same* statements on the comment page maintained by the *Wall Street Journal* in its online edition. In that case, Section 230 grants full immunity from liability to the paper because the letter is third-party content. Odder still, it does so even though the online comment may get much wider circulation and may do more damage than the letter in the print edition.

These problems have driven two kinds of responses. One, discussed in Chapter 4, comes in the form of public demands for greater voluntary content control by social media platforms. Critics point out that those entities enjoy Section 230's expansive immunity precisely because Congress hoped and anticipated that it would incentivize them to take down offensive and potentially harmful content. To the extent they fail to do so, the argument goes, they are abusing the immunity the statute provides to them.

The other response has consisted of calls for the revision, or even wholesale repeal, of Section 230. Moderate tinkering with the statute may sound like a good idea, but trying to devise a surgical fix to the largest dilemmas caused by Section 230 proves extraordinarily difficult. Some of the more ambitious approaches that members of Congress have proposed would not only gut the statute but would run afoul of the First Amendment. One was described by a conservative political commentator as an "unwise, unconstitutional mess."[13]

[13] David French, *Josh Hawley's Internet Censorship Bill Is an Unwise, Unconstitutional Mess*, National Review (June 20, 2019), https://www.nationalreview.com/2019/06/josh-hawley-internet-censorship-bill-unconstitutional/.

A wholesale repeal of Section 230 is legally possible (the First Amendment does not require its existence), but for the foreseeable future it seems socially and politically unworkable. At least in the United States, people have become accustomed to an open and unrestrained online environment – for better and for worse. A seismic shift in potential liability for third-party content providers would likely change the internet landscape in dramatic ways, including in some we cannot anticipate. Indeed, efforts to restrain content flow on the internet have proven controversial and difficult to maintain even in countries that have a preexisting history of imposing such restrictions.[14]

The uninhibited and largely unregulated online environment that Section 230 helps create inspires in many people a curious mixture of passion, addiction, concern, and outrage. This is unremarkable, given that free speech generally inspires those sorts of conflicting feelings and that the internet is, in some sense, the marketplace of ideas writ large. But those contradictory impulses can lead us into deep and dangerous places of confusion and can result in wild and irrational swings in public policy.

An example of this dynamic comes in the complicated relationship between former President Donald Trump and Twitter. During his candidacy and well into his administration, President Trump proved himself a prolific – sometimes even relentless – user of the social media site. While his first impeachment trial was ongoing, he sent out 142 tweets in a single day. He later eclipsed that record in the midst of the social unrest and protests that took place over the murder of George Floyd by tweeting or retweeting 200 messages in one twenty-four-hour period.[15]

And he was as provocative as he was prodigious. Over the years, he sent out tweets that were criticized as false,[16] offensive,[17] cyberbullying,[18] racist,[19]

[14] *See, e.g.*, Vindu Goel and Salman Masood, *Facebook, Google and Twitter Rebel against Pakistan's Censorship Rules*, New York Times (Feb. 27, 2020), https://www.nytimes.com/2020/02/27/technology/pakistan-internet-censorship.html; Nir Kshetri, *Chinese Internet Users Turn to the Blockchain to Fight against Government Censorship*, The World (Feb. 25, 2019), https://www.pri.org/stories/2019–02–25/chinese-internet-users-turn-blockchain-fight-against-government-censorship.

[15] Connor Perret, *Trump Broke His All-Time Tweeting Record amid Nationwide Protests, Sending More Tweets in a Single Day than He Did during His Impeachment Trial*, Insider.com (June 6, 2020), https://www.insider.com/trump-breaks-record-most-tweets-in-a-single-day-2020–6.

[16] *See, e.g.*, Linda Qiu, *Hey @jack, Here Are More Questionable Tweets from @realdonaldtrump*, New York Times (June 3, 2020), https://www.nytimes.com/2020/06/03/us/politics/trump-twitter-fact-check.html.

[17] *See, e.g.*, *Donald Trump's Ten Most Offensive Tweets*, Forbes, https://www.forbes.com/pictures/flji45elmm/donald-trumps-10-most-of/#ef8ce8670df3.

[18] *See, e.g.*, Nancy Jo Sales, *Why Is the President of the United States Cyberbulling a 16-Year-Old Girl?*, The Guardian (Dec. 14, 2019), https://www.theguardian.com/commentisfree/2019/dec/14/trump-president-greta-thunberg-bullying.

[19] *See, e.g.*, Colin Dwyer, *"Go Back Where You Came From": The Long Rhetorical Roots of Trump's Racist Tweets*, NPR (July 15, 2019), https://www.npr.org/2019/07/15/741827580/go-back-where-you-came-from-the-long-rhetorical-roots-of-trump-s-racist-tweets.

sexist,[20] an obstruction of justice,[21] witness tampering,[22] pushing debunked conspiracy theories,[23] and likely to incite violence.[24] Name calling and making derogatory comments about specific individuals and institutions became common fare on the President's Twitter feed.

Although some of his supporters may have enjoyed (or at least been indifferent to) his fiery online persona, critics questioned why Twitter did not enforce its generally applicable content standards against the President. For years, Twitter resisted doing so because the fact that a major political figure engages in online misconduct is *itself* a matter of public interest and concern. If an average citizen tweets out an obvious lie or a debunked conspiracy theory, then that usually does not tell the public anything they need to know. If the titular leader of the free world posts such a message, then it does.

In May of 2020, Twitter departed from its policy of leaving the President's tweets alone. Late in that month, Trump posted a message saying that "There is NO WAY (ZERO!) that Mail-In Ballots [*sic*] will be anything less than substantially fraudulent." The President cited no data in support of this claim. In fact, abundant evidence to the contrary existed.

Facing mounting pressure to take the President to task for his online misbehavior, Twitter decided it needed to respond. As a result, it put a warning label on the tweet and linked it to a page that showed the claim to be unsubstantiated. Twitter did not remove the President's tweet or terminate his account. To the contrary, his post remained on the site and anyone wishing to view it could easily do so. Twitter just made sure that anyone who read the tweet had access to additional information.

Twitter's actions drew a swift and angry rebuke from the President. Trump declared that Twitter had silenced him in violation of his right to freedom of expression and vowed that he would take prompt action against social media

[20] *See, e.g.*, Daniel Politi, *Trump Shares Sexist Messages about Prominent Female Democrats in Twitter Spree*, SLATE (May 24, 2020), https://slate.com/news-and-politics/2020/05/trump-sexist-messages-female-democrats-hillary-clinton.html.

[21] *See, e.g.*, Deanna Paul, *Trump's Latest Tweets Cross Clear Lines, Experts Say: Obstruction of Justice and Witness Tampering*, WASHINGTON POST (Dec. 3, 2018), https://www.washingtonpost.com/politics/2018/12/03/trumps-latest-tweets-cross-clear-lines-experts-say-obstruction-justice-witness-tampering/.

[22] *Id.*

[23] *See, e.g.*, Cat Zakrzewski, *The Technology 202: President Trump's Conspiracy Theories Are Putting Pressure on Twitter to Change Its Policies*, WASHINGTON POST (June 10, 2020), https://www.washingtonpost.com/news/powerpost/paloma/the-technology-202/2020/06/10/the-technology-202-president-trump-s-conspiracy-theories-are-putting-pressure-on-twitter-to-change-its-policies/5edfe562602ff12947e888d1/.

[24] *See, e.g.*, Rebecca Shabad, *"Racist President": Democrats Accuse Trump of Inciting Violence in Minneapolis*, NBC NEWS (May 29, 2020), https://www.nbcnews.com/politics/politics-news/racist-president-democrats-accuse-trump-inciting-violence-minneapolis-n1217871.

companies.[25] Within days, he issued an Executive Order that, among other things, argued for a narrowing of the interpretation of Section 230.[26] Given that the legislative branch passes laws and the judicial branch construes them, it was unclear what (if any) actual impact the order would have. Some commentators dismissed it as "political theater."[27]

If President Trump intended the Order to persuade Twitter to leave his posts alone, it did not have that effect. Within a day, he had tweeted out a message regarding the protests going on in Minneapolis regarding the murder of George Floyd that said: "These THUGS are dishonoring the memory of George Floyd, and I won't let that happen. Just spoke to Governor Tim Walz and told him that the Military is with him all the way. Any difficulty and we will assume control but, when the looting starts, the shooting starts. Thank you!"[28]

Again, Twitter did not delete the message or terminate the President's account. Instead, it posted an advisory stating: "This tweet violated the Twitter Rules about glorifying violence. However, Twitter has determined that it may be in the public's interest for the Tweet to remain available." Anyone interested in seeing the tweet could do so by clicking past the notice, but the move further infuriated the President.

The President's characterization of Twitter's conduct obviously was wrong on the facts: at that point, Twitter had not censored or silenced him. To the contrary, anyone inclined to read his tweets remained free to do so and to ignore whatever Twitter had to say about them. After the January 6, 2021, attack on the Capitol, Twitter would indeed suspend the President's account – but it hadn't done so yet.

For our purposes, however, the more important point is that President Trump was also wrong on the law. His most fundamental mistake was failing to recognize that Twitter could not have violated his right to free speech under the First Amendment because it is a private entity, not an arm of the government, and therefore not subject to the First Amendment's constraints. Nothing in First Amendment doctrine prevented Twitter from deleting the offending tweets altogether or unceremoniously

[25] *See* Shannon Bond, *Trump Threatens to Shut Down Social Media after Twitter Adds Warning to His Tweets*, NPR (May 27, 2020), https://www.npr.org/2020/05/27/863011399/trump-threatens-to-shut-down-social-media-after-twitter-adds-warning-on-his-twee.

[26] *See* Executive Order on Preventing Online Censorship (May 28, 2020), https://www.whitehouse.gov/presidential-actions/executive-order-preventing-online-censorship/.

[27] Bobby Allyn, *Stung by Twitter, Trump Signs Executive Order to Weaken Social Media Companies*, NPR (May 28, 2020), https://www.npr.org/2020/05/28/863932758/stung-by-twitter-trump-signs-executive-order-to-weaken-social-media-companies.

[28] The phrase "when the looting starts, the shooting starts" echoed language used by a Miami police chief in the late 1960s. Trump's use of the phrase was swiftly condemned by a variety of commentators and some Twitter users reported it to the company as a rule violation. *See* Brian Stelter and Donie O'Sullivan, *Trump Tweets Threat that "Looting" Will Lead to "Shooting"*, CNN (May 29, 2020), https://www.cnn.com/2020/05/29/tech/trump-twitter-minneapolis/index.html.

throwing the President off of the site, as it later did. But this error, although foundational, pales in comparison to an even more extravagant mistake of law.

As this book has suggested, the President did not just get the law wrong; he got it exactly backwards. After all, if anything about this sequence of events raised red flags under the First Amendment, then it was that the head of the executive branch of the federal government wanted to use the power of his office to retaliate against a private entity for expressing a viewpoint. The offense to free speech doctrine did not come from Twitter's labels. It came from the President's Executive Order.

Still, if the Executive Order departed from the legal principles we have outlined in this book, then it also had considerable resonance with a different idea that we discussed: the Everyday First Amendment. As you'll recall, the Everyday First Amendment is the phrase we use to describe the popular impulse to apply free expression principles where the law does not require it. In Chapter 4, we explored some of the ways in which this phenomenon may call useful and important questions, like whether we should protect the free speech rights of whistleblowers who are punished by the private companies whose wrongdoing they report. Nevertheless, as we noted there, the Everyday First Amendment brings with it some concerns, particularly in the realm of online speech and in connection with the service providers and social media platforms that dominate it.

President Trump's Executive Order was an outsized example of the problems with the Everyday First Amendment. On the one hand, the order traded on the language of the law of free expression. It began with the sentence "Free speech is the bedrock of American democracy" and repeatedly invoked the connection between expression, debate, and the democratic form of government. The Order described social media platforms as "a 21st century equivalent of the public square," bemoaned the market power that these platforms hold, and set the President up as the defender of free speech against their assaults. On a superficial reading, it might sound uncontroversial, perhaps even noble and constitutionally vigilant.

But, of course, none of this has anything to do with the First Amendment. To the contrary, under the guise of protecting the First Amendment, the order did precisely what the First Amendment protects *against* – a public official punishing a private party for saying something that he didn't like. As we discussed earlier, it is only natural given the compelling values that underlie our free speech principles that we should want to apply them even where the law does not command it. This Executive Order, however, offers a powerful cautionary tale about the confusions and misunderstandings into which an unmoored Everyday First Amendment can lead us.

A deep irony at work here adds an additional dimension. After all, one can sensibly argue that no one benefited more from Section 230, the open nature of the internet, and the hesitancy of social media platforms to limit speech and speakers than President Trump. The last thing he actually would have wanted would have been a dramatic rollback of Section 230. That would have put him out of the business of doing something he very much enjoyed, sometimes to the tune of hundreds of times a day.

Perhaps President Trump knew that, and he issued the Executive Order (most of which was without force) for other, strategic reasons. If that's the case, then we can see yet another risk inherent in an Everyday First Amendment untethered from legal doctrine: people can manipulate it to their own ends, covering pernicious agendas with a thin but shiny constitutional lacquer. It presents a wolf as a sheep – or, worse, as a shepherd.

To return to where we started, the internet did not change everything. But, among other novelties, it has added fresh risks to free expression by inviting new modes of discourse that actually undermine the very values they purport to promote. These developments require a vigilance in the protection of First Amendment freedoms that is as creative as it is persistent.

We conclude by noting one additional respect in which the internet puts pressure on free speech rights. Internet platforms, like Google, make content available not just in the United States but around the world. In this country, those platforms enjoy the protections of the First Amendment and Section 230. But other nations have different standards that may apply when these platforms "do business" there.

This issue came to the foreground in 2014 in the so-called Google Spain case. In 2009, Spanish citizen Mario Consteja Gonzalez discovered that a Google search of his name quickly revealed a 1998 newspaper article reporting that he had been forced to sell a property in order to settle a debt. He found the article embarrassing and no longer relevant to his current situation because the debt had been discharged over a decade earlier. He contacted the newspaper and Google and asked them to remove the article and the links to it, but he met with no success and so pursued claims against them.

A series of legal skirmishes brought the case to the Court of Justice of the European Union, which ruled in his favor as against Google. Much of the Court's opinion dealt with a number of technical questions about the applicability of European data protection law. For our purposes, the critical aspects of its ruling relate to the structure of its reasoning and the obligation that it recognized on the part of data processors like Google.

The European model of free expression is a relativist one. It recognizes the public interest in receiving information and the right of companies like Google to make it available. But it balances those interests against others that are viewed as equal in importance.

Here, those competing interests were embodied in various provisions of the European Union Charter of Fundamental Rights, including Article 7 (respect for private and family life) and Article 8 (protection of personal data). After weighing these considerations, the Court concluded that Consteja Gonzalez had an enforceable right to demand that Google deindex the story about him. More broadly, the Court concluded that anyone who had a legitimate interest in doing so could object to the continued circulation of data about them, and the "data controller" would have to remove the information if it was inadequate, no longer relevant, or excessive.[29]

This was promptly labeled as a "right to be forgotten" although that is plainly inaccurate. After all, the ruling did not force the newspaper to delete the article from its archives or gag anyone from speaking about the underlying facts. Instead, it just made the information harder to find because it would not show up in response to an inquiry conducted on the world's most famously efficient internet search engine. It gives those who object *more* privacy but not *complete* privacy.

Those limitations notwithstanding, in the United States a law to this effect plainly would not pass constitutional muster. Indeed, a prohibition against publishing information because someone objected to it as "no longer relevant" offends multiple principles that we have discussed in this book. It is hopelessly vague; it is overly broad; it does not include the necessary breathing room for good faith error. And the "relevance" of any given piece of data can change – for example, financial information about a real estate developer becomes more "relevant" if he goes on to become a high-profile public figure and, then, President of the United States.

A comprehensive review of subsequent developments and of the current state of European data protection and privacy law lies well beyond the scope of this book. What matters here is that a company headquartered in the United States discovered that it was not immune from the effects of European laws that take a very different approach to freedom of speech. Consider: the decision was issued in 2014; by August of 2016, Google had received more than half a million requests for data removal and had reviewed more than 1.5 million URLs in connection with those requests, taking hundreds of thousands down.[30]

But the internet has not just brought pressure to bear on the First Amendment rights of search engines like Google. It has also done so with respect to traditional news media, like newspapers and magazines, and the journalists who work with them. Many such news outlets have become *online* publishers and, thereby, *international* publishers. In the 1980s, a daily major market newspaper was lucky to have readers throughout the entire state; now, they commonly have readers on the other side of the world. In some instances, this gives rise to the risk that they, their journalists, or their sources will be sued over their content in a country that is much less solicitous of freedom of speech than the United States.

For a number of years, the phenomenon of "libel tourism" made this risk more than hypothetical. An aggrieved party pursuing such a strategy might, for example,

29 For a more detailed overview of the case and the issues addressed, *see* Lydia F de la Torre, *Google Spain v. AEPD: Remembering the Right to Be Forgotten*, MEDIUM (June 17, 2019), https://medium.com/golden-data/google-v-spain-the-right-to-be-forgotten-aaee50dae43c.

30 Guy Vassall-Adams and Jacob Goldstein, *Google Spain and the Right to Be Forgotten Two Years Later*, MEDIA LAW (July, 2016), http://www.medialaw.org/component/k2/item/3538-google-spain-andthe-right-to-be-forgotten-two-years-later.

bring a libel case in England, where the demanding *New York Times Co.* v. *Sullivan* standard does not apply and the claim is easier to prove. A plaintiff who secured a large libel judgment overseas could enforce it there, if the defendant had assets in that jurisdiction, or try to do so here, if the defendant did not.

To guard against the latter possibility, in 2010 the United States Congress passed the SPEECH Act (standing for Securing the Protection of our Enduring and Established Constitutional Heritage). Under the Act, which was signed into law by President Barack Obama, foreign libel judgments are unenforceable in United States court unless the law of the foreign jurisdiction offers at least as much protection to speech as the First Amendment or, alternatively, the defendant would have been found liable under United States law. (A number of individual states have passed similar laws.) The SPEECH Act was largely inspired by the experience of author Rachel Ehrenfeld, a United States citizen who lived in New York and who was sued in the United Kingdom by a Saudi billionaire who claimed to have been libeled by one of her books.

For these reasons, it might be said that the internet has set us on a free speech collision course. On the one hand, it has exponentially expanded the capacity of every person to share ideas, opinions, and information – not just locally but globally. On the other hand, for precisely that reason, the internet increases the likelihood that our approach to free expression will come into conflict with the approaches of other countries. A world that becomes smaller by definition becomes more crowded. The likelihood of friction increases correspondingly.

Conclusion

Our Hazardous Freedom

Imagine that a free speech absolutist and a free speech relativist enter into the sort of reasoned discussion that the marketplace of ideas envisions. Under the conventional framing of the marketplace of ideas model, their goal is to arrive at the truth. In the end, one will persuade the other that their view is the right one. Participants in debates over free expression often approach things in just such a manner.

This conventional framing, however, misses a different function that the marketplace of ideas performs. It is preliminary but essential. That function is especially important where the debate concerns a complicated and nuanced collection of issues, as freedom of expression undoubtedly does. It is this: before the marketplace of ideas provides an opportunity for the participants in a discussion to arrive at the *truth*, it provides an opportunity for them to arrive at *understanding*.

Sometimes understanding is the best we can do. Even after a long and exploratory conversation, important differences remain. But understanding has real value. It fosters deeper and more complex thinking on our part. It allows discussion to progress, even if it does not point toward some certain, inescapable, and universally endorsed truth at the end of the inquiry.

In this book, we have not presumed to offer the "truth" about free expression, if anything like that actually exists. Instead, we have tried to offer tools to build understanding as between those in the absolutist and relativist camps. We might summarize those tools by reference to the *Tinker* Court's wonderful description of the First Amendment as a "hazardous freedom."

We have invited those inclined toward the absolutist view to understand the *hazards* that free expression creates. Speech has consequences – sometimes dire ones. It can harm individuals and institutions. It can be weaponized by the forces of oppression, distortion, and hate. Speech is worth protecting precisely because of its power, but like every power this one is subject to abuse. And its burdens and abuses do not fall equally upon all of us. An absolutist doctrine that does not acknowledge these realities will be callously disconnected from the lived experience of countless persons.

At the same time, we have invited those inclined toward the relativist view to understand the importance of *this freedom*. It serves the foundational values we discussed in the opening chapters. It has had a signal place in the amplification of minority voices and the advancement of noble causes. And efforts to limit it are often vague, overreaching, and subject to abuses of their own. A relativist doctrine that does not acknowledge these realities will leave room for tyrannies great and small and, as *Barnette* warned, may ultimately yield only the "unanimity of the graveyard."

Even with this enhanced understanding, debates about free speech will not always leave us in satisfactory places. It is certain that reasonable disagreements will remain. But it is equally certain that, without doing the hard work of seeking to understand the competing viewpoint, there is no rational hope of making whatever progress can be achieved.

We hope that the tools offered here will help foster better informed and more productive conversations about freedom of expression. We shall see. After all, what Justice Holmes said of the marketplace of ideas theory holds true for this book as well: "It is an experiment. As all life is an experiment."

Index